Temple of Apollo at Corinth.
Photo by Andrew Gillis.

These are the ruins of an archaic Greek temple of Apollo that was built in Corinth around 550 B.C. It remained the foremost center of worship in that city until 146 B.C., when Roman troops under the command of the consul Lucius Mummius Achaicus marched on Corinth. Mummius broke up the Achaean League, which Corinth headed at that time, destroyed the city, and shipped its art treasures to Rome.

Frederick Williams

Elementary Classical

Greek

ἡ Ἑλληνικὴ γλῶττα

Revised Edition

Southern Illinois University Press

Carbondale

Library of Congress Cataloging-in-Publication Data

Williams, Frederick (Frederick L.)
    Elementary classical Greek=hē Hellēnikē glōtta/
Frederick Williams.—Rev. ed.
        p.   cm.
    Includes bibliographical references and indexes.
    1. Greek language—Grammar—1950 . I. Title.
    II. Title: Hellēnikē glōtta.
    PA258.W74 1991
    488.82'421—dc20
    ISBN 0-8093-1795-8   91-19763
    ISBN 0-8093-2577-2 (pbk. : alk. paper)   CIP

Printed on recycled paper. ♻

The paper used in this publication meets the minimum requirements of
American National Standard for Information Sciences—Permanence of
Paper for Printed Library Materials, ANSI Z39.48-1992. ⊚

For Marty

θάλλει δ' ὑπ' αὐτῆς κἀπαέξεται βίος

Contents

Illustrations

Preface to the Revised Edition

Those who are familiar with the first edition of this text will notice
three principal differences in the revised edition. First, nearly one
hundred reading passages from ancient authors have been more
fully identified, with standard book, section, and paragraph refer-
ences (for prose selections) and line numbers (for poetry). The ben-
efit, for both the instructor and the student, seems to outweigh any
objection to full citation. Second, in response to student and instructor requests, further exercises have been added to the sections
on participles and conditions. And third, errors have been corrected
throughout. My thanks are due to those who have made suggestions
for this revision, and also to those who have helped to make it
possible; I am particularly indebted to Joan O'Brien, Ladislaus
Bolchazy, John Guyon, Kenney Withers, Curtis Clark, and to my
wife, Brigitte, for her patience, her understanding, and her wisdom.

Frederick Williams

Preface

Two principles controlled the composition of this text: 1) that it is still possible even for an average American student to learn classical Greek; and 2) that the most important thing for *any* student of Greek to learn is the Greek verb.

Some of the readings in this book, which would normally seem impenetrable to beginners, are presented first in simpler, then in more complex language, leading gradually to the actual words of the ancient author (all within the same lesson). This elementary device helps bridge many of the difficult gaps between modern English and ancient Greek and can also be used profitably by the individual instructor for other reading passages which have not been graduated.

The six principal parts of Greek verbs (including blanks for deponent and defective verbs) are presented and should be learned from the outset (lesson 6). If they learn only the principal parts they are able to conjugate, both average and better students seem to have more difficulty with the forms presented later on. The verbs given in lesson vocabularies in full are to be memorized. Some verbs, of course, are more important than others, and a few individual forms are given in some vocabularies, without accompanying principal parts, in order to facilitate reading the Greek sentences for that lesson.

As the students learn more about Greek verbs, they should *do* more with them. Partial synopses, including all the forms presented up to a given point, should become a regular part of verb review. A complete synopsis of γράφω is provided in Appendix C as an example.

The book is designed for a college course that meets four or five times a week for two semesters; a course that meets less frequently will be able to do less drill in class. Each lesson should take about four or five days, depending on the length and complexity of the material: one day for an introduction to each topic, one or two days reading the Greek sentences aloud in Greek and translating them into good English, and another day or two for drill (the "Practice" section of each lesson) and writing in Greek ("Composition"). More difficult topics (-μι verbs, participles) will come slower, and easier ones (purpose clauses, adjectives in -ης) more quickly. But over the first three years that this arrangement was used, the beginning class finished the material in time to read all of the Supplementary Readings provided after lesson 24.

There is a vocabulary with every lesson, with nouns, verbs, and adjectives each presented separately, followed by the other parts of speech grouped together. These vocabularies should be learned with their lessons, but there are also general vocabularies (Greek-English, English-Greek) in the back for easy reference.

The composition exercises have been patterned after the Greek sentences in each lesson, and students should be encouraged early to imitate them in making their own Greek sentences. If time permits, it is valuable to have students present their compositions for corrections and discussion in class (on a blackboard, if possible, and repeated orally).

The Supplementary Readings are meant to be read with the assistance of two other works: H. G. Liddell and Robert Scott, eds., *An Abridged Greek-English Lexicon* (Oxford University Press, 1957), and H. W. Smyth, *Greek Grammar,* rev. ed. Gordon M. Messing (Cambridge: Harvard University Press, 1956). It is useful to have students begin to consult these essential tools midway through the second semester. Notes to the Supplementary Readings are keyed to Smyth and to the abridged Liddell and Scott.

I owe a debt of gratitude to many, but I wish especially to offer my thanks to a few: to William Huie Hess, who taught me how to read Greek; to Gordon Kirkwood, Stuart Small, and Joan O'Brien, who gave me encouragement when I was right and corrected me when I was wrong; to Alan Cohn for his consistently good advice; to Peter Kuniholm for assistance with the art treasures at Cornell; to Andrew Gillis and Michael Vendl for their superb photography; to my students and to Charles Speck and my other colleagues at SIU, who have encouraged me for the last three years; and finally, to my wife, Marty, for making this not merely possible but enjoyable.

Frederick Williams

Elementary Classical Greek

1. Two Wrestlers (*Pancratiasts*).

A third-century B.C. sculpture in the Uffizi Gallery, Florence; from a copy in the H. W. Sage Collection of Casts of Ancient Sculpture at Cornell University; photo by Andrew Gillis.

The Greeks often viewed life as a conflict between more or less evenly matched opponents, and the Olympics (and other festival games) are only one manifestation of their love of competition. These two athletes, mistakenly called ''wrestlers,'' are really engaged in another Olympic sport, the παγκράτιον, or all-out contest of strength—a full-contact competition in which only biting and gouging were prohibited, and which ended only when the loser raised his hand as a signal of defeat. By contrast, wrestling in ancient Greece was a more simple matter of throwing one's opponent to the ground three times.

Lesson 1

The Alphabet

1. The classical Greek alphabet has twenty-four letters:

form		pronunciation	Greek name
A	α	papa	ἄλφα
B	β	biography	βῆτα
Γ	γ	glucose	γάμμα
Δ	δ	diameter	δέλτα
E	ε	epitaph	ἒ ψιλόν
Z	ζ	heads up	ζῆτα
H	η	plane	ἦτα
Θ	θ	theory	θῆτα
I	ι	idiot	ἰῶτα
K	κ	kaleidoscope	κάππα
Λ	λ	logic	λάμβδα
M	μ	metropolis	μῦ
N	ν	neon	νῦ
Ξ	ξ	axiom	ξῖ
O	ο	ornithology	ὂ μικρόν
Π	π	period	πῖ
P	ρ	rhapsody	ῥῶ
Σ	σ ς	symbol	σίγμα
T	τ	telephone	ταῦ
Y	υ	German ü	ὖ ψιλόν
Φ	φ	philosophy	φῖ
X	χ	German ch	χῖ
Ψ	ψ	rhapsody	ψῖ
Ω	ω	omen	ὦ μέγα

2. a. The pronunciations indicated above are traditional, but students should also know that contemporary scholarship suggests different pronunciations for some letters in the classical period: ζ, Tuesday; η, pet; θ, hothouse; φ, uphill; and ω, awful.

b. When γ immediately precedes κ, ξ, χ, or another γ in the same word, it sounds like the *ng* in lo*ng:* ἄγκυρα, σῦριγξ, ἔγχος, ἄγγελος. γ is never soft, like the *g* in *George:* γεωργός, γίγνομαι.

c. The form ς of the letter sigma occurs as the last letter in a word, σ everywhere else: σεισμός.

3. The principal diphthongs in Greek are

αι	*I*
αυ	c*ow*
ει	r*ei*gn
ευ	*e* of r*e*d + *ue* of bl*ue*
οι	t*oy*
ου	s*ou*p
υι	*we*

4. The initial sound designated by the letter *h-* in English also exists in Greek, but it is not represented by a Greek letter. Instead, the sign ʽ (called a *rough breathing*) is placed over the first vowel (or the second vowel of an initial diphthong): ἱέναι, αὑτόν. The sign ʼ (called a *smooth breathing*) indicates that the *h-* sound is not pronounced: ἰέναι, αὐτόν.

Initial υ- and ρ- always have a rough breathing: ὕβρις, υἱός, ῥᾳδίου. Words beginning with consonants (other than ρ) do not use breath marks; words beginning with vowels and ρ always do.

5. The letter iota sometimes appears in a diminutive form (ͺ) beneath α, η, or ω, and is silent. It represents a sound that was once noticeable, however, and it is often the only written clue to the particular inflection (case, person, mood) of a word, so it must not be overlooked. When it is in this position, it is called *iota subscript:* ἡμέρᾳ, διδῷ, ἔχῃ.

6. ε and ο are always *short* in quantity, while η, ω, and the diphthongs are always *long.* α, ι, and υ are short in some words, long in others. Knowing the length of vowels is useful primarily in reading Greek poetry, which is distinguished from Greek prose not by rhyme but by the regular alternation of short and long syllables.

7. Punctuation in Greek is as follows:

period	. (as in English)
comma	, (as in English)
colon or semicolon	· (top half of English colon)
question mark	; (like English semicolon)
exclamation point	none
quotation marks	none; first letter of direct quotation is capitalized

8. Capital letters are used in Greek for proper names, to begin direct quotations, and to begin a long section in a literary work, such as a chapter. Capitals are not used at the beginning of each sentence.

Practice saying and writing the following sentences in Greek:

1. τὸ μέγα βιβλίον ἴσον τῷ μεγάλῳ κακῷ. — Callimachus
   A big book is the same as a big pain.

2. βρεκεκεκὲξ κοὰξ κοάξ,
   βρεκεκεκὲξ κοὰξ κοάξ,
   λιμναῖα κρηνῶν τέκνα,
   ξύναυλον ὕμνων βοὰν
   φθεγξώμεθ᾽, εὔγηρυν ἐμὰν
   ἀοιδάν, κοὰξ κοάξ. — Aristophanes, *Frogs*
   Brekekekex koax koax,
   Brekekekex koax koax,
   Come, sons of the swamp,
   You watery waifs,
   Let's croak a cappella these
   Sweet-sounding melodies,
   Blending our voices in
   Song, koax koax.

3. νῦν δὲ ποῖ με χρὴ μολεῖν; — Sophocles, *Electra*
   And now where should I go?

4. ποδαπός ἐστιν οὗτος, ὅτι καὶ οἱ ἄνεμοι καὶ ἡ θάλαττα
ὑπακούουσιν αὐτῷ;—Saint Matthew
What kind of man is this, that both the winds and the sea
obey him?

5. διψῇ δὲ πρᾶγος ἄλλο μὲν ἄλλου,
ἀεθλονικία δὲ μάλιστ' ἀοιδὰν φιλεῖ,
στεφάνων ἀρετᾶν τε δεξιωτάταν ὀπαδόν.—Pindar,
Nemean Ode 3
Every achievement has a different thirst,
And above all, gold-medal victory loves song,
The most adroit accompanist to crowns and to success.

6. χαλεπὸν τὸ μὴ φιλῆσαι,
χαλεπὸν δὲ καὶ φιλῆσαι·
χαλεπώτερον δὲ πάντων
ἀποτυγχάνειν φιλοῦντα.—Anacreon
It's hard not to fall in love,
And hard to fall in love, too;
But harder than everything
Is to be in love and lose.

7. καὶ ποιμένες ἦσαν ἐν τῇ χώρᾳ τῇ αὐτῇ ἀγραυλοῦντες
καὶ φυλάττοντες φυλακὰς τῆς νυκτὸς ἐπὶ τὴν ποίμνην
αὐτῶν. καὶ ἄγγελος Κυρίου ἐπέστη αὐτοῖς, καὶ δόξα
Κυρίου περιέλαμψεν αὐτούς· καὶ ἐφοβήθησαν φόβον
μέγαν. καὶ εἶπεν αὐτοῖς ὁ ἄγγελος, Μὴ φοβεῖσθε.—
Saint Luke
And there were in the same country shepherds abiding in
the field and keeping watch over their flock by night. And
an angel of the Lord came upon them, and the glory of the
Lord shone round about them, and they were sore afraid.
And the angel said unto them, "Fear not."

8. ὅπως μοι, ὦ ἄνθρωπε, μὴ ἐρεῖς ὅτι ἔστιν τὰ δώδεκα δὶς
ἕξ.—Plato, *Republic*
Mind you, Sir, don't tell me 12 is 2 times 6!

9. λέγω ὑμῖν, ὅτι παντὶ τῷ ἔχοντι, δοθήσεται· ἀπὸ
   δὲ τοῦ μὴ ἔχοντος, καὶ ὃ ἔχει ἀρθήσεται ἀπ' αὐτοῦ.—
   Saint Luke
   I say unto you, that unto every one who has shall be
   given; but from him who has not, even what he has shall
   be taken from him.

10. ζητεῖτε ἄλλο τι ἢ ἐν οἷς ζῶμεν.—Thucydides
    You seek a different world than that in which we live.

Lesson 2

Accent

There are only three written accents in Greek: the *acute* (´), the *grave* (`), and the *circumflex* (˜). The rules governing their placement are as follows.

1. *a*. The number of syllables in a Greek word is equal to the number of vowels and diphthongs in that word.
   b. Only the last three syllables of Greek words bear written accents.
   c. The last syllable in a word is called the *ultima,* the next-to-last is called the *penult,* and the third from the end is called the *antepenult.*

2. *a*. The acute stands either on *long* or on *short* syllables; it may appear on the ultima, the penult, or the antepenult, but it appears on the antepenult only of those words that have a short ultima: κακός, λέγω, δίδωμι.
   b. The grave accent appears only on the ultima and takes the place of an acute when another word follows immediately, with no punctuation mark separating them: καὶ τὰ καλά.
   c. The circumflex accent stands only on long syllables; it may appear on the ultima or the penult, but it appears on the penult only of those words that have a short ultima. An accented long penult followed by a short ultima *must* bear a circumflex accent—it cannot bear an acute: τιμᾶν, ἑταῖρος.
   d. An accent of any type is written above the vowel it governs, and above the second vowel of a diphthong: πρός, μοίρας, καί, πλοῦτος.

3. *a*. A word with an acute (or grave) on the ultima is called an *oxytone:* τούς, περί, κατασκευήν.
   b. A word with an acute on the penult is called a *paroxytone:* δαίμων, λόγος, μέλλει.

   c. A word with an acute on the antepenult is called a *proparoxytone:* Σώκρατες, ἄνθρωπος, μακάριος.

   d. A word with a circumflex on the ultima is called a *perispomenon:* ποῖ, τῆς, ἡμῶν, ἀργυροῦς.

   e. A word with a circumflex on the penult is called a *properispomenon:* δοῦναι, γυναῖκες, φιλοῦντα.

4. *a.* The accent of the inflected forms of nouns and adjectives tends to stay on the syllable accented in the nominative singular and is therefore called *persistent.* The nominative singular form will be given in the paradigms, vocabularies, and in a lexicon (dictionary) and must be memorized.

   b. The accent of conjugated forms of verbs (those forms with personal endings) tends to move as far to the left as the length of the ultima will allow and is therefore called *recessive.* The position of the accent on infinitives is fixed and will be learned as each tense and voice is presented.

5. *a.* A syllable with a short vowel is *short.*

   b. A syllable with a long vowel or a diphthong is *long.*

   c. The diphthongs -αι and -οι, as the *last two letters* of a Greek word, are considered short for purposes of accent, except in contractions (lessons 3 and 13) and the optative mood (lesson 17): ἄνθρωποι, ἄρισται, but ἀνθρώποις, ἀρίσταις, δηλοῖ, νοῖ, δώσοι.

Practice

1. Identify the following words according to the terms in paragraph 3:

ἄριστος	τῷ
ἀγαθόν	δῶρον
ἐπιμαχώτατα	κατὰ
μολεῖν	ἀνθρώπους
λόγων	λιμναῖα

2. Write the following words with proper accents:

λαμβανουσι (proparoxytone)
ἀνθρωποι (proparoxytone)
ψυχη (oxytone)
ψυχης (perispomenon)
φιλια (paroxytone)
ἀγω (paroxytone)
εἰπον (properispomenon)
στησαι (properispomenon)
ἁ (oxytone)
ᾠ (perispomenon)

3. Write each word in sentence 7 of lesson 1, separately, and identify each one according to accent (the words ὁ and ἐν are *proclitics* and have no accent; see lesson 5).

Lesson 3

The Definite Article,
Regular Adjectives,
Second-Declension Nouns

1. *a*. Nouns, pronouns, and adjectives in Greek are *inflected* (changed, in spelling and often in accent) to indicate different grammatical and syntactical relations. The inflections, or changes, in these words must be memorized in order to recognize and understand them in Greek literature.

   b. The inflections for nouns, pronouns, and adjectives are called *declensions* and are arranged into a few easily learned patterns that provide models for every such word in the language.

   c. The *paradigm* (model, example) of each declensional pattern is representative of a group of words similarly declined.

2. Every Greek noun has a specific grammatical *gender: masculine, feminine,* or *neuter;* three *numbers: singular, dual,* and *plural;* and five *cases: nominative, genitive, dative, accusative,* and *vocative.*

   a. Gender: The gender of a noun is fixed by convention and does not change.

   b. Number: The singular is used for one, the dual for two, and the plural for two or more persons, places, or things. Only the singular and plural are normally used, the dual being reserved for emphasis, for a few rare prose instances of natural pairs (eyes, hands, etc.), and for poetry.

   c. Case: The cases in Greek indicate a wide variety of syntactical relationships and special grammatical uses that will be presented throughout the year. The cases and some typical uses are as follows:

Nominative: the subject of a sentence.
Genitive: possessor; origin; separation.
Dative: indirect object; means; instrument.
Accusative: direct object; subject of infinitives.
Vocative: direct address.

The genitive, dative, and accusative are very commonly used as objects of prepositions, as well.

3. *Adjectives,* words that modify nouns or pronouns, also have gender, number, and case in order that they may satisfy the main rule of their existence: *every adjective must agree, in number, gender, and case, with the noun that it modifies.* For that reason, each adjective has all five cases, all three numbers, and all three genders.

4. *a.* Inflected words have what may be called *principal parts,* which are given in vocabulary lists or dictionaries and must be memorized for each word. The principal parts, combined with the *paradigm* inflections, will give the student access to every regularly inflected word in Greek.

   b. The three principal parts of a Greek noun are 1) *nominative singular,* 2) *genitive singular,* and 3) *the nominative singular definite article* that agrees with the noun in gender:
   φίλος, φίλου, ὁ
   ὁδός, ὁδοῦ, ἡ
   ἱερόν, ἱεροῦ, τό

   c. The three principal parts of a Greek adjective are 1) *masculine nominative singular,* 2) *feminine nominative singular,* and 3) *neuter nominative singular:*
   καλός, καλή, καλόν

5. Learn the declension of the *definite article,* ὁ, ἡ, τό, *the:*

	SINGULAR		
	masculine	*feminine*	*neuter*
n	ὁ	ἡ	τό
g	τοῦ	τῆς	τοῦ
d	τῷ	τῇ	τῷ
a	τόν	τήν	τό
(no v)			

PLURAL

n	οἱ	αἱ	τά
g	τῶν	τῶν	τῶν
d	τοῖς	ταῖς	τοῖς
a	τούς	τάς	τά

(*no v*)

6. Learn the declensions of the following five *second-declension* nouns, paying close attention both to the spelling changes and to the changes in accent. It will help to memorize these paradigms with their corresponding definite articles as they are presented here:

ἱερόν, ἱεροῦ, τό *temple* (*oxytone*)

	singular	*plural*
n	τὸ ἱερόν	τὰ ἱερά
g	τοῦ ἱεροῦ	τῶν ἱερῶν
d	τῷ ἱερῷ	τοῖς ἱεροῖς
a	τὸ ἱερόν	τὰ ἱερά
v	ἱερόν	ἱερά

φίλος, φίλου, ὁ *friend* (*paroxytone*)

n	ὁ φίλος	οἱ φίλοι
g	τοῦ φίλου	τῶν φίλων
d	τῷ φίλῳ	τοῖς φίλοις
a	τὸν φίλον	τοὺς φίλους
v	φίλε	φίλοι

στέφανος, στεφάνου, ὁ *crown* (*proparoxytone*)

n	ὁ στέφανος	οἱ στέφανοι
g	τοῦ στεφάνου	τῶν στεφάνων
d	τῷ στεφάνῳ	τοῖς στεφάνοις
a	τὸν στέφανον	τοὺς στεφάνους
v	στέφανε	στέφανοι

νοῦς, νοῦ, ὁ *mind* (*perispomenon;*
rare in this declension)

n	ὁ νοῦς	οἱ νοῖ
g	τοῦ νοῦ	τῶν νῶν
d	τῷ νῷ	τοῖς νοῖς
a	τὸν νοῦν	τοὺς νοῦς
v	νοῦ	νοῖ

ψῆφος, ψήφου, ἡ *pebble, ballot* (*properispomenon*)

n	ἡ ψῆφος	αἱ ψῆφοι
g	τῆς ψήφου	τῶν ψήφων
d	τῇ ψήφῳ	ταῖς ψήφοις
a	τὴν ψῆφον	τὰς ψήφους
v	ψῆφε	ψῆφοι

7. Learn the declension of the following adjective:

ἄριστος, ἀρίστη, ἄριστον *best*

SINGULAR

	masculine	feminine	neuter
n	ἄριστος	ἀρίστη	ἄριστον
g	ἀρίστου	ἀρίστης	ἀρίστου
d	ἀρίστῳ	ἀρίστῃ	ἀρίστῳ
a	ἄριστον	ἀρίστην	ἄριστον
v	ἄριστε	ἀρίστη	ἄριστον

PLURAL

	masculine	feminine	neuter
n	ἄριστοι	ἄρισται	ἄριστα
g	ἀρίστων	ἀρίστων	ἀρίστων
d	ἀρίστοις	ἀρίσταις	ἀρίστοις
a	ἀρίστους	ἀρίστας	ἄριστα
v	ἄριστοι	ἄρισται	ἄριστα

8. *a.* An adjective in the *attributive position,* between the article and the noun, is an attribute of the noun:

   ὁ ἄριστος νοῦς *the best mind*
   ἡ καλὴ ὁδός *the beautiful road*

   b. An adjective in the *predicate position,* outside the article-noun group, is a quality predicated of the noun, and together with the noun and article, it can form a complete simple sentence, with the verb "is" or "are" understood:

   ὁ νοῦς ἄριστος. *The mind is best.*
   καλὴ ἡ ὁδός. *The road is beautiful.*

9. The definite article in Greek has many of the same uses that the definite article has in English; but it is also used where we do not normally use an article in English:

a. with proper names: εἴδομεν τὸν Σωκράτη. *We saw Socrates.*

b. generically: οἱ ἄνθρωποι πολλοί, ὀλίγοι οἱ φίλοι. *People are abundant, friends are few.*

c. in place of a possessive adjective (where the identity of the possessor is clear from the context): ἔλιπε τὰ βιβλία. *She left her books.*

10. In a copulative sentence where one noun is identified with another, the subject is usually accompanied by a definite article, and the predicate noun usually is not:

    ὄνειρος ὁ βίος. *Life is a dream.*

11. The dative case, without a preposition, can be used to express the person *to whom* or *for whom* something is valid. This use is called the *dative of relation:*

    τὸ ἔργον χαλεπὸν τοῖς παιδίοις. *The work is difficult for the children.*

Vocabulary

NOUNS

ἄνθρωπος, ἀνθρώπου, ὁ *man; human being, person*
ἀρχῇ *beginning* (feminine dative singular; see lesson 4)
δῶρον, δώρου, τό *gift*
ἔργον, ἔργου, τό *work, deed*
θεός, θεοῦ, ὁ *god*
ἰατρός, ἰατροῦ, ὁ *healer, physician*
ἱερόν, ἱεροῦ, τό *temple*
λόγος, λόγου, ὁ *account, word, speech, explanation, reason, story; in New Testament, Christ*
μητράσι *mothers* (dative plural; see lesson 6)
νοῦς, νοῦ, ὁ *mind*
ὁδός, ὁδοῦ, ἡ *road, way*
παιδίον, παιδίου, τό *child* (*under seven years of age*)
πατράσι *fathers* (dative plural; see lesson 6)
πόνος, πόνου, ὁ *work, toil; trouble, pain*

στέφανος, στεφάνου, ὁ *crown, wreath*
φίλος, φίλου, ὁ *friend*
χρόνος, χρόνου, ὁ *time*
ψῆφος, ψήφου, ἡ *pebble; ballot, vote*

VERBS

ἐστί *is* (usually written ἐστίν before a vowel or at the end of a
sentence; enclitic—see lesson 5)
ἦν *was*

ADJECTIVES

ἄριστος, ἀρίστη, ἄριστον *best*
ἕκαστος, ἑκάστη, ἕκαστον *each*
ἕτερος, ἑτέρα, ἕτερον *another;* (with article) *one or the other
of two*
καλός, καλή, καλόν *beautiful, fine; good*
κρυπτός, κρυπτή, κρυπτόν *hidden, secret*
ξένος, ξένη, ξένον *strange, foreign, unusual*
ὁ, ἡ, τό *the*
οὐδέν *nothing* (literally, *not one . . . ;* neuter nominative singular;
see Appendix B)
σοφός, σοφή, σοφόν *wise, learned; skilled, clever*
φανερός, φανερά, φανερόν *visible; open*
χαλεπός, χαλεπή, χαλεπόν *difficult, dangerous, harsh,
troublesome*

OTHER

γάρ *for, because* (postpositive conjunction—*not* a preposition)
ἐγώ *I* (nominative personal pronoun; see lesson 13)
ἐν *in, among, on* (preposition; always takes its objects in the *dative*
case; proclitic—see lesson 5)
ἐνταῦθα *here* (adverb)
ἤ *or; than* (conjunction)
ἡμῶν *of us* (genitive personal pronoun; see lesson 13)
καί *and* (conjunction)

ποῦ *where?* (interrogative adverb)
πρός (+ *dative* objects) *near, close to;* (+ *accusative* objects)
  beside, with, in the presence of; toward (preposition)

Practice

Decline fully, singular and plural, with definite articles:
1. foreign god
2. beautiful friend
3. difficult road
4. wise child

Reading

Read aloud in Greek and translate:
  1. χαλεπὴ ἡ ὁδός.
  2. κρυπτὴ ἦν ἡ ψῆφος, ἢ φανερά;
  3. καλόν ἐστι τὸ δῶρον.
  4. καλὸν τὸ τοῦ ἀρίστου παιδίου δῶρον.
  5. ὁ νοῦς θεός ἐστιν.
  6. ὁ γὰρ νοῦς θεός.
  7. ὁ γὰρ νοῦς ἡμῶν ἐν ἑκάστῳ θεός.
  8. ὁ φίλος ἕτερος ἐγώ.—Aristotle, *Magna Moralia*
  9. ἰατρός ἐστιν ὁ χρόνος.
 10. ἰατρὸς τῶν πόνων ἐστὶν ὁ χρόνος.
 11. ἰατρὸς τῶν πόνων ἀνθρώποις ὁ χρόνος.
 12. στέφανος τὰ παιδία.
 13. στέφανος τοῖς πατράσι καὶ ταῖς μητράσι τὰ παιδία.
 14. οὐδὲν ξένον ἐστίν.
 15. τῷ σοφῷ ἀνθρώπῳ οὐδὲν ξένον ἐστίν.
 16. τῷ σοφῷ ξένον οὐδέν.
 17. ποῦ ἐστι τὸ ἱερόν;
 18. πρὸς τῇ ὁδῷ ἐστι τὸ ἱερόν.
 19. ἐν ἀρχῇ ἦν ὁ λόγος, καὶ ὁ λόγος ἦν πρὸς τὸν θεόν, καὶ
    θεὸς ἦν ὁ λόγος.—Saint John

Composition

Write in Greek:
1. The physician is a fine human being.
2. The child's friend (the friend of the child) was in the road.
3. The mind in each of the children is a gift of the gods.
4. Beside the road lives (οἰκεῖ) a strange man.

Lesson 4

First-Declension Nouns, Some
Uses of the Genitive and Dative,
Adjectives as Abstract Nouns

1. *a.* In *accent,* nouns of the first declension differ from nouns of the second declension only in one particular: the *genitive plural* of every first-declension noun is always *perispomenon.*
   b. Spelling changes, however, show many distinct differences between the two declensions.

2. *a.* The *plural endings* of first-declension nouns are as follows (for both masculine and feminine):

n	-αι
g	-ῶν
d	-αις
a	-ας
v	-αι

   b. There are no neuter nouns in the first declension.

3. There are five categories of the *singular endings* of the first declension:
   a. feminines declined like νίκη;
   b. feminines with stems that end in ε, ι, or ρ, and that have -α- where class a) has -η-: χώρα (long α), μοῖρα (short α);
   c. feminines with stems that do *not* end in ε, ι, or ρ, and that have -α- in the nominative and accusative, -η- in the genitive and dative: δόξα;
   d. masculines declined like πολίτης; and
   e. masculines with stems that end in ε, ι, or ρ, and that have -α- where class d) has -η-: νεανίας.

4. Learn the following nouns:

νίκη, νίκης, ἡ *victory*

ἡ νίκη	αἱ νῖκαι
τῆς νίκης	τῶν νικῶν
τῇ νίκῃ	ταῖς νίκαις
τὴν νίκην	τὰς νίκας
νίκη	νῖκαι

χώρα, χώρας, ἡ *place*

ἡ χώρα	αἱ χῶραι
τῆς χώρας	τῶν χωρῶν
τῇ χώρᾳ	ταῖς χώραις
τὴν χώραν	τὰς χώρας
χώρα	χῶραι

μοῖρα, μοίρας, ἡ *lot, fate*

ἡ μοῖρα	αἱ μοῖραι
τῆς μοίρας	τῶν μοιρῶν
τῇ μοίρᾳ	ταῖς μοίραις
τὴν μοῖραν	τὰς μοίρας
μοῖρα	μοῖραι

δόξα, δόξης, ἡ *opinion*

ἡ δόξα	αἱ δόξαι
τῆς δόξης	τῶν δοξῶν
τῇ δόξῃ	ταῖς δόξαις
τὴν δόξαν	τὰς δόξας
δόξα	δόξαι

πολίτης, πολίτου, ὁ *citizen*

ὁ πολίτης	οἱ πολῖται
τοῦ πολίτου	τῶν πολιτῶν
τῷ πολίτῃ	τοῖς πολίταις
τὸν πολίτην	τοὺς πολίτας
πολῖτα	πολῖται

νεανίας, νεανίου, ὁ *young man*

ὁ νεανίας	οἱ νεανίαι
τοῦ νεανίου	τῶν νεανιῶν
τῷ νεανίᾳ	τοῖς νεανίαις
τὸν νεανίαν	τοὺς νεανίας
νεανία	νεανίαι

5. A noun may stand in the genitive case if it is the object of action implicit in another noun. This use is called the *objective genitive,* and it takes the predicate position:

αἰσχρὰ ἡ ἐπιθυμία τῶν ἡδονῶν. *The love of pleasures is shameful.*

6. The *possessor* may stand in the genitive case, either in the attributive position (for nouns) or in the predicate position (for personal pronouns):

πολλὰ τὰ τοῦ διδασκάλου βιβλία. *The teacher's books are many.*
ἀγαθοὶ οἱ φίλοι ἡμῶν. *Our friends are noble.*

7. The *partitive genitive* (also called *genitive of the whole*) expresses the entire group or class of which one or more specific substantives is a member. It occurs in the predicate position:

ἕκαστος τῶν Ἀθηναίων παρῆν. *Each of the Athenians was present.*

8. The genitive case can be used alone, without a preposition, to denote the *origin* or *source* of something:

ἡ ὑγίεια δῶρον τῶν θεῶν. *Health is a gift from the gods.*

9. The dative case alone, without a preposition, may be used to express the person in whose *interest* or to whose *advantage* (or *disadvantage*) the statement of the predicate applies:

τὰ χρήματα τοῖς ἀνθρώποις κακόν. *Money is a pain for people.*

10. A neuter adjective (singular or plural), together with the appropriate definite article, is often used to express the quality of the adjective as an abstract noun:

τὸ καλόν *the good*
τὸ κακόν *the bad*
τὰ σοφά *wisdom*
τὰ καλά *beauty*

Vocabulary

βίος, βίου, ὁ *life*
βροτός, βροτοῦ, ὁ *mortal*
γνώμη, γνώμης, ἡ *opinion, intelligence, judgment*
δόξα, δόξης, ἡ *opinion, reputation*
θελκτήριον, θελκτηρίου, τό *charm, spell*
λύπη, λύπης, ἡ *pain*
μοῖρα, μοίρας, ἡ *lot, portion; fate*
νεανίας, νεανίου, ὁ *young man*
νίκη, νίκης, ἡ *victory*
πολίτης, πολίτου, ὁ *citizen, member of the* πόλις
χώρα, χώρας, ἡ *place; land, country*
ψυχή, ψυχῆς, ἡ *soul*

ἔστιν *there is* (accent different from that of ἐστίν)
ἔχει *has* (third-person singular indicative—see lesson 6)

ἀγαθός, ἀγαθή, ἀγαθόν *good, noble, brave*
ἀθάνατος, ἀθάνατον *immortal, deathless* (a two-ending adjective,
    like most other compound adjectives. It has only two sets of
    endings: one for masculine or feminine, and the other for
    neuter.)
ἀνεόρταστος, ἀνεόρταστον *without holidays*
ἀπανδόκευτος, ἀπανδόκευτον *without an inn to rest at*
κακός, κακή, κακόν *bad, evil; ugly; base*
μακρός, μακρά, μακρόν *long, large*
μόνος, μόνη, μόνον *alone, only*
οὗτος *this* (masculine nominative singular—see lesson 11)
χρηστός, χρηστή, χρηστόν *good, kind, useful*

οὐ *no, not* (written οὐκ before a smooth breathing, and οὐχ before
    a rough breathing)
χωρίς *without* (adverb used as a preposition + *genitive* objects)

Practice

Decline the following first-declension nouns fully:
1. ψυχή, ψυχῆς, ἡ *soul*
2. στρατιώτης, στρατιώτου, ὁ *soldier*

3. θεά, θεᾶς, ἡ *goddess*
4. γλῶττα, γλώττης, ἡ *tongue, language*
5. θάλαττα, θαλάττης, ἡ *sea*
6. γνώμη, γνώμης, ἡ *opinion, intelligence, judgment*
7. ταμίας, ταμίου, ὁ *treasurer*
8. φιλία, φιλίας, ἡ *friendship, love*

Reading

1. σοφὴ ἡ γνώμη.
2. σοφὴ ἡ τοῦ ἀγαθοῦ πολίτου γνώμη.
3. οὐκ ἔστιν οὐδὲν τοῖς βροτοῖς χωρὶς θεῶν.
4. λύπης ἰατρός ἐστιν ὁ χρηστὸς φίλος.
5. λύπης ἰατρός ἐστιν ἀνθρώποις λόγος,
   ψυχῆς γὰρ οὗτος μόνος ἔχει θελκτήρια.—Menander
6. ὁ βίος ὁδός ἐστιν.
7. ὁ βίος μακρὰ ὁδός.
8. βίος ἀνεόρταστος μακρὰ ὁδὸς ἀπανδόκευτος.—Democritus

Composition

1. The reputation of good men is immortal.
2. The opinions of the goddesses give (διδόασι + *accusative* direct object and *dative* indirect object) victory to noble mortals.
3. The long road is best for the soldiers.
4. There is nothing for the citizens without a victory.
5. The young man's soul is beautiful.

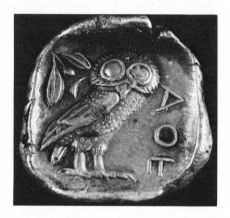

2. Athena and the Owl.

From the Cornell University Collection of Ancient Coins; photo by Andrew Gillis.

This silver tetradrachm (449–413 B.C.) shows the patron goddess of Athens, Athena, on the obverse, and on the reverse, the owl (and a spray of olive) with which she was so often connected in religious cult during classical times. The letters AΘE are the first three letters of Ἀθῆναι and Ἀθήνη; the letter H was not used in Athens until the end of the fifth century B.C. (see illustration 9). The areas of human life over which Athena had sovereignty included war (although she was a defensive fighter and not wantonly aggressive like the god of war, Ares), agriculture (it was Athena who "invented" the olive tree that flourishes so well in Greece), and many arts and crafts, such as weaving, spinning, pottery, and metalworking.

Lesson 5

Proclitics and Enclitics

1. Certain words in Greek do not normally have written accents of their own. Such a word relies instead on the word either immediately *preceding* it or immediately *following* it for its accent.

2. The ten words listed below are *proclitics,* and they are said to lean forward to the next word in the sentence for their accent:

ὁ *the*	ἐκ (ἐξ) *out of, from*
ἡ *the*	εἰς *into*
οἱ *the*	εἰ *if*
αἱ *the*	οὐ (οὐκ, οὐχ) *no, not*
ἐν *in, among, on*	ὡς *that, as, so that*

If a proclitic is the last word in a sentence, or if it is followed immediately by an enclitic, it bears an *acute* accent; otherwise, it bears no accent:

οὔ τις τῶν ἐν τέλει *No one of those in power*
οὐχ οἱ θεοί, ἡμεῖς δὲ οὔ. *Not the gods, and not us.*

3. Some words in Greek are *enclitics,* and are said to lean back upon the preceding word in the sentence for their accent. Enclitics are of two types: *monosyllabic* (of one syllable) and *disyllabic* (of two syllables). The rules governing the accent of both types of enclitics are as follows:

   a. An *oxytone* keeps its accent *acute* when it is followed by either a monsyllabic or a disyllabic enclitic, and the following enclitic bears no accent:

   ἀγαθός ἐστιν
   ὁδός τις

   b. A *perispomenon* remains unchanged before either type of enclitic, and the following enclitic bears no accent:

   στρατιωτῶν τινων
   ὑμῖν που

    c. An *extra acute* accent is added to the ultima of a *proparoxytone* and of most *properispomena* (see [*d*] below) before either type of enclitic, and the following enclitic bears no accent:

        θάλαττά τις
        θάλατταί τινες
        γνῶμαί τινες
        πολῖτά τε

    d. A *paroxytone* (or a *properispomenon* ending in -ξ or -ψ) remains unchanged before either type of enclitic; a following monosyllabic enclitic bears no accent, but a following *disyllabic* enclitic keeps its accent (always on the ultima):

        λόγος μοι
        κῆρυξ τις
        λόγων τινῶν
        γνώμας τινάς

    e. When an enclitic is followed immediately by one or more other enclitics, only the last of the series bears no accent:

        εἴ πού τινές ποτε ἤκουσαν

4. *a.* Learn the declension of the *interrogative pronoun/adjective* τίς, τί *who? which? what?* Note that the accent of this word is always *acute* (except for the alternative genitive and dative singular forms) and always on the first syllable. *None* of the forms of the interrogative is enclitic:

		masculine/feminine	*neuter*
		τίς *who? which?*	τί *what?*
sg.		τίνος or τοῦ	τίνος or τοῦ
		τίνι or τῷ	τίνι or τῷ
		τίνα	τί
pl.		τίνες	τίνα
		τίνων	τίνων
		τίσι	τίσι
		τίνας	τίνα

    b. The letter -ν may be added to the end of certain words when they are followed by a word beginning with a vowel. This letter is then called ν-*movable*. It may be added to any word

ending in -σι, to third-person singular verbs ending in -ε, and
to the word ἐστί:

τίσιν αὐτῶν
τίσι τῶν ἀνθρώπων

5. Learn the declension of the *indefinite pronoun/adjective* τις, τι
any(one), some(one), any(thing), some(thing), (a) certain . . .
Note that the forms of this word are accented on the *last* syllable, and that this word is *postpositive* (never comes first in a
sentence and follows, rather than precedes, words that it directly
modifies or emphasizes). *All* of the forms of the indefinite are
enclitic (including the alternative forms):

	masculine/feminine	*neuter*
	τίς *any(one), etc.*	τί *any(thing), etc.*
sg.	τινός or τοῦ	τινός or τοῦ
	τινί or τῷ	τινί or τῷ
	τινά	τί
	τινές	τινά
pl.	τινῶν	τινῶν
	τισί	τισί
	τινάς	τινά

6. A word that ends in a short vowel may *elide* (drop, omit) that
vowel before a word that begins with a vowel, and an *apostrophe (')* is then written in its place. If this elision causes a voiceless, unaspirated mute (π, τ, or κ) in the elided word to be
followed immediately by a rough breathing, the mute is changed
to the aspirated form of its class (φ, θ, or χ, respectively):

τίς ἄρ' οὗτός ἐστιν for τίς ἄρα οὗτός ἐστιν
ἐφ' οἷς for ἐπὶ οἷς
οὐκ ἔσθ' ὅπως for οὐκ ἔστι(ν) ὅπως

7. A noun in the dative or accusative may specify the respect in
which something is so. This use is called the *dative* (or *accusative) of respect:*

τοῖς ἔργοις καλή *beautiful in her deeds*
δεινοὶ μάχην *terrifying in battle*

8. Sometimes, for emphasis or clarification, an attribute follows its noun, and the definite article is repeated between the two. This is called the *formal attributive* position:

ὁ ἄνθρωπος ὁ σοφός *the wise man*
τῇ στρατιᾷ τῇ τῶν Ἀθηναίων *to the army of the Athenians*

Vocabulary

Ξενοφῶν, Ξενοφῶντος, ὁ *Xenophon, an Athenian historian of the late fifth/early fourth centuries B.C., who accompanied the expedition of the younger Cyrus first as a private citizen, and later as its leader in retreat, and wrote about it in his memoirs, called* The Anabasis
ὄμματα *eyes* (neuter accusative plural — see lesson 8)
ὀργή, ὀργῆς, ἡ *impulse; anger, wrath*
στρατιά, στρατιᾶς, ἡ *army*
στρατιώτης, στρατιώτου, ὁ *soldier*
ταμίας, ταμίου, ὁ *treasurer*
ὦτα *ears* (neuter accusative plural — see lesson 8)

εἶ *you are* (second-person singular — see lesson 6)
ἦν *there was* (as the first word in a sentence)

Ἀθηναῖος, Ἀθηναία, Ἀθηναῖον *Athenian; of, from Athens*
δεινός, δεινή, δεινόν *fearful, terrible; marvelous; clever, skillful*
ποδαπός, ποδαπή, ποδαπόν *from what country? of what sort?*
τίς, τί *who? which? what?* (interrogative)
τις, τι *any(one), some(one), any(thing), some(thing), (a) certain . . .* (indefinite)
τυφλός, τυφλή, τυφλόν *blind*

τε *and* (postpositive, enclitic conjunction)
τε . . . καί *both . . . and*
τε . . . τε *both . . . and*

Practice

Decline fully the following nouns (singular and plural) with the appropriate indefinite adjective:

1. ψυχή	6. λόγος
2. πολίτης	7. δόξα
3. ἄνθρωπος	8. βίος
4. δῶρον	9. ταμίας
5. νοῦς	10. παιδίον

Reading

1. δεινή ἐσθ' ἡ πολιτῶν τινων ὀργή.
2. τίς ἐστιν οὗτος; ποδαπός ἐστιν οὗτος; στρατιώτης τε καὶ ταμίας ἐστίν.
3. τυφλὸς εἶ.
4. τυφλὸς εἶ τὰ ὄμματα.
5. τυφλὸς τά τε ὦτα τά τε ὄμματα εἶ.
6. τυφλὸς τά τ' ὦτα τόν τε νοῦν τά τ' ὄμματ' εἶ. — Sophocles, *Oedipus the King* 371.
7. ἦν τις ἐν τῇ στρατιᾷ, Ξενοφῶν Ἀθηναῖος.
8. ἀγαθή ἐστιν ἡ δόξα ἡ τῶν Ἀθηναίων πολιτῶν.

Composition

1. Who is the Athenian in the road?
2. Certain soldiers in the army (are) brave.
3. The opinion of the good physician is wise.
4. The opinion of some physicians is wise.
5. A certain Xenophon was in the temple.

Lesson 6

Regular Verbs, Present, Future, and Imperfect Indicative

1. *a*. The inflections for verbs are called *conjugations* and, like declensions, are arranged in easily learned patterns.
   b. There are six *principal parts* for every regular Greek verb, which must be committed to memory as vocabulary items. There are certain similarities among the various parts of any given verb, and these similarities may help you learn the principal parts. But beware of trying to predict one principal part of a verb from the form of another: the similarities do *not* exist for all verbs.

2. The first two principal parts of regular verbs are
   I. *first-person singular, present indicative active*
   II. *first-person singular, future indicative active*
   For the other four principal parts, see lessons 9, 21, 22, 23, and Appendix C.

I	II
λύω *I set free, destroy*	λύσω *I will set free*
πέμπω *I send*	πέμψω *I will send*
γράφω *I write*	γράψω *I will write*
παιδεύω *I teach*	παιδεύσω *I will teach*

   but:

φέρω *I carry, bear*	οἴσω *I will carry*
ἐλαύνω *I march*	ἐλῶ *I will march*

3. The *personal endings* for the first two principal parts of regular verbs are the same. They are added to the *stem* of the verb, present or future, to form the full conjugation. Subject pronouns are used in Greek only for emphasis or clarification.

-ω *I* (first-person singular)

-εις *you* (second-person singular)

-ει *he, she, it* (third-person singular)

-ομεν *we* (first-person plural)

-ετε *you* (second-person plural)

-ουσι *they* (third-person plural)

The *stem* is discovered by removing the letter -ω from the ending of the first or second principal part:

	I	II
	λυ-	λυσ-
	πεμπ-	πεμψ-
	φερ-	οἰσ-

Learn the following present and future indicative active conjugations:

λύω *I set free, destroy, loose*   λύσω *I will set free*

λύεις *you set free, etc.*   λύσεις *you will set free*

λύει *he, she, it sets free*   λύσει *he, she, it will set free*

λύομεν *we set free*   λύσομεν *we will set free*

λύετε *you set free*   λύσετε *you will set free*

λύουσι *they set free*   λύσουσι *they will set free*

πέμπω *I send*   πέμψω *I will send*

πέμπεις *you send*   πέμψεις *you will send*

πέμπει *he, she, it sends*   πέμψει *he, she, it will send*

πέμπομεν *we send*   πέμψομεν *we will send*

πέμπετε *you send*   πέμψετε *you will send*

πέμπουσι *they send*   πέμψουσι *they will send*

φέρω *I bear, carry*   οἴσω *I will bear*

φέρεις *you bear, etc.*   οἴσεις *you will bear*

φέρει *he, she, it bears*   οἴσει *he, she, it will bear*

φέρομεν *we bear*   οἴσομεν *we will bear*

φέρετε *you bear*   οἴσετε *you will bear*

φέρουσι *they bear*   οἴσουσι *they will bear*

4. The *present* and *future active infinitives* are formed by adding the ending -ειν to the stem of the first or second principal part:

λύειν *to loose*	λύσειν *to be going to loose*
πέμπειν *to send*	πέμψειν *to be going to send*
φέρειν *to carry*	οἴσειν *to be going to carry*

5. Remember that a ν-movable may be added to the personal ending -ε, or to any word ending in -σι, either at the end of a sentence or immediately before a word beginning with a vowel:
    τοὺς πολεμίους λύσουσιν. *They will destroy the enemy.*
    τοὺς φίλους πέμπουσιν εἰς ᾿Αθήνας. *They are sending their friends into Athens.*
    τὰ παιδία ἔπεμπεν εἰς ᾿Αθήνας. *She used to send her children into Athens.*

6. Most transitive verbs in Greek take direct objects in the accusative case. The equivalents of some transitive *English* verbs, however, are not transitive in Greek, and they require a genitive or dative to express the connection. These verbs will be identified in the vocabularies when they are introduced. If not otherwise noted, verbs should be assumed to take their direct complements in the accusative case:
    καινοὺς λόγους μανθάνω. *I am learning new words.*
    ὁ νεανίας φιλεῖ τὴν μητέρα. *The young man loves his mother.*
but:
    ἀεὶ πιστεύομεν τοῖς φίλοις. *We always trust our friends.*

7. Learn the present indicative conjugation of εἰμί, *be:*

εἰμί *I am*	ἐσμέν *we are*
εἶ *you are*	ἐστέ *you are*
ἐστί *he, she, it is*	εἰσί *they are*
εἶναι *to be*	

All the present indicative forms of this verb are enclitic except εἶ. The present infinitive, εἶναι, is not enclitic. When the third-person singular form is accented ἔστι, it can mean either *there is* or *it is possible,* and it is then not enclitic.

8. The *imperfect* tense is a past tense, usually referring to habitual or repeated action or to an act in progress:
    ἐνομίζομεν *we used to think*

ἐπέμπετε *you (regularly) sent*
ἔφερες *you were carrying*
The imperfect is formed by adding an *augment* (either a prefixed letter, ἐ-, or by lengthening the initial vowel of verbs whose first principal part begins with a vowel) and the endings listed below to the stem of the first principal part:
λύω → stem λυ- → imperfect ἔλυον
The endings for the imperfect active are

-ον	-ομεν
-ες	-ετε
-ε	-ον

The present infinitive is used for both present and imperfect. There is no separate imperfect infinitive.

9. Learn the imperfect conjugations of λύω and ἄγω. Remember that the accent of finite forms of Greek verbs is recessive (lesson 2):

ἔλυον *I was destroying,*		ἦγον *I used to lead,*	
ἔλυες	*etc.*	ἦγες	*etc.*
ἔλυε		ἦγε	
ἐλύομεν		ἤγομεν	
ἐλύετε		ἤγετε	
ἔλυον		ἦγον	

10. Neuter subjects in Greek regularly take singular verbs:
τὸ παιδίον γράφει. *The child is writing.*
τὰ παιδία γράφει. *The children are writing.*

11. Learn the declension of αὐτός, αὐτή, αὐτό, which has three separate meanings:
   a. In the *attributive* position, the forms of αὐτός mean *same:*
   τὸ αὐτὸ βιβλίον *the same book*
   b. In the *predicate* position, it is the intensive modifier *-self:*
   οἱ νόμοι αὐτοί *the laws themselves*
   αὐτὴ ἡ γυνή *the woman herself*
   c. Alone, it is the *third-person personal pronoun* (genitive, dative, and accusative only):
   πέμπομεν αὐτούς. *We are sending them.*
   γράψω αὐτό. *I will write it.*

	masculine	*feminine*	*neuter*
sg.	αὐτός	αὐτή	αὐτό
	αὐτοῦ	αὐτῆς	αὐτοῦ
	αὐτῷ	αὐτῇ	αὐτῷ
	αὐτόν	αὐτήν	αὐτό
pl.	αὐτοί	αὐταί	αὐτά
	αὐτῶν	αὐτῶν	αὐτῶν
	αὐτοῖς	αὐταῖς	αὐτοῖς
	αὐτούς	αὐτάς	αὐτά

12. Learn the declensions of μήτηρ, *mother,* and πατήρ, *father:*

ἡ μήτηρ	ὁ πατήρ
τῆς μητρός	τοῦ πατρός
τῇ μητρί	τῷ πατρί
τὴν μητέρα	τὸν πατέρα
μῆτερ	πάτερ
αἱ μητέρες	οἱ πατέρες
τῶν μητέρων	τῶν πατέρων
ταῖς μητράσι	τοῖς πατράσι
τὰς μητέρας	τοὺς πατέρας
μητέρες	πατέρες

Other words that indicate family relationships are as follows:

ἀνήρ, ἀνδρός, ὁ *man; husband* (see lesson 8)

γυνή, γυναικός, ἡ *woman; wife* (see lesson 8)

παῖς, παιδός, ὁ or ἡ *child (over seven years of age)* (see lesson 8)

ἀδελφός, ἀδελφοῦ, ὁ *brother*

ἀδελφή, ἀδελφῆς, ἡ *sister*

κασίγνητος, κασιγνήτου, ὁ *brother*

κασιγνήτη, κασιγνήτης, ἡ *sister*

πάππος, πάππου, ὁ *grandfather*

τήθη, τήθης, ἡ *grandmother*

υἱός, υἱοῦ, ὁ *son*

θυγατήρ, θυγατρός, ἡ *daughter* (declined like πατήρ, with vocative singular θύγατερ)

ὑϊδοῦς, ὑϊδοῦ, ὁ *grandson*

ὑϊδῆ, ὑϊδῆς, ἡ *granddaughter*

Vocabulary

ἀδελφή, ἀδελφῆς, ἡ *sister*
ἀδελφός, ἀδελφοῦ, ὁ *brother*
Ἀθῆναι, Ἀθηνῶν, αἱ *Athens* (always plural)
γλῶττα, γλώττης, ἡ *tongue, language*
εὔκλεια, εὐκλείας, ἡ *good reputation, glory*
μήτηρ, μητρός, ἡ *mother*
νόμος, νόμου, ὁ *law, custom*
πατήρ, πατρός, ὁ *father*
πολέμιοι, πολεμίων, οἱ *enemy (military)*

(Starting with this lesson, verbs in the vocabularies will be listed with all principal parts. They should be memorized as each verb is introduced, even though they will not all be used immediately. A dash indicates that a verb does not have that particular principal part. The imperfect will be given in parentheses for verbs that begin with a vowel.)

ἄγω, ἄξω, ἤγαγον, ἦχα, ἦγμαι, ἤχθην (imperfect ἦγον) *lead, drive*
γράφω, γράψω, ἔγραψα, γέγραφα, γέγραμμαι, ἐγράφην *write*
εἰμί, ἔσομαι, —, —, —, — (imperfect ἦν; see lesson 7) *be*
ἐθέλω, ἐθελήσω, ἠθέλησα, ἠθέληκα, —, — (imperfect ἤθελον) *want, wish*
λέγω, λέξω, ἔλεξα, εἴρηκα, λέλεγμαι, ἐλέχθην *say, tell*
λύω, λύσω, ἔλυσα, λέλυκα, λέλυμαι, ἐλύθην *set free, loose; destroy*
μανθάνω, μαθήσομαι, ἔμαθον, μεμάθηκα, —, — *learn*
νομίζω, νομιῶ, ἐνόμισα, νενόμικα, νενόμισμαι, ἐνομίσθην *think, believe; believe in, honor*
παιδεύω, παιδεύσω, ἐπαίδευσα, πεπαίδευκα, πεπαίδευμαι, ἐπαιδεύθην *teach, educate*
πέμπω, πέμψω, ἔπεμψα, πέπομφα, πέπεμμαι, ἐπέμφθην *send*
πιστεύω, πιστεύσω, ἐπίστευσα, πεπίστευκα, πεπίστευμαι, ἐπιστεύθην *trust* (+ *dative*)
φέρω, οἴσω, ἤνεγκον, ἐνήνοχα, ἐνήνεγμαι, ἠνέχθην *bear, carry*

αὐτός, αὐτή, αὐτό *same; -self; him, her, it, them*
καινός, καινή, καινόν *new, fresh*

ἀεί *always* (adverb)
εἰς *into* (preposition + *accusative*)
πολλάκις *often* (adverb)
ὡς *as* (conjunction)

Practice

Conjugate five regular Greek verbs fully, in the present, imperfect, and future (indicative and infinitive).

Reading

1. ἀεὶ ἐθέλομεν νομίζειν τοὺς θεούς.
2. αὐτοὶ οἱ σοφοὶ τὰ παιδία εἰς Ἀθήνας οἴσουσιν.
3. πόνος πόνῳ πόνον φέρει. — Sophocles, *Ajax* 866
4. ὁ πόνος πατήρ ἐστι τῆς εὐκλείας.
5. πόνος γάρ, ὡς λέγουσιν, εὐκλείας πατήρ. — Euripides
6. οἱ νόμοι τοὺς ἀνθρώπους ἐπαίδευον.
7. πιστεύομεν τοῖς τῶν φίλων λόγοις.
8. πολλάκις γράφει τὰ αὐτά.
9. πολλάκις γράφει τὰ αὐτὰ ἡ μήτηρ.
10. πολλάκις γὰρ ἔγραφε τὰ αὐτὰ τοῖς παιδίοις ἡ μήτηρ.

Composition

1. Will you write to your sister?
2. They always trust their mother.
3. Do you (plural) trust your friends?
4. We want to trust the gods.
5. I want to send the same gifts to my father.
6. For who will want to learn languages?
7. We often carry useful things (τὰ χρηστά; a word for *things* is rarely expressed in such phrases).
8. The young man was learning the charms of the gods.
9. Glory is a custom for the Athenians.
10. I will carry the new laws into Athens.

Lesson 7

Regular Third-Declension Nouns, Time within Which, Imperfect of εἰμί

1. The third declension includes masculine, feminine, and neuter nouns, whose endings vary according to the *stem*. The stem of a regular third-declension noun can be discovered by removing the -ος ending from the *genitive singular:*
   ἄρχων, ἄρχοντος, ὁ *ruler;* stem: ἀρχοντ-
   ἐλπίς, ἐλπίδος, ἡ *hope;* stem: ἐλπιδ-
Learn the following third-declension paradigms:

κύων, κυνός, ὁ or ἡ *dog*

ὁ κύων	οἱ κύνες
τοῦ κυνός	τῶν κυνῶν
τῷ κυνί	τοῖς κυσί
τὸν κύνα	τοὺς κύνας
κύον	κύνες

ἐλπίς, ἐλπίδος, ἡ *hope*

ἡ ἐλπίς	αἱ ἐλπίδες
τῆς ἐλπίδος	τῶν ἐλπίδων
τῇ ἐλπίδι	ταῖς ἐλπίσι
τὴν ἐλπίδα	τὰς ἐλπίδας
ἐλπί	ἐλπίδες

χάρις, χάριτος, ἡ *favor, grace*

ἡ χάρις	αἱ χάριτες
τῆς χάριτος	τῶν χαρίτων
τῇ χάριτι	ταῖς χάρισι
τὴν χάριν	τὰς χάριτας
χάρι	χάριτες

ποιμήν, ποιμένος, ὁ *shepherd*

ὁ ποιμήν	οἱ ποιμένες
τοῦ ποιμένος	τῶν ποιμένων
τῷ ποιμένι	τοῖς ποιμέσι
τὸν ποιμένα	τοὺς ποιμένας
ποιμήν	ποιμένες

δαίμων, δαίμονος, ὁ *divinity*

ὁ δαίμων	οἱ δαίμονες
τοῦ δαίμονος	τῶν δαιμόνων
τῷ δαίμονι	τοῖς δαίμοσι
τὸν δαίμονα	τοὺς δαίμονας
δαῖμον	δαίμονες

κῆρυξ, κήρυκος, ὁ *messenger*

ὁ κῆρυξ	οἱ κήρυκες
τοῦ κήρυκος	τῶν κηρύκων
τῷ κήρυκι	τοῖς κήρυξι
τὸν κήρυκα	τοὺς κήρυκας
κῆρυξ	κήρυκες

ἄρχων, ἄρχοντος, ὁ *ruler*

ὁ ἄρχων	οἱ ἄρχοντες
τοῦ ἄρχοντος	τῶν ἀρχόντων
τῷ ἄρχοντι	τοῖς ἄρχουσι
τὸν ἄρχοντα	τοὺς ἄρχοντας
ἄρχον	ἄρχοντες

2. *a.* Third-declension oxytones with stems that end in a dental mute (τ, δ, θ) are declined like ἐλπίς, with the accusative singular ending -α added to the stem. See the declension of ἐλπίς above.

  b. Dental-mute stems that are *not* oxytone in the nominative singular are declined like χάρις and drop the dental mute (τ, δ, θ) before adding the accusative singular ending -ν. See the declension of χάρις above.

  c. Third-declension nouns with monosyllabic stems accent the ultima of *genitive* and *dative* (both singular and plural). See the declension of κύων (stem κυν-) above.

d. In the *dative plural,* the ending -σι causes the stem to change according to more-or-less regular patterns that cannot always be predicted for each noun. Study the declensions above. Remember that before a word beginning with a vowel, the dative plural of the third declension has ν-movable:

τοῖς ἄρχουσι γράφουσιν. *They are writing the rulers.*
τοῖς ἄρχουσιν ἔγραφον. *They were writing the rulers.*

e. As with first- and second-declension nouns, third-declension *vocatives* and *nominatives* are often different in the singular but are always identical in the plural. See the declensions above.

3. Learn the *imperfect* conjugation of εἰμί. None of the forms of the imperfect is enclitic, and as with other verbs, there is no separate imperfect infinitive.

ἦν or ἦ *I was*   ἦμεν *we were*
ἦσθα *you were*   ἦτε *you were*
ἦν *he, she, it was*   ἦσαν *they were*

4. The genitive case alone, without a preposition, can be used to express the *time within which* something occurs:

ἄξουσι τοὺς πολίτας εἰς Δελφοὺς ὀκτὼ ἡμερῶν. *They will lead the citizens to Delphi within eight days.*
τῆς νυκτὸς οἱ πολέμιοι ἔλυον τὴν ὁδόν. *During the night the enemy were destroying the road.*

5. The word *thing* (or *things*) is rarely expressed in Greek when modified by an attributive adjective. Instead, the neuter adjective is used alone, with or without a definite article:

τὰ αὐτά *the same things*
καλόν *a fine thing*

6. The infinitive can be used as a verbal noun, equivalent to the gerund in English, and in this use it is called the *articular infinitive.* It is always *neuter singular* and may be accompanied by a definite article:

χαλεπὸν τὸ γράφειν. *Writing is difficult.*

Vocabulary

Ἀγαμέμνων, Ἀγαμέμνονος, ὁ *Agamemnon*
ἄρχων, ἄρχοντος, ὁ *ruler*
δαίμων, δαίμονος, ὁ or ἡ *divinity, divine power; god*
Δελφοί, Δελφῶν, οἱ *Delphi* (always plural)
ἐλπίς, ἐλπίδος, ἡ *hope*
ἡγεμών, ἡγεμόνος, ὁ *leader, commander*
ἡμέρα, ἡμέρας, ἡ *day*
Ἰλιάς, Ἰλιάδος, ἡ *The Iliad*
κῆρυξ, κήρυκος, ὁ *messenger*
κύων, κυνός, ὁ or ἡ *dog*
λαός, λαοῦ, ὁ *people* (often used in the plural)
νύξ, νυκτός, ἡ *night*
Ὅμηρος, Ὁμήρου, ὁ *Homer*
πεδίον, πεδίου, τό *plain*
ποιητής, ποιητοῦ, ὁ *poet*
ποιμήν, ποιμένος, ὁ *shepherd*
πόλεμος, πολέμου, ὁ *war*
σοφία, σοφίας, ἡ *wisdom; skill, cleverness*
χάρις, χάριτος, ἡ *favor, grace*

ἁμαρτάνω, ἁμαρτήσομαι, ἥμαρτον, ἡμάρτηκα, ἡμάρτημαι,
   ἡμαρτήθην (imperfect ἡμάρτανον) *miss; make a mistake*
ἔστιν *it is possible* (+ complementary infinitive)
ἔφη *he, she, it said* (imperfect of φημί; see lesson 24)
ὀνομάζω, ὀνομάσω, ὠνόμασα, ὠνόμακα, ὠνόμασμαι,
   ὠνομάσθην (imperfect ὠνόμαζον) *name, specify; call* something
   such-and-such (+ two *accusatives*)

δίς *twice* (adverb)
ἡμῖν *to us, for us* (see lesson 13)
ὥσπερ *just as* (adverb or conjunction)

Practice

Decline five third-declension nouns fully (singular and plural), with
the appropriate definite article and an attributive adjective.

Reading

1. ὁ ἄρχων Ἀγαμέμνων ποιμὴν ἦν τῶν λαῶν, ὡς ἔφη ὁ Ὅμηρος ἐν τῇ Ἰλιάδι.
2. ὁ ποιητὴς τὸν Ἀγαμέμνονα ὠνόμαζε ποιμένα λαῶν.
3. ἦσαν ποιμένες ἐν τῷ πεδίῳ τῆς νυκτός.
4. τοῖς ἀγαθοῖς ἐστιν ἡ τῶν θεῶν χάρις.
5. τὰ δῶρα οἴσουσιν οἱ κήρυκες εἰς Δελφούς.
6. καλόν ἐστι μανθάνειν.
7. καλόν ἐστι τοῖς ἄρχουσι μανθάνειν σοφά.
8. οὐκ ἔστιν ἐν πολέμῳ δὶς ἁμαρτάνειν. —Plutarch
9. οἱ γὰρ ποιηταὶ ἡμῖν ὥσπερ πατέρες τῆς σοφίας εἰσὶ καὶ ἡγεμόνες. —Plato, *Lysis* 214a

Composition

1. The poets call Agamemnon a good ruler.
2. Hope was a fine thing for the soldiers.
3. Dogs trust the brave shepherds.
4. And shepherds will trust their brave dogs.
5. The night used to destroy (imperfect) our hopes.
6. The messengers lead the new rulers to the divinities.

3. King Lysimachus.

From a copy in the author's collection; photo by Michael Vendl.

*Lysimachus was a general under Alexander the Great and became the king
(βασιλεύς) of Thrace when Alexander died in 323 B.C. This silver tetradrachm was
minted sometime in the late fourth century or early third century B.C. and has the
face of Alexander on the obverse, and on the reverse (shown here), the goddess
Athena (identifiable by her helmet and shield) seated and holding in her hand
the minor goddess Νίκη, or winged Victory, who was usually associated closely
with Athena. The inscription names the source of the coin, the man who issued it:
βασιλέως Λυσιμάχου.*

Lesson 8

Irregular and Neuter Nouns of the Third Declension

1. Learn the declension of the following paradigms, each of which represents a small but important group of nouns:

βασιλεύς, βασιλέως, ὁ *king*

ὁ βασιλεύς	οἱ βασιλεῖς
τοῦ βασιλέως	τῶν βασιλέων
τῷ βασιλεῖ	τοῖς βασιλεῦσι
τὸν βασιλέα	τοὺς βασιλέας
βασιλεῦ	βασιλεῖς

πόλις, πόλεως, ἡ *city, state*

ἡ πόλις	αἱ πόλεις
τῆς πόλεως	τῶν πόλεων
τῇ πόλει	ταῖς πόλεσι
τὴν πόλιν	τὰς πόλεις
πόλι	πόλεις

μάθημα, μαθήματος, τό *lesson*

τὸ μάθημα	τὰ μαθήματα
τοῦ μαθήματος	τῶν μαθημάτων
τῷ μαθήματι	τοῖς μαθήμασι
τὸ μάθημα	τὰ μαθήματα
μάθημα	μαθήματα

ἔτος, ἔτους, τό *year*

τὸ ἔτος	τὰ ἔτη
τοῦ ἔτους	τῶν ἐτῶν
τῷ ἔτει	τοῖς ἔτεσι
τὸ ἔτος	τὰ ἔτη
ἔτος	ἔτη

2. *a.* The accent of the *genitive* of πόλις (singular and plural) violates the rules for accenting words with long ultima. The accent of the singular form became fixed at an early stage,

before a shift took place in the length of the last two syllables, from πόληος to πόλεως, and the accent of the plural was attracted to the antepenult by analogy with the singular: πόλεων.

b. ἔτος is typical of a group of nouns called σ-*stem neuters,* all of which originally had a stem ending in σ: ἐτεσ-. Between two vowels, the -σ- disappeared, and in Attic Greek, the resultant two vowels contracted into a diphthong or long vowel:

> *genitive singular:* ἔτεσ-ος → ἔτε-ος → ἔτους
> *nominative plural:* ἔτεσα → ἔτεα → ἔτη
> *genitive plural:* ἐτέσων → ἐτέων → ἐτῶν

3. Learn the declension of the following nouns:

γυνή, γυναικός, ἡ *woman, wife*

ἡ γυνή	αἱ γυναῖκες
τῆς γυναικός	τῶν γυναικῶν
τῇ γυναικί	ταῖς γυναιξί
τὴν γυναῖκα	τὰς γυναῖκας
γύναι	γυναῖκες

ἀνήρ, ἀνδρός, ὁ *man, husband*

ὁ ἀνήρ	οἱ ἄνδρες
τοῦ ἀνδρός	τῶν ἀνδρῶν
τῷ ἀνδρί	τοῖς ἀνδράσι
τὸν ἄνδρα	τοὺς ἄνδρας
ἄνερ	ἄνδρες

παῖς, παιδός, ὁ or ἡ *child (boy or girl over seven)*

ἡ παῖς	αἱ παῖδες
τῆς παιδός	τῶν παίδων
τῇ παιδί	ταῖς παισί
τὴν παῖδα	τὰς παῖδας
παῖ	παῖδες

Σωκράτης, Σωκράτους, ὁ *Socrates*

> ὁ Σωκράτης
> τοῦ Σωκράτους
> τῷ Σωκράτει
> τὸν Σωκράτη or Σωκράτην
> Σώκρατες

Σοφοκλῆς, Σοφοκλέους, ὁ *Sophocles*
ὁ Σοφοκλῆς
τοῦ Σοφοκλέους
τῷ Σοφοκλεῖ
τὸν Σοφοκλέα
Σοφόκλεις

4. Review the declension of πατήρ, *father,* and μήτηρ, *mother.*

5. The possessor may be expressed by the *dative* case without a preposition, and the thing possessed is the subject of a verb of being:

τῷ Σωκράτει εἰσὶν ἀγαθοὶ φίλοι. *Socrates has good friends* (literally, *good friends exist for Socrates*).

Vocabulary

ἀγάπη, ἀγάπης, ἡ *love, affection*
αἴνιγμα, αἰνίγματος, τό *riddle*
ἀνήρ, ἀνδρός, ὁ *man, husband*
ἀρχή, ἀρχῆς, ἡ *beginning, origin*
βάρος, βάρους, τό *weight*
βασιλεύς, βασιλέως, ὁ *king*
γένεσις, γενέσεως, ἡ *origin, source, creation*
γυνή, γυναικός, ἡ *woman, wife*
δρᾶμα, δράματος, τό *deed, action; drama*
εἶδος, εἴδους, τό *form, shape; (human) figure*
ἔσοπτρον, ἐσόπτρου, τό *mirror*
ἔτος, ἔτους, τό *year*
Εὐριπίδης, Εὐριπίδου, ὁ *Euripides*
ἱερεύς, ἱερέως, ὁ *priest*
κάτοπτρον, κατόπτρου, τό *mirror*
μάθημα, μαθήματος, τό *lesson*
μάθησις, μαθήσεως, ἡ *learning, education*
Οἰδίπους, Οἰδίποδος or Οἰδίπου, ὁ *Oedipus*
οἶνος, οἴνου, ὁ *wine*
ὄψις, ὄψεως, ἡ *appearance; face, countenance*
παῖς, παιδός, ὁ or ἡ *child (over seven years of age)*
πεῖρα, πείρας, ἡ *trial, attempt*

πίστις, πίστεως, ἡ *faith, trust*
ποίησις, ποιήσεως, ἡ *production, creating*
πόλις, πόλεως, ἡ *city, state*
πρᾶξις, πράξεως, ἡ *action, doing*
πρόσωπον, προσώπου, τό *face; mask, dramatic character*
Σοφοκλῆς, Σοφοκλέους, ὁ *Sophocles*
Σφίγξ, Σφιγγός, ἡ *Sphinx (mythical beast, half-bird, half-woman)*
Σωκράτης, Σωκράτους, ὁ *Socrates*
σῶμα, σώματος, τό *body; corpse*
χαλκός, χαλκοῦ, ὁ *copper, bronze; a metal mirror*
χρυσός, χρυσοῦ, ὁ *gold*

βλέπω, βλέψομαι, ἔβλεψα, βέβλεφα, βέβλεμμαι, ἐβλέφθην *see,
  look*
ἔχω, ἕξω or σχήσω, ἔσχον, ἔσχηκα, ἔσχημαι, ἐσχέθην
  (imperfect εἶχον) *have, hold*
μένω, μενῶ, ἔμεινα, μεμένηκα, —, — *remain, stay*

δίπους, δίπουν *two-footed*
μέγιστος, μεγίστη, μέγιστον *very large, very great* (see
  lesson 10)
μείζων *greater* (feminine nominative singular—see lesson 10)
τετράπους, τετράπουν *four-footed*
τούτων *of these* (feminine genitive plural—see lesson 11)
τρία *three (things)* (neuter nominative plural—see Appendix B)
τρίπους, τρίπουν *three-footed*

ἄρτι *just now, right now* (adverb)
δέ *and; but* (postpositive conjunction)
διά *through, by means of* (preposition + *genitive*)
νῦν *now* (adverb)
τοι *let me tell you* (enclitic particle, indicating an impression
  frequently conveyed in English by emphasis or tone rather than
  by separate words; usually introduces a general sentiment or
  maxim; postpositive)
τότε *then, at that time* (adverb)

Practice

Decline ten nouns fully (singular and plural) from the vocabulary of
this lesson, with the appropriate definite article.

Reading

1. τὰς γνώμας οὐ γράψομεν.
2. τὰς τῶν ποιητῶν γνώμας οὐκ ἐμανθάνομεν.
3. πεῖρά ἐστιν ἡ ἀρχή.
4. πεῖρά τοι μαθήσεως ἀρχή. — Alcman
5. ἔβλεπε τὰ πρόσωπα ὁ Σοφοκλῆς.
6. νῦν βλέπει τὰ τοῦ δράματος πρόσωπα ὁ Εὐριπίδης.
7. τότε ὁ Οἰδίπους ἐμάνθανε τὸ τῆς Σφιγγὸς αἴνιγμα· Τί ἐστι τὸ αὐτὸ τετράπουν καὶ δίπουν καὶ τρίπουν;
8. ἔχει μέγιστον βάρος ὁ χρυσός.
9. ὁ τῶν σοφῶν νοῦς, ὥσπερ χρυσός, βάρος ἔχει μέγιστον. — Demophilus
10. κάτοπτρον εἴδους χαλκός ἐστ', οἶνος δὲ νοῦ. — Aeschylus
11. οὐ βλέπετε τοὺς κύνας ἐν τῇ πόλει;
12. οἱ γὰρ κύνες οὐ μένουσιν ἐν ταῖς Ἀθήναις.
13. ὁ βίος πρᾶξις, οὐ ποίησις. — Aristotle, *Politics* 1254a7
14. ὡς ἐν σώματι ὄψις, ἐν ψυχῇ νοῦς. — Aristotle, *Nicomachean Ethics* 1096b30
15. βλέπομεν γὰρ ἄρτι διὰ ἐσόπτρου ἐν αἰνίγματι, τότε δὲ πρόσωπον πρὸς πρόσωπον. μένει δὲ τρία· πίστις, ἐλπὶς, ἀγάπη. μείζων δὲ τούτων ἡ ἀγάπη. — Saint Paul, First Letter to the Corinthians (abridged)

Composition

1. The king trusts his wife in the city.
2. Sophocles teaches the citizens through his dramas.
3. The riddle is strange to the men and the women.
4. We do not see our children in the mirror right now.
5. What is the lesson of the play (drama)?
6. We want to see our boy in a new play.

Lesson 9

First and Second Aorist of Regular Verbs, Infinitive in Indirect Statement

1. The *aorist* tense is the tense of simple action in the past in Greek. In the indicative mood, it is equivalent to the French simple past or Spanish preterite tenses. The terms *first* and *second* refer to different forms, not different tenses, and are used to classify different sets of conjugational spellings in this tense.

2. The first-person singular, aorist indicative active is the *third principal part* of regular Greek verbs, and it must be learned for each verb. It cannot be predicted from any other principal part.

3. Learn the *first aorist indicative active* of λύω and νομίζω below. As in the imperfect tense, the aorist indicative has an *augment:* usually the syllable ἐ- prefixed to the aorist stem; or, for verbs whose aorist stem begins with a vowel, the augment consists of a lengthening of that vowel. The personal endings of the first aorist indicative active are as follows:

-α	-αμεν
-ας	-ατε
-ε(ν)	-αν

These endings are added to the *augmented* aorist stem of verbs with a first aorist conjugation. The stem is the *unaugmented* third principal part, with the final -α removed:

ἐνόμισα: aorist stem, νομισ-
ἔμεινα: aorist stem, μειν-
ἔλυσα: aorist stem, λυσ-

ἔλυσα *I destroyed*
ἔλυσας *you destroyed*
ἔλυσε *he, she, it destroyed*

ἐλύσαμεν *we destroyed*
ἐλύσατε *you destroyed*
ἔλυσαν *they destroyed*

ἐνόμισα *I thought*
ἐνόμισας *you thought*
ἐνόμισε *he, she, it thought*

ἐνομίσαμεν *we thought*
ἐνομίσατε *you thought*
ἐνόμισαν *they thought*

4. Most first aorists have a stem ending in -σ, but many others end in a liquid (λ, μ, ν, or ρ) and are thus called *liquid first aorists*. They are conjugated in the same way:

ἔμεινα *I stayed*
ἔμεινας *you stayed*
ἔμεινε *he, she, it stayed*

ἐμείναμεν *we stayed*
ἐμείνατε *you stayed*
ἔμειναν *they stayed*

5. The first aorist *infinitive* active is formed by adding -αι to the *unaugmented* aorist stem. The accent is always on the penult:

        λῦσαι *to destroy*   νομίσαι *to think*
        μεῖναι *to remain*   παιδεῦσαι *to teach*

The infinitive does not always keep its *time* in Greek; more often it keeps its *aspect*. So a present infinitive often indicates a continuous or progressive action or state, while an aorist infinitive indicates a single act:

ἐθέλω βλέπειν τὴν πόλιν. *I want to see, keep seeing, the city.*
ἐθέλω βλέψαι τὴν πόλιν. *I want to (take one) look at the city.*

6. The *second aorist* conjugation is formed by adding the *imperfect* endings to the *augmented* second aorist stem. The stem is the *unaugmented* third principal part, with the final -ον removed:

ἤνεγκον: aorist stem, ἐνεγκ-
ἔμαθον: aorist stem, μαθ-
ἤγαγον: aorist stem, ἀγαγ-

Some verbs have a first aorist; some have a second aorist. Which ones have which must be learned from the vocabulary entry. If the third principal part ends in -α, the verb has a first aorist; if it ends in -ον, it has a second aorist.

Learn the *second aorist indicative active* of φέρω and μανθάνω below:

ἤνεγκον *I carried*   ἔμαθον *I learned*
ἤνεγκες *you carried*   ἔμαθες *you learned*
ἤνεγκε *he, she, it carried*   ἔμαθε *he, she, it learned*

ἠνέγκομεν *we carried*   ἐμάθομεν *we learned*
ἠνέγκετε *you carried*   ἐμάθετε *you learned*
ἤνεγκον *they carried*   ἔμαθον *they learned*

Confusion between the imperfect and second aorist tenses in Greek can be avoided because, although the endings are identical, the *stems* of the two are always different:

ἐμανθάνομεν *we were learning, used to learn*
ἐμάθομεν *we learned*

7. The second aorist *infinitive* active is formed by adding -εῖν to the unaugmented second aorist stem. The accent is always perispomenon:

ἐνεγκεῖν *to carry*
μαθεῖν *to learn*
ἀγαγεῖν *to lead, to drive*

8. Certain words of *saying* and *thinking,* such as λέγω, ἔφη, and νομίζω, govern an *indirect statement* construction in which the *subject* of the indirect statement is *accusative,* and the *verb* of the indirect statement is *infinitive.* This pattern for indirect statement is sometimes called the *accusative/infinitive construction.* Study the examples below.

ὁ βασιλεὺς πιστεύσει τῷ κήρυκι. *The king will trust his herald.* (direct statement)

ἔλεγον τὸν βασιλέα πιστεύσειν τῷ κήρυκι. *They used to say that the king would trust his herald.*
νομίζομεν τὸν βασιλέα πιστεύσειν τῷ κήρυκι. *We think that the king will trust his herald.*
ἔφη τὸν βασιλέα πιστεύσειν τῷ κήρυκι. *He said that the king would trust his herald.*

Notice that the *tense* of the original verb is kept in the indirect statement: if the direct statement was future, the infinitive will be future; if it was present, the infinitive will be present, *regardless of the tense of the introductory verb* (ἔλεγον, νομίζομεν, etc.).

Notice also that only the *subject, its predicate modifiers,* and the *verb* of the direct statement are changed in the indirect statement; direct and indirect objects, prepositional phrases, adverbial modifiers, all remain unchanged.

If the subject of the introductory verb and the subject of the indirect statement are the same, the accusative is not used; instead, the subject remains nominative and only the original verb is changed (to the infinitive of its original tense):

ὁ βασιλεὺς Ἀθηναῖός ἐστιν. *The king is an Athenian.*
ἔφη ὁ βασιλεὺς Ἀθηναῖος εἶναι. *The king said that he was an Athenian.*

9. Learn the conjugation of οἶδα, *I know.* It is really a *perfect* tense conjugation of the verb εἴδω, *I see,* but it is used as the *present* tense of the verb *know* (*I have seen; therefore, I know*).

οἶδα *I know*
οἶσθα *you know*
οἶδε(ν) *he, she, it knows*

ἴσμεν *we know*
ἴστε *you know*
ἴσασι *they know*

εἰδέναι *to know* (infinitive)

10. The *genitive* case is used, alone or with the preposition ἐκ (ἐξ before vowels), to indicate the *origin* of a thing:

ἔμαθον δὲ τοῦ πατρὸς πάντα. *And I learned everything from my father.*

Vocabulary

αἰών, αἰῶνος, ὁ *a person's lifetime; an age, epoch*
θάνατος, θανάτου, ὁ *death*
θησαυρός, θησαυροῦ, ὁ *treasure-house, treasury*
μορφή, μορφῆς, ἡ *shape, form*
ὄνομα, ὀνόματος, τό *name*
οὔνομα, οὐνόματος, τό *poetic spelling of* ὄνομα
τέλος, τέλους, τό *fulfillment, completion, end*
τόλμα, τόλμης, ἡ *courage, nerve, boldness*
τύχη, τύχης, ἡ *luck, fortune*
ὕπνος, ὕπνου, ὁ *sleep*
φύσις, φύσεως, ἡ *nature, character*

ἀμείβω, ἀμείψω, ἤμειψα, —, ἤμειμμαι, ἠμείφθην (imperfect
  ἤμειβον) *change, alter*
βάλλω, βαλῶ, ἔβαλον, βέβληκα, βέβλημαι, ἐβλήθην *throw,*
  cast, hurl
ἐκβάλλω, ἐκβαλῶ, ἐξέβαλον, ἐκβέβληκα, ἐκβέβλημαι,
  ἐξεβλήθην *throw out; cast aside; produce*
οἶδα *know; know how to* (+ complementary *infinitive*)

δολιχός, δολιχή, δολιχόν *long*
κύριος, κυρία, κύριον *authoritative, supreme; having authority or*
  power over something (+ *genitive*)
μικρός, μικρά, μικρόν *small*
πάντα *every(thing)* (neuter accusative plural—see lesson 14)
πονηρός, πονηρά, πονηρόν *wicked, evil*

ἐκ (ἐξ before vowels) *out of, from* (preposition + *genitive*)
ἠδέ *and* (poetic word, = καί)
καί *also, even, merely* (adverb)

Practice

Conjugate five regular verbs fully, in the present, future, imperfect,
and aorist, indicative and infinitive.

Reading

1. καὶ οἱ μικροὶ νόμοι τοὺς ἀνθρώπους παιδεύουσιν.
2. ἔφη καὶ τοὺς μικροὺς νόμους τοὺς ἀνθρώπους παιδεύειν.
3. καλόν ἐστι χρηστοὺς φίλους ἔχειν.
4. νομίζουσιν οἱ ἄνθρωποι καλὸν εἶναι χρηστοὺς φίλους ἔχειν.
5. νομίζετε τὸν θάνατον κακὸν εἶναι τοῖς ἀνθρώποις;
6. ἡ τόλμα ἀρχή ἐστιν.
7. τόλμα πράξεως ἀρχή, τύχη δὲ τέλους κυρία. — Democritus
8. ὁ θάνατος ὕπνος ἐστίν.
9. οἱ σοφοὶ νομίζουσι τὸν θάνατον ὕπνον εἶναι.
10. ἔφη τοὺς σοφοὺς νομίζειν τὸν θάνατον ὕπνον εἶναι.
11. χάρις χάριν φέρει.
12. ὁ ἀγαθὸς ἄνθρωπος ἐκ τοῦ ἀγαθοῦ θησαυροῦ ἐκβάλλει ἀγαθά· καὶ ὁ πονηρὸς ἄνθρωπος ἐκ τοῦ πονηροῦ θησαυροῦ ἐκβάλλει πονηρά. — Saint Matthew xii.35
13. ἡ γυνὴ καλή ἐστιν.
14. ὁ βασιλεὺς τὴν γυναῖκα καλὴν εἶναι νομίζει.
15. ἔφη τὸν βασιλέα τὴν γυναῖκα καλὴν εἶναι νομίζειν.
16. αἰὼν πάντα φέρει· δολιχὸς χρόνος οἶδεν ἀμείβειν
οὔνομα καὶ μορφὴν καὶ φύσιν ἠδὲ τύχην. — Plato

Composition

1. Sleep is beautiful.
2. The shepherds think that sleep is evil.
3. I will not change my nature.
4. Mother knows everything.
5. She said that mother knew everything.
6. Mother said that she (mother) knew everything.
7. We used to think that luck was a small (thing).

4. Menander.

From a copy of a Hellenistic double herm of Aristophanes and Menander in the H. W. Sage Collection of Casts of Ancient Sculpture at Cornell University; photo by Andrew Gillis.

Born in Athens around 342 B.C., Menander wrote and produced over a hundred comic plays, of which several fragments and only one complete play, Δύσκολος [The Grouch], survive. The Latin playwrights Plautus and Terence translated and adapted several of Menander's plays for Roman audiences, and some of their Latin adaptations have also survived (for example, Plautus' Bacchides, *Terence's* Brothers *and* The Eunuch). *His plays were situation comedies, almost always involving young lovers who ended up happily married.*

Lesson 10

Comparative and Superlative Adjectives and Adverbs

1. As in English, there are three *degrees* to the Greek adjective and adverb: *positive, comparative,* and *superlative:*

   σοφός *wise*   σοφῶς *wisely*
   σοφώτερος *wiser*   σοφώτερον *more wisely*
   σοφώτατος *wisest*   σοφώτατα *most wisely*

2. The adjectives σοφός and πονηρός have a so-called regular comparison; that is, in the comparative degree, they add -ότερος or -ώτερος to the stem of the positive degree; and in the superlative, they add -ότατος or -ώτατος to the positive stem. The positive stem is the first principal part of the adjective, with -ος removed. If the last syllable of the positive stem is *long,* the comparative and superlative endings beginning with -ο are used; if the last syllable of the positive stem is *short,* the endings beginning with -ω are used:

   σοφός, positive stem σοφ-: σοφώτερος, σοφώτατος
   πονηρός, positive stem πονηρ-: πονηρότερος,
   πονηρότατος

3. Learn the declension of σοφώτερος, *wiser,* and σοφώτατος, *wisest, very wise.* All regular adjectives are declined like this, unless the last syllable of the positive stem is long, in which case -ο- is substituted for -ω- as the first letter of the ending.

σοφώτερος	σοφωτέρα	σοφώτερον
σοφωτέρου	σοφωτέρας	σοφωτέρου
σοφωτέρῳ	σοφωτέρᾳ	σοφωτέρῳ
σοφώτερον	σοφωτέραν	σοφώτερον
σοφώτεροι	σοφώτεραι	σοφώτερα
σοφωτέρων	σοφωτέρων	σοφωτέρων
σοφωτέροις	σοφωτέραις	σοφωτέροις
σοφωτέρους	σοφωτέρας	σοφώτερα

σοφώτατος	σοφωτάτη	σοφώτατον
σοφωτάτου	σοφωτάτης	σοφωτάτου
σοφωτάτῳ	σοφωτάτη	σοφωτάτῳ
σοφώτατον	σοφωτάτην	σοφώτατον
σοφώτατοι	σοφώταται	σοφώτατα
σοφωτάτων	σοφωτάτων	σοφωτάτων
σοφωτάτοις	σοφωτάταις	σοφωτάτοις
σοφωτάτους	σοφωτάτας	σοφώτατα

4. Many adjectives have a so-called irregular comparison, with comparatives ending in -ων and superlatives ending in -ιστος. Many, though not all, of these adjectives also use a different stem for each of the three degrees. These declensions have *recessive,* not persistent, accent in the comparative and superlative. Learn the declension of ἀμείνων, *better,* and review the declension of ἄριστος, *best* (lesson 3):

masculine/feminine	*neuter*
ἀμείνων	ἄμεινον
ἀμείνονος	ἀμείνονος
ἀμείνονι	ἀμείνονι
ἀμείνονα or ἀμείνω	ἄμεινον
ἀμείνονες or ἀμείνους	ἀμείνονα or ἀμείνω
ἀμεινόνων	ἀμεινόνων
ἀμείνοσι	ἀμείνοσι
ἀμείνονας or ἀμείνους	ἀμείνονα or ἀμείνω

5. Learn and practice the three degrees of the following adjectives:
   ἀγαθός *good, brave:* ἀμείνων, ἄμεινον
      ἄριστος, ἀρίστη, ἄριστον
   ἀγαθός *good, noble:* βελτίων, βέλτιον
      βέλτιστος, βελτίστη, βέλτιστον
   ἀγαθός *good, strong:* κρείττων, κρεῖττον
      κράτιστος, κρατίστη, κράτιστον
   δίκαιος *just:* (regular comparison)
   κακός *bad, evil:* κακίων, κάκιον
      κάκιστος, κακίστη, κάκιστον
   καλός *good, pretty:* καλλίων, κάλλιον
      κάλλιστος, καλλίστη, κάλλιστον

μέγας *big, great* (see lesson 14): μείζων, μεῖζον
    μέγιστος, μεγίστη, μέγιστον
μικρός *small:* ἐλάττων, ἔλαττον
    ἐλάχιστος, ἐλαχίστη, ἐλάχιστον
νέος *new, young:* (regular comparison)
πονηρός *evil, wicked:* (regular comparison)
ῥᾴδιος *easy:* ῥᾴων, ῥᾷον
    ῥᾷστος, ῥᾴστη, ῥᾷστον
φίλος *dear, beloved:* φιλίων, φίλιον
    φίλτατος, φιλτάτη, φίλτατον

6. The positive degree of regular adverbs is formed by changing the
   final -ν of the *masculine genitive plural* adjective to -ς:
       κακῶν *bad* → κακῶς *badly*
       σοφῶν *wise* → σοφῶς *wisely*
       δικαίων *just* → δικαίως *justly*

7. The comparative adverb is the *neuter accusative singular* of the
   comparative adjective; the superlative adverb is the *neuter accusative plural* of the superlative adjective:

ἄμεινον *more bravely*	ἄριστα *most bravely*
σοφώτερον *more wisely*	σοφώτατα *most wisely*
δικαιότερον *more justly*	δικαιότατα *most justly*

8. The second member of an unequal comparison may be introduced two different ways: either by the conjunction ἤ, *than,*
   or with no conjunction at all. If ἤ is used, the second member
   of the comparison is in the *same case* as the first member; if *no*
   conjunction is used, the second member is in the *genitive case.*
   This use of the genitive is called *genitive of unequal comparison.*
       οὐκ οἶδα κρείττονα ἄνδρα ἤ τὸν τύραννον. *I do not know
   a stronger man than the king.*
       οὐκ οἶδα κρείττονα ἄνδρα τοῦ τυράννου. *I do not know a
   stronger man than the king.*

9. The *degree of difference* in an unequal comparison is expressed
   by the *dative case* alone, without a preposition:
       κεφαλῇ ἐλάττων *a head shorter (shorter by a head)*
       μακρῷ ἄριστα *the best by far*

10. Sometimes the comparative degree of the adjective or adverb has the force of *too* or *rather.* Sometimes the superlative degree is best translated by *very.*

> μείζων ἦν ὁ θυμός, ἔλαττον δὲ τὸ σῶμα. *His spirit was too great, and his body too small.*
> ὁ πατὴρ σοφώτατος ἀνήρ. *My father is a very wise man.*

11. The *genitive of distinction* is used with verbs meaning *to differ:*

> ἄρχων ἀγαθὸς οὐ διαφέρει πατρὸς ἀγαθοῦ. *A good ruler is not different from a good father.*

Vocabulary

ἄνθος, ἄνθους, τό *blossom, bloom; flower* (poetic nominative/accusative plural ἄνθεα)

δημοκρατία, δημοκρατίας, ἡ *democracy*

ἥμισυ, ἡμίσεος, τό *half* (from adjective ἥμισυς — see lesson 16)

κτῆμα, κτήματος, τό *possession*

μελέτη, μελέτης, ἡ *practice, exercise; habit*

πενία, πενίας, ἡ *poverty*

πῦρ, πυρός, τό *fire* (singular only; no plural in use)

τυραννίς, τυραννίδος, ἡ *tyranny*

τύραννος, τυράννου, ὁ *king; tyrant, absolute ruler*

ὕδωρ, ὕδατος, τό *water*

ὕμνος, ὕμνου, ὁ *hymn of praise, ode*

φροντίς, φροντίδος, ἡ *thought, reflection, speculation*

αἴνει *praise* (imperative, second-person singular — see lesson 24)

ἄρχω, ἄρξω, ἦρξα, ἦρχα, ἦργμαι, ἤρχθην (imperfect ἦρχον) *rule, govern* (usually + *genitive*); *begin* (in middle voice — see lesson 19)

διαφέρειν *are different from* (+ *genitive*; subject is τοὺς εὐδαίμονας)

φασι *they say* (present of φημί; enclitic; see lesson 23)

χρή *it is necessary (that)* (impersonal verb + *accusative/infinitive* complement)

ἄθλιος, ἀθλία, ἄθλιον *struggling, wretched, miserable*

ἀμείνων, ἄμεινον *better, braver*

ἀναγκαῖος, ἀναγκαία, ἀναγκαῖον *necessary, indispensable*
βέλτιστος, βελτίστη, βέλτιστον *best, most noble*
βελτίων, βέλτιον *better, nobler*
δεύτερος, δευτέρα, δεύτερον *second*
διάδηλος, διάδηλον *distinguishable*
δίκαιος, δικαία, δίκαιον *just*
ἐλάττων, ἔλαττον *smaller; less; worse*
ἐλάχιστος, ἐλαχίστη, ἐλάχιστον *smallest; least; worst*
εὐδαίμων, εὔδαιμον *blessed, fortunate; happy* (declined like
    ἀμείνων)
κάκιστος, κακίστη, κάκιστον *worst, most evil*
κακίων, κάκιον *worse, more evil*
κάλλιστος, καλλίστη, κάλλιστον *most beautiful; best*
καλλίων, κάλλιον *more beautiful; better*
κράτιστος, κρατίστη, κράτιστον *strongest; best*
κρείττων, κρεῖττον *stronger; better*
μέγας *big, large, great* (see lesson 14)
μέγιστος, μεγίστη, μέγιστον *largest, greatest*
μείζων, μεῖζον *larger, greater*
νέος, νέα, νέον *new, young*
οἰκεῖος, οἰκεία, οἰκεῖον *kindred; dear; personal, one's own*
παλαιός, παλαιά, παλαιόν *old, aged; ancient*
πάντων *all* (masculine genitive plural of πᾶς; see lesson 14)
πλείων, πλεῖον *more* (comparative of πολύς; see lesson 14)
ῥᾴδιος, ῥᾳδία, ῥᾴδιον *easy*
ῥᾷστος, ῥᾴστη, ῥᾷστον *easiest*
ῥᾴων, ῥᾷον *easier*
συγγενές *akin;* (as abstract noun) *kinship* (from adjective
    συγγενής—see lesson 16)
συμπαθής *sympathetic* (feminine nominative singular—see
    lesson 16)
φιλίων, φίλιον *dearer, more beloved*
φίλτατος, φιλτάτη, φίλτατον *dearest, most beloved*

εὖ *well* (adverb of ἀγαθός)
ἥκιστα *least* (adverb)
κἄν = καὶ ἐν
κατά (elided to κατ᾽ before a smooth, καθ᾽ before a rough breath-
    ing) *down into; by; against* (+ *genitive* objects); *throughout;*
    in; during (+ *accusative* objects) (preposition)

λίαν *too much, too; very* (adverb)
μεγάλως *largely, greatly* (adverb)
μέν . . . δέ *on the one hand* . . . *on the other hand* (particles, both
    postpositive, used to indicate contrast or opposition between two
    phrases or clauses)
ὅθεν *whence, from where; for which reason* (relative adverb)
οὐδέ *and not; nor* (conjunction); *not even* (adverb)
πως *somehow; in some way* (enclitic, postpositive adverb)
ὡς (+ superlative adjective or adverb) *as . . . as possible*

Practice

Form adverbs, positive, comparative, and superlative, from the
following adjectives (see pars. 6 and 7 above):

1. φίλος   5. καλός
2. ἀγαθός *brave* (positive εὖ)   6. πονηρός
3. μικρός   7. δίκαιος
4. μέγας (positive μεγάλως)   8. νέος

Reading

1. οὐκ ἔστι πενίας οὐδὲν μεῖζον κακόν.
2. πονηρότατα τῶν πολιτῶν ἦρχεν ὁ τύραννος.
3. σοφὸς Σοφοκλῆς, σοφώτερος δ᾽ Εὐριπίδης,
    ἀνδρῶν δὲ πάντων Σωκράτης σοφώτατος.
4. τί ἐστι τὸ ἄριστον κτῆμα ἀνδρί;
5. ἄριστον ἀνδρὶ κτῆμα συμπαθὴς γυνή. — Hippothoon
6. τί ἐστιν ἡ ἀρχὴ τῶν κακῶν;
7. ἀρχὴ μεγίστη τῶν ἐν ἀνθρώποις κακῶν
    ἀγαθά, τά λίαν ἀγαθά. — Menander
8. οὐ βελτίστη ἡ τυραννίς, οὐδὲ ῥᾴστη ἡ δημοκρατία.
9. πυρὸς καὶ ὕδατος ὁ φίλος ἀναγκαιότερος. — Plutarch
10. ἐνόμιζεν ὁ Σωκράτης τὸν θάνατον βελτίονα εἶναι τοῦ
    πονηροῦ βίου.
11. νεώτερος τῆς ἀδελφῆς εἰμι.
12. ἐλάττω ἔφη τὸν πατέρα εἶναι ἢ τὴν μητέρα.

13. τὸ συγγενὲς γὰρ δεινόν, ἔν τε τοῖς κακοῖς
    οὐκ ἔστιν οὐδὲν κρεῖττον οἰκείου φίλου.—Euripides,
    Andromache 985–6
14. ὁ κύων τοῖς ἀνδράσι φίλτατός ἐστιν.
15. ἐκ τίνος εἰσὶν ἀγαθοὶ οἱ ἄνθρωποι;
16. ἐκ μελέτης πλείους ἢ φύσεως ἀγαθοί.—Critias
17. σοφωτέρους γὰρ χρὴ βροτῶν εἶναι θεούς.—Euripides,
    Hippolytus 120
18. κἂν βροτοῖς
    αἱ δεύτεραί πως φροντίδες σοφώτεραι.—Euripides,
    Hippolytus 435–6
19. αἴνει δὲ παλαιὸν μὲν οἶνον, ἄνθεα δ' ὕμνων
    νεωτέρων.—Pindar, *Olympian Ode* 9. 48–9
20. ὁ ἀγαθὸς καὶ κακὸς ἥκιστα διάδηλοι καθ' ὕπνον, ὅθεν
    φασὶν οὐδὲν διαφέρειν τὸ ἥμισυ τοῦ βίου τοὺς εὐδαίμονας
    τῶν ἀθλίων.—Aristotle, *Nicomachean Ethics* 1102b5

Composition

(Write each comparison two different ways; see par. 8 above.)
1. The mother is more beautiful than the child.
2. He said that tyranny was the worst (thing) for the Athenians.
3. A just woman always speaks very wisely.
4. Nothing is more beloved than a young dog.
5. The king is younger by far than his wife.

Lesson 11

Demonstratives, Relative Pronoun, Indirect Statement with ὅτι or ὡς

1. Learn the declension of οὗτος, αὕτη, τοῦτο, *this, these:*

οὗτος	αὕτη	τοῦτο
τούτου	ταύτης	τούτου
τούτῳ	ταύτῃ	τούτῳ
τοῦτον	ταύτην	τοῦτο
οὗτοι	αὗται	ταῦτα
τούτων	τούτων	τούτων
τούτοις	ταύταις	τούτοις
τούτους	ταύτας	ταῦτα

2. Learn the declension of ἐκεῖνος, ἐκείνη, ἐκεῖνο, *that, those:*

ἐκεῖνος	ἐκείνη	ἐκεῖνο
ἐκείνου	ἐκείνης	ἐκείνου
ἐκείνῳ	ἐκείνῃ	ἐκείνῳ
ἐκεῖνον	ἐκείνην	ἐκεῖνο
ἐκεῖνοι	ἐκεῖναι	ἐκεῖνα
ἐκείνων	ἐκείνων	ἐκείνων
ἐκείνοις	ἐκείναις	ἐκείνοις
ἐκείνους	ἐκείνας	ἐκεῖνα

3. Learn the declension of ὅδε, ἥδε, τόδε, *this/that, these/those:*

ὅδε	ἥδε	τόδε
τοῦδε	τῆσδε	τοῦδε
τῷδε	τῇδε	τῷδε
τόνδε	τήνδε	τόδε
οἵδε	αἵδε	τάδε
τῶνδε	τῶνδε	τῶνδε
τοῖσδε	ταῖσδε	τοῖσδε
τούσδε	τάσδε	τάδε

4. All three demonstrative words may be used alone as *pronouns,* or they may be used as *adjectives* to modify nouns directly. When they are used as adjectives, they occupy the *predicate position:*

τῷδε τῷ βασιλεῖ πιστεύομεν. *We trust that king.*
κακά ἐστι τὰ φάρμακα ταῦτα. *These drugs are harmful.*

5. ὅδε is a weaker demonstrative than either οὗτος or ἐκεῖνος and is formed by adding the *enclitic suffix* -δε (to be distinguished from the conjunction δέ, which is *not* enclitic) to the *definite article:*

ὁ + δε = ὅδε   τοῦ + δε = τοῦδε
αἱ + δε = αἵδε   ταῖς + δε = ταῖσδε

6. οὗτος often points *backward,* while ὅδε often points *forward;* so when forms of these two demonstratives are contrasted, they often mean more than simply *this* or *that:*

ἐνόμιζε δὲ ταῦτα· ἀλλὰ τάδε ἔλεξεν. *And he was thinking this (these things, just mentioned); but he said this (these things, the following things).*

7. When οὗτος and ἐκεῖνος are contrasted after a list of two or more persons or things, οὗτος often means *the latter* (i.e., the nearer, the one most recently mentioned), while ἐκεῖνος often means *the former* (i.e., the one farthest away).

8. Learn the declension of ὅς, ἥ, ὅ, the relative pronoun *who, which, that:*

ὅς	ἥ	ὅ
οὗ	ἧς	οὗ
ᾧ	ᾗ	ᾧ
ὅν	ἥν	ὅ
οἵ	αἵ	ἅ
ὧν	ὧν	ὧν
οἷς	αἷς	οἷς
οὕς	ἅς	ἅ

The relative pronoun agrees with its *antecedent* only in *gender* and *number;* its *case* is determined by the syntax of its own clause, although a relative pronoun that would normally stand in the *accusative* is often attracted into the case of its antecedent if the antecedent is *genitive* or *dative.* A demonstrative antecedent is often omitted (understood), as occasionally in English:

μικρὰ ἦν ἡ πόλις ἣν ἐλύσαμεν. *The city that we destroyed was small.*

πιστεύομεν τῷ φίλῳ ᾧ βλέπομεν (for ὃν βλέπομεν). *We trust the friend whom we see.*

ὃν οἱ θεοὶ φιλοῦσιν ἀποθνῄσκει νέος (for οὗτος ὃν . . .). *(He) whom the gods love dies young.*

9. λέγω and several similar verbs also introduce indirect statement with the conjunctions ὅτι or ὡς, *that,* with the subject and verb of the indirect statement unchanged from their original (direct) forms. Compare the accusative/infinitive construction:

ἡ μήτηρ ἀγαθή ἐστιν. *My mother is brave.*

ἐνόμιζε τὴν μητέρα ἀγαθὴν εἶναι. *He thought that his mother was brave.*

ἔλεγεν ὅτι ἡ μήτηρ ἀγαθή ἐστιν. *He said that his mother was brave.*

10. The *dative* case alone can be used to express the *means* or *instrument* by which something is done:

ἔβαλλον ἐμὲ τοῖς λίθοις. *They hit me with stones.*

τὴν πόλιν εἷλε τῇ μαχαίρᾳ. *He captured the city with his sword.*

Vocabulary

ἄνεμος, ἀνέμου, ὁ *wind*
θάλαττα, θαλάττης, ἡ *sea*
κακόν, κακοῦ, τό *trouble, problem*
λόγος (ἐστί) = λέγουσι (+ *accusative/infinitive*)
πολυπραγμοσύνη, πολυπραγμοσύνης, ἡ *curiosity, inquisitiveness*
πτερόν, πτεροῦ, τό *feather* (usually in plural)

φιλομάθεια, φιλομαθείας, ἡ *love of learning or knowing*
  (+ objective *genitive*)

ἀποθνῇσκω, ἀποθανοῦμαι, ἀπέθανον, τέθνηκα, —, — (imperfect
  ἀπέθνῃσκον) *die*
ἀποτυγχάνειν *to lose* (present infinitive)
θαυμάζω, θαυμάσομαι, ἐθαύμασα, τεθαύμακα, τεθαύμασμαι,
  ἐθαυμάσθην *wonder, marvel (at)*
λέγοντες *saying* (masculine nominative plural participle—see
  lesson 14)
πείθω, πείσω, ἔπεισα, πέπεικα and πέποιθα, πέπεισμαι,
  ἐπείσθην *persuade;* (middle voice) *obey* (+ *dative*)
ὑπακούω, ὑπακούσομαι, ὑπήκουσα, —, —, — (imperfect
  ὑπήκουον) *listen to, obey* (+ *genitive* or *dative*)
φιλῆσαι *to fall in love* (aorist infinitive—see lesson 13)
φιλοῦντα *being in love, when one is in love* (masculine accusative
  singular participle—see lesson 14)

ἀλλότριος, ἀλλοτρία, ἀλλότριον *someone else's*
ἐκεῖνος, ἐκείνη, ἐκεῖνο *that, those; the former*
ἐμός, ἐμή, ἐμόν *my, mine*
μυρίος, μυρία, μυρίον *numberless, countless, infinite*
ὅδε, ἥδε, τόδε *this/that, these/those; the following*
οὗτος, αὕτη, τοῦτο *this, these; the latter, foregoing*
πάντων *everything* (neuter genitive plural of πᾶς; see lesson 14)

ἀλλά *but* (conjunction)
μή *no, not* (the negative of *will* and *thought,* as οὐ is the negative
  of *fact* and *statement;* μή is usually used to negate the *imperative*
  mood, the dependent *subjunctive* and *optative* moods, and the
  infinitive, except in indirect statement)
μοι *to me, for me* (dative personal pronoun, enclitic; see lesson 13)
ὅς, ἥ, ὅ *who, which, that* (relative pronoun)
ὅτι *that* (conjunction)
ὡς *that* (conjunction)

Practice

1. Decline three nouns, one from each gender, fully (singular and plural) with the appropriate definitive article and the demonstrative adjective οὗτος, αὕτη, τοῦτο.
2. Do the same with three different nouns and the demonstrative adjective ὅδε, ἥδε, τόδε.
3. Do the same with three different nouns and the demonstrative adjective ἐκεῖνος, ἐκείνη, ἐκεῖνο.
4. Rewrite page 53, sentences 2, 10, and 15, using λέγω ὅτι instead of ἔφη.

Reading

1. οἱ δὲ ἄνθρωποι ἐθαύμασαν λέγοντες, Ποδαπός ἐστιν οὗτος, ὅτι καὶ οἱ ἄνεμοι καὶ ἡ θάλαττα ὑπακούουσιν αὐτῷ;—Saint Matthew viii.27
2. τί ἐστιν ἡ πολυπραγμοσύνη;
3. ἡ πολυπραγμοσύνη φιλομάθειά τίς ἐστιν ἀλλοτρίων κακῶν.—Plutarch
4. δῶρα πείθει τοὺς ἀνθρώπους.
5. λόγος ἐστὶ τὰ δῶρα πείθειν καὶ τοὺς θεούς.
6. πείθειν δῶρα καὶ θεοὺς λόγος·
   χρυσὸς δὲ κρείττων μυρίων λόγων βροτοῖς.—Euripides, *Medea* 964–5
7. καὶ τοῦτό μοι ἑτέρα λύπη, τὸ τοῖς ἐμοῖς πτεροῖς ἀποθνήσκειν.—Aesop (the Eagle speaking, after having been shot with an arrow)
8. χαλεπὸν τὸ μὴ φιλῆσαι,
   χαλεπὸν δὲ καὶ φιλῆσαι·
   χαλεπώτερον δὲ πάντων
   ἀποτυγχάνειν φιλοῦντα.—Anacreon

Composition

1. These winds are stronger than those.

2. He said that these winds are stronger than those. (use λέγω
   + ὅτι or ὡς)
3. He said that those winds are stronger than these. (use ἔφη
   + accusative/infinitive)
4. It is not difficult to lose.
5. The gold which they had was very beautiful.
6. You will not persuade the king with those gifts.

Lesson 12

-μι Verbs

1. Most of the verbs that you have learned so far have been *thematic* verbs; that is, they employ a *thematic vowel* between the verb stem and the verb ending. Normally, the thematic vowel is o before an ending that begins with a nasal (μ or ν), and ε elsewhere. They are lengthened to ω and η, respectively, in the subjunctive mood and are replaced by a separate "modal sign" in the optative mood, so their status is not consistent or permanent throughout the Greek verbal system. But for verbs that employ them, thematic vowels provide one means of identifying and classifying verbs, at least in certain moods.

   But there is also another group of verbs, small but very important, that do not employ this thematic vowel and are thus called *nonthematic* verbs. Since this group is also characterized by a first-person present indicative active ending in -μι, instead of the -ω of regular verbs, they are also, more often, called -μι verbs.

2. -μι verbs are almost always irregular, in some form or tense, and for that reason must be treated like irregular verbs. That is, they must be learned *individually* and *very carefully*. Apparent similarities must be treated with caution and each verb memorized as if it were unique.

   Fortunately, there are very few -μι verbs; but they and their compounds are extremely important in Greek literature.

3. -μι verbs fall into three classes:
   a. root class, with endings added to the verb root. εἰμί is a root-class -μι verb.
   b. present reduplicating class, with endings added to a stem in the present and imperfect tenses that has "reduplicated" the initial consonant sound of the verb root. δίδωμι (root δο-), τίθημι (root θε-), and ἵστημι (root στα-) are present-reduplicating-class -μι verbs.

c. -νυμι *class,* with the syllable -νυ- between the stem and the ending of the present and imperfect tenses. δείκνυμι is a -νυμι class -μι verb.

4. Learn the following conjugations:

δίδωμι *give*

present	*imperfect*
δίδωμι *I give, etc.*	ἐδίδουν *I was giving, etc.*
δίδως	ἐδίδους
δίδωσι	ἐδίδου
δίδομεν	ἐδίδομεν
δίδοτε	ἐδίδοτε
διδόασι	ἐδίδοσαν

διδόναι (infinitive)

future	*second aorist*
(Notice that in the future, -μι verbs are thematic and regular.)	(Irregular, as are many so-called second aorists of -μι verbs.)
δώσω *I will give, etc.*	ἔδωκα *I gave, etc.*
δώσεις	ἔδωκας
δώσει	ἔδωκε
δώσομεν	ἔδομεν
δώσετε	ἔδοτε
δώσουσι	ἔδοσαν
δώσειν (infinitive)	δοῦναι (infinitive)

τίθημι *place, put, make*

present	*imperfect*
τίθημι	ἐτίθην
τίθης	ἐτίθεις
τίθησι	ἐτίθει
τίθεμεν	ἐτίθεμεν
τίθετε	ἐτίθετε
τιθέασι	ἐτίθεσαν

τιθέναι (infinitive)

future	*second aorist*
θήσω	ἔθηκα
θήσεις	ἔθηκας
θήσει	ἔθηκε
θήσομεν	ἔθεμεν
θήσετε	ἔθετε
θήσουσι	ἔθεσαν
θήσειν (infinitive)	θεῖναι (infinitive)

ἵημι *release, let go, throw*

present	*imperfect*
ἵημι	ἵην
ἵης	ἵεις
ἵησι	ἵει
ἵεμεν	ἵεμεν
ἵετε	ἵετε
ἱᾶσι	ἵεσαν

ἱέναι (infinitive)

future	*second aorist*
ἥσω	ἧκα
ἥσεις	ἧκας
ἥσει	ἧκε
ἥσομεν	εἷμεν
ἥσετε	εἷτε
ἥσουσι	εἷσαν
ἥσειν (infinitive)	εἷναι (infinitive)

ἵστημι *make to stand, set up* (*transitive* in meaning,
in the present, imperfect, future, and *first* aorist
tenses); *stand, stand firm, stand still* (*intransitive*
in meaning, in the *second* aorist and perfect tenses)

present	*imperfect*
ἵστημι	ἵστην
ἵστης	ἵστης
ἵστησι	ἵστη
ἵσταμεν	ἵσταμεν
ἵστατε	ἵστατε
ἱστᾶσι	ἵστασαν

ἱστάναι (infinitive)

future	*first aorist*
στήσω	ἔστησα
στήσεις	ἔστησας
στήσει	ἔστησε
στήσομεν	ἐστήσαμεν
στήσετε	ἐστήσατε
στήσουσι	ἔστησαν
στήσειν (infinitive)	στῆσαι (infinitive)

second aorist

ἔστην
ἔστης
ἔστη

ἔστημεν
ἔστητε
ἔστησαν

στῆναι (infinitive)

δείκνυμι *show, point out*

present	*imperfect*
δείκνυμι	ἐδείκνυν
δείκνυς	ἐδείκνυς
δείκνυσι	ἐδείκνυ
δείκνυμεν	ἐδείκνυμεν
δείκνυτε	ἐδείκνυτε
δεικνύασι	ἐδείκνυσαν

δεικνύναι (infinitive)

future	*first aorist*
δείξω	ἔδειξα
δείξεις	ἔδειξας
δείξει	ἔδειξε
δείξομεν	ἐδείξαμεν
δείξετε	ἐδείξατε
δείξουσι	ἔδειξαν
δείξειν (infinitive)	δεῖξαι (infinitive)

5. Review the following forms of εἰμί, *be:*

present	imperfect
εἰμί	ἦν or ἦ
εἶ	ἦσθα
ἐστί	ἦν
ἐσμέν	ἦμεν
ἐστέ	ἦτε
εἰσί	ἦσαν

εἶναι (infinitive)

Remember that the present indicative of εἰμί is *enclitic* in all forms except εἶ.

6. The richness, strength, and variety of -μι verbs in Greek come from their many *compounds*. While it is possible for *any* verb or group of verbs to form compounds with prepositional prefixes, in practice, only -μι verbs form compounds with nearly every preposition in the language (see Appendix A). The resultant compound verbs increase the reader's vocabulary and illustrate the importance of learning the simple, uncompounded verbs well first.

The following orthographic rules apply to the formation of compound verbs of the regular type as well as of -μι verbs. The meanings of some compound verbs can be guessed successfully from the elements of the compound: for example, κατατίθημι, from the preposition κατά, *down,* and τίθημι, *place,* means *place down, pay down, deposit.* But many others must be learned from a lexicon (dictionary) or vocabulary list: προδίδωμι, for example, from the preposition πρό, *before,* and δίδωμι, *give,* means *give beforehand, pay in advance,* meanings that can be easily derived from the two parts of the compound; but it also, more frequently, means *betray, forsake, abandon* — meanings that are not so obvious.

7. *a.* When a preposition ending in a vowel is prefixed to a verb that *begins* with a vowel, the final vowel of the preposition is elided:

διά + τίθημι → διατίθημι (*arrange, distribute*)
but διά + ἐτίθει → διετίθει

b. If the uncompounded verb begins with a rough breathing, and if either π or τ is the last letter of the elided prepositional prefix, then the π will become φ, and the τ will become θ:

ἀπ(ό) + ἵημι → ἀφίημι (*allow, forgive*)

κατ(ά) + ἵστημι → καθίστημι (*appoint, settle down*)

c. Compound verbs are augmented between the prefix and the verb; that is, prefixes are added to (and elided, if necessary, before) the augmented verb form:

ἐπιγράφω (*inscribe*): ἐπέγραφον, ἐπεγράψατε, etc.

d. A consonant that was changed because of a rough breathing reverts to its original form before a smooth breathing:

καθίστημι, καθίστασαν, but κατέστην, κατέστησας

e. A vowel that was elided (before a verb beginning with a vowel) is replaced before a verb beginning with a consonant:

καθίστημι, κατέστην, but καταστήσει, καταστῆναι

f. The letter ν undergoes the following changes:

before π, β, φ, or μ, it becomes μ: ἐμβαίνω;

before γ, κ, or χ, it becomes γ: συγκομίζω;

before λ, it becomes λ: ἐλλείπω; and

before σ or ζ, it disappears: συσπεύδω.

g. The prepositions περί and πρό never elide, but πρό often combines with the vowel ε to form the diphthong ου:

περιίστημι, προίημι, but προύδωκα, προυδίδουν

h. The accent of compound verbs never recedes to the left of the augment:

ἀφῆκα, ἀφεῖμεν (*not* ἄφηκα, ἄφειμεν, as might be expected from the recessive accent rule).

i. The accent of compounds of enclitic verbs *is* recessive but only on those forms for which the uncompounded verb is enclitic:

πάρειμι, ἔξεστι, but παρεῖναι, ἐξῆν.

8. Learn and practice the following compound verbs:

κατατίθημι, καταθήσω, κατέθηκα, κατατέθηκα, κατατέθειμαι, κατετέθην *set down, establish; deposit*

πάρειμι, παρέσομαι *be present*

προδίδωμι, προδώσω, προύδωκα, προδέδωκα, προδέδομαι, προυδόθην *betray, forsake, abandon*

ἀφίημι, ἀφήσω, ἀφῆκα, ἀφεῖκα, ἀφεῖμαι, ἀφείθην *allow, forgive; set free, dismiss; divorce*

διατίθημι, διαθήσω, διέθηκα, διατέθηκα, διατέθειμαι, διετέθην
distribute, manage, arrange
συνίστημι, συστήσω, συνέστησα and συνέστην, συνέστηκα,
συνέσταμαι, συνεστάθην I. (in *transitive* tenses) *combine,
organize, put together; contrive; compose; introduce (friends);*
II. (in *intransitive* tenses) *come together (in battle); band
together (as friends); come into existence; be healthy, firm, solid*

Vocabulary

Ἕλληνες, Ἑλλήνων, οἱ *Greeks, Hellenes*
Μαραθών, Μαραθῶνος, ὁ *Marathon,* on the northeast coast
of Attica, where the Greeks first defeated the Persians (490 B.C.)
μέλος, μέλους, τό *song, poem*
μοναρχία, μοναρχίας, ἡ *monarchy*
Πέρσης, Πέρσου, ὁ *a Persian*
πολιτεία, πολιτείας, ἡ *government*

ἀφίημι, ἀφήσω, ἀφῆκα, ἀφεῖκα, ἀφεῖμαι, ἀφείθην (imperfect
ἀφίην) *allow, forgive; set free, dismiss; divorce*
γνοίης *you could recognize* (second-person singular aorist optative;
see lesson 17)
γνώσῃ *you will know, recognize* (second-person singular future; see
lessons 15, 19)
δείκνυμι, δείξω, ἔδειξα, δέδειχα, δέδειγμαι, ἐδείχθην *show,
point out*
διατίθημι, διαθήσω, διέθηκα, διατέθηκα, διατέθειμαι, διετέθην
distribute, manage, arrange
δίδωμι, δώσω, ἔδωκα, δέδωκα, δέδομαι, ἐδόθην *give*
ἵημι, ἥσω, ἧκα, εἷκα, εἷμαι, εἵθην (imperfect ἵην) *throw, release,
let go*
ἵστημι, στήσω, ἔστησα and ἔστην, ἕστηκα, ἕσταμαι, ἐστάθην
(imperfect ἵστην) *cause to stand, set up* (in present, imperfect, future, and *first* aorist); *stand, stand firm, stand still* (in
passive voice and *second* aorist, perfect)
κατατίθημι, καταθήσω, κατέθηκα, κατατέθηκα, κατατέθειμαι,
κατετέθην *set down, establish, deposit*
νικᾶν *to conquer, to win* (infinitive; see lesson 13)
πάρειμι, παρέσομαι, —, —, —, — *be present*

προδίδωμι, προδώσω, προύδωκα, προδέδωκα, προδέδομαι,
προυδόθην *betray, forsake, abandon*
συνίστημι, συστήσω, συνέστησα and συνέστην, συνέστηκα,
συνέσταμαι, συνεστάθην (see par. 8 above)
τίθημι, θήσω, ἔθηκα, τέθηκα, τέθειμαι, ἐτέθην *place, put, make*

ἐσθλός, ἐσθλή, ἐσθλόν *good, brave, noble*
μιᾷ *one* (feminine dative singular; see Appendix B)
πολλοί *many* (masculine nominative plural; see lesson 14)

ἄν (untranslatable particle used with certain verbal constructions
    [here with γνοίης]; see lessons 15, 17)
ἀσφαλῶς *firmly, with certainty* (adverb)
ἐμέ *me* (accusative singular pronoun; see lesson 13)
ἐπεί *since, because; when* (conjunction)
ἐπί *on, upon; at* (preposition + *dative*)
κἄν = καὶ ἄν
σοι *to you* (dative singular pronoun; see lesson 13)

Practice

1. Conjugate each simple -μι verb in this lesson fully, in every
   tense so far presented, both indicative and infinitive.
2. Conjugate five compound -μι verbs fully, in every tense so far
   presented, both indicative and infinitive.

Reading

1. τοῦτο τὸ μέλος ὡς χάριν σοι καταθήσω.
2. οὐ παρῆν ἐγώ, καὶ οἱ φίλοι προύδοσαν ἐμέ.
3. ἐνταῦθα γὰρ κακὸς φίλος εἶ.
4. οὔκ,
    ἀλλ᾽ ἐν χρόνῳ γνώσῃ τάδ᾽ ἀσφαλῶς, ἐπεί
    χρόνος δίκαιον ἄνδρα δείκνυσιν μόνος,
    κακὸν δὲ κἄν ἐν ἡμέρᾳ γνοίης μιᾷ. — Sophocles,
    Oedipus the King 613–15
5. πολλοὶ Πέρσαι παρῆσαν ἐν τῷ πεδίῳ ἐπὶ τῷ Μαραθῶνι·
    ἐνταῦθα δὲ ἔστησαν οἱ Ἕλληνες, καὶ οὐκ ἀφεῖσαν αὐτοὺς
    νικᾶν.

6. χρὴ συνιστάναι τὴν πολιτείαν ἐκ μὲν μοναρχίας, ὥσπερ οἱ Πέρσαι, ἐκ δὲ δημοκρατίας, ὥσπερ οἱ Ἀθηναῖοι.
7. οὗτος ὁ πολίτης διαθήσει κράτιστα τὴν πολιτείαν.
8. ῥᾷον ἐξ ἀγαθοῦ θεῖναι κακόν, ἢ ἐκ κακοῦ ἐσθλόν.— Theognis

Composition

1. Were you present when the women were distributing gifts?
2. Certain Greeks used to believe that the army betrayed the government.
3. Who will establish laws for these citizens?
4. We banded together at Marathon.
5. I do not want to forgive the Persians.

Lesson 13

Contract Verbs, Personal Pronouns

1. Learn the declension of ἐγώ, the first-person personal pronoun:

ἐγώ *I*   ἡμεῖς *we*
ἐμοῦ (μου) *my; me*   ἡμῶν *our; us*
ἐμοί (μοι) *me*   ἡμῖν *us*
ἐμέ (με) *me*   ἡμᾶς *us*

   The forms in parentheses are enclitic and less emphatic.

2. Learn the declension of σύ, the second-person personal pronoun:

σύ *you*   ὑμεῖς *you* (plural)
σοῦ (σου) *your; you*   ὑμῶν *your; you*
σοί (σοι) *you*   ὑμῖν *you*
σέ (σε) *you*   ὑμᾶς *you*

   The forms in parentheses are enclitic and less emphatic.

3. Remember that the oblique cases (genitive, dative, and accusative) of αὐτός, αὐτή, αὐτό are used as the regular third-person personal pronouns (see lesson 6).

4. Three fairly common groups of verbs have present stems that end in a vowel that is contracted in Attic Greek with the verb endings of the present and imperfect tenses. These three groups are consequently known as *contract verbs,* and the rules for their formation are given below in graphic form, followed by a paradigm for each group.
   a. Present *stems* of the first group end in α, and the verbs are called -αω *contracts.* νικάω, *conquer,* is an -αω contract.
   b. Present *stems* of the second group end in ε, and the verbs are called -εω *contracts.* ποιέω, *do, make,* is an -εω contract.

c. Present *stems* of the third group end in o, and the verbs are called -οω *contracts*. δηλόω, *show, reveal,* is an -οω contract.

These verbs do *not* contract in any tense other than the present and imperfect.

5. Below is a graph of the contractions that occur in each group. On the left are the stem endings, across the top are the possible vowels with which they contract (including any diphthong that contains the letter ι), and in the graph are the resultant contractions (for example, α- contracts with -ο into ω):

	-ε	-ο	-ου	-ω	-η	-ι-*diphthong*
α-	α	ω	ω	ω	α	ᾳ (pres. infin.: α)
ε-	ει	ου	ου	ω	η	ι-*diphthong*
ο-	ου	ου	ου	ω	ω	οι (pres. infin.: ου)

6. Learn the present and imperfect conjugations of νικάω. The forms in parentheses are the uncontracted forms and are provided only for your information. They need not be memorized. In some dialects of Greek literature, however, it is the *uncontracted* forms that are used, and all contract verbs are listed in vocabularies and the Greek-English lexicon in their uncontracted form. This year, we will use only the contracted forms:

present		*imperfect*	
νικῶ	(νικάω)	ἐνίκων	(ἐνίκαον)
νικᾷς	(νικάεις)	ἐνίκας	(ἐνίκαες)
νικᾷ	(νικάει)	ἐνίκα	(ἐνίκαε)
νικῶμεν	(νικάομεν)	ἐνικῶμεν	(ἐνικάομεν)
νικᾶτε	(νικάετε)	ἐνικᾶτε	(ἐνικάετε)
νικῶσι	(νικάουσι)	ἐνίκων	(ἐνίκαον)

νικᾶν (νικάειν)

7. Learn the present and imperfect conjugations of ποιέω:

	present		*imperfect*
ποιῶ	(ποιέω)	ἐποίουν	(ἐποίεον)
ποιεῖς	(ποιέεις)	ἐποίεις	(ἐποίεες)
ποιεῖ	(ποιέει)	ἐποίει	(ἐποίεε)
ποιοῦμεν	(ποιέομεν)	ἐποιοῦμεν	(ἐποιέομεν)
ποιεῖτε	(ποιέετε)	ἐποιεῖτε	(ἐποιέετε)
ποιοῦσι	(ποιέουσι)	ἐποίουν	(ἐποίεον)

ποιεῖν (ποιέειν)

8. Learn the present and imperfect conjugations of δηλόω:

	present		*imperfect*
δηλῶ	(δηλόω)	ἐδήλουν	(ἐδήλοον)
δηλοῖς	(δηλόεις)	ἐδήλους	(ἐδήλοες)
δηλοῖ	(δηλόει)	ἐδήλου	(ἐδήλοε)
δηλοῦμεν	(δηλόομεν)	ἐδηλοῦμεν	(ἐδηλόομεν)
δηλοῦτε	(δηλόετε)	ἐδηλοῦτε	(ἐδηλόετε)
δηλοῦσι	(δηλόουσι)	ἐδήλουν	(ἐδήλοον)

δηλοῦν (δηλόειν)

9. As in English, so in Greek two words may be contracted into one, with a resultant loss of a vowel or a diphthong. This process is called *crasis* and joins only a word that *ends* with a vowel and a following word that *begins* with a vowel. An apostrophe is placed over the contracted syllable:

τὰ αὐτά → ταὐτά

καὶ ἐν → κἀν

A rough breathing can precipitate other orthographic changes as well:

καὶ ὁ → χὠ

10. The *possessive* genitive may also be used in the predicate to designate the person or thing to whom or to which something belongs as a *characteristic* or *duty,* especially with an articular infinitive as the subject of the sentence. These special uses are sometimes called *genitive of characteristic* or *genitive of duty:*

ἀνδρὸς τὸ πολεμεῖν, γυναικὸς δὲ μένειν. *It is (characteristic, or the duty,) of man to make war, and of woman to wait.*

Vocabulary

ἀνάμνησις, ἀναμνήσεως, ἡ *memory, remembering, recall*
ἀρετή, ἀρετῆς, ἡ *virtue*
ἀστράγαλος, ἀστραγάλου, ὁ *neck bone, knucklebone;* (in plural)
  bones used as *dice, dice game*
γέλως, γέλωτος, ὁ *laughter*
δίκαια, δικαίων, τά *rights*
ἔαρ, ἔαρος or ἦρος, τό *spring* (the season); *springtime*
ἐγγυητής, ἐγγυητοῦ, ὁ *guarantor, security, guarantee*
εὐτέλεια, εὐτελείας, ἡ *simplicity; little expense, economy*
ἐχθρός, ἐχθροῦ, ὁ *enemy* (personal, not military)
μαλακία, μαλακίας, ἡ *softness; moral weakness*
Μοῦσα, Μούσης, ἡ *a Muse, one of the sovereign deities of*
  poetry, literature, music, and dance
ὅρκος, ὅρκου, ὁ *oath; sworn compact*
Πλάτων, Πλάτωνος, ὁ *Plato*
συνθήκη, συνθήκης, ἡ *agreement, covenant, compact*
χελιδών, χελιδόνος, ἡ *swallow* (the bird)

γελάω, γελάσομαι, ἐγέλασα, —, γεγέλασμαι, ἐγελάσθην *laugh*
γίγνεται *becomes* (third-person singular *deponent;* see lesson 19)
δεῖ *it is necessary (that)* (impersonal verb + *accusative/infinitive*
  complement)
δηλόω, δηλώσω, ἐδήλωσα, δεδήλωκα, δεδήλωμαι, ἐδηλώθην
  show, reveal
δοκέω, δόξω, ἔδοξα, δέδοχα, δέδογμαι, ἐδόχθην *expect; think;*
  seem, pretend (+ *infinitive*); *seem, seem best to* someone
  (+ *dative* of the person, complementary *infinitive*)
ἐξαπατάω, ἐξαπατήσω, ἐξηπάτησα, ἐξηπάτηκα, ἐξηπάτημαι,
  ἐξηπατήθην (imperfect ἐξηπάτων) *cheat, deceive*
ἐπαινέω, ἐπαινέσομαι, ἐπήνεσα, ἐπήνεκα, ἐπήνημαι, ἐπηνέθην
  (imperfect ἐπήνουν) *praise*
ἐράω (imperfect ἤρων) *love, be in love with* (+ *genitive*) (tenses
  other than present and imperfect are supplied by the deponent
  verb ἔραμαι)
καλέω, καλῶ, ἐκάλεσα, κέκληκα, κέκλημαι, ἐκλήθην *call,*
  summon, name
κελεύω, κελεύσω, ἐκέλευσα, κεκέλευκα, κεκέλευσμαι,

ἐκελεύσθην *urge; order, command* (+ *accusative/infinitive*)

νικάω, νικήσω, ἐνίκησα, νενίκηκα, νενίκημαι, ἐνικήθην *win, conquer*

οἰκέω, οἰκήσω, ᾤκησα, ᾤκηκα, ᾤκημαι, ᾠκήθην (imperfect ᾤκουν) *inhabit, dwell (in), live (in)*

πάσχω, πείσομαι, ἔπαθον, πέπονθα, —, — *suffer, experience; be treated* well, badly, etc. (+ *adverb*)

ποιέω, ποιήσω, ἐποίησα, πεποίηκα, πεποίημαι, ἐποιήθην *do, make*

πολεμέω, πολεμήσω, ἐπολέμησα, πεπολέμηκα, πεπολέμημαι, ἐπολεμήθην *fight, make war on* (+ *dative*)

πράττω, πράξω, ἔπραξα, πέπραχα and πέπραγα, πέπραγμαι, ἐπράχθην *achieve, manage, effect; do, act*

συμφήσουσι *will agree with* (future of σύμφημι; + *dative*)

τυγχάνω, τεύξομαι, ἔτυχον, τετύχηκα, τέτευγμαι, ἐτεύχθην *meet, come upon* (+ *genitive*)

ὑγιαίνειν *to be healthy* (present infinitive)

φιλοκαλέω, φιλοκαλήσω, ἐφιλοκάλησα, —, —, — *love beauty, love what is beautiful*

φιλοσοφέω, φιλοσοφήσω, —, πεφιλοσόφηκα, —, — *love knowledge, pursue wisdom*

αἰσχρός, αἰσχρά, αἰσχρόν *shameful, disgraceful; ugly*

ἀλλήλων *one another, each other* (reciprocal, used only in the oblique cases, with no singular in use; declined like the plural of ἄριστος)

ἥδιστος, ἡδίστη, ἥδιστον *sweetest, very sweet*

λῶστος, λῴστη, λῶστον *most desirable, very desirable*

μακάριος, μακαρία, μακάριον *blessed, happy; prosperous*

οἷος, οἵα, οἷον *such as; of what sort*

οἷος or οἷός τε (+ *infinitive*) *fit, able to*

ὀλίγος, ὀλίγη, ὀλίγον *little, small, short; few*

ἄγαν *very much, too much, to excess* (adverb)

ἄνευ *without* (preposition + *genitive*)

ἐγώ *I* (personal pronoun)

εἰς *before, in the presence of* (preposition + *accusative*)

εὖ *well* (adverb of ἀγαθός)

ἧττον *less* (adverb)

μᾶλλον *more, rather* (adverb, comparative of μάλα, *very*)

μετά *with* (preposition + *genitive*)

μηδέν *nothing* (used for οὐδέν in constructions where μή would be used instead of οὐ; see Appendix B)

οὔκουν . . . ; (particle used to introduce impatient or excited questions; its force is conveyed more by tone in English than by separate words; almost equivalent to οὐ, but more emphatic and urgent)

οὕτω (οὕτως before a vowel, and sometimes even before a consonant) *thus, so, in this way* (adverb of οὗτος)

σύ *you* (personal pronoun)

Practice

Conjugate three contract verbs fully (one from each group), in the present, imperfect, future, and aorist indicative active, and give the present, future, and aorist active infinitives for each verb.

Reading

1. ὁ ποιητὴς χαλεπὴν ἐκάλει τῆς ἀρετῆς τὴν ὁδόν.
2. μία χελιδὼν ἔαρ οὐ ποιεῖ. —Cratinus (fifth-century B.C. writer of comedy)
3. μία γὰρ χελιδὼν ἔαρ οὐ ποιεῖ, οὐδὲ μία ἡμέρα· οὕτω δὲ οὐδὲ μακάριον καὶ εὐδαίμονα μία ἡμέρα οὐδ' ὀλίγος χρόνος. —Aristotle, *Nicomachean Ethics* 1098a
4. ἐδόκει τοῖς Ἀθηναίοις στῆναι ἐνταῦθα καὶ πολεμεῖν.
5. ὁ Πλάτων τὰς Μούσας ἔφη τὰς τῶν ἀρίστων ψυχὰς οἰκεῖν.
6. χαλεπὸν τὸ ποιεῖν, τὸ δὲ κελεῦσαι ῥᾴδιον. —Philemon
7. μηδὲν ἄγαν.
8. οὕτω τὸ λίαν ἧττον ἐπαινῶ
   τοῦ μηδὲν ἄγαν·
   καὶ συμφήσουσι σοφοί μοι. —Euripides, *Hippolytus* 264–6
9. φιλοκαλοῦμέν τε μετ' εὐτελείας καὶ φιλοσοφοῦμεν ἄνευ μαλακίας. —Thucydides 2.40
10. γίγνεται ὁ νόμος συνθήκη καὶ ἐγγυητὴς ἀλλήλοις τῶν δικαίων, ἀλλ' οὐχ οἷος ποιεῖν ἀγαθοὺς καὶ δικαίους τοὺς πολίτας. —Aristotle, *Politics* 1280b10

11. κάλλιστον τὸ δικαιότατον, λῷστον δ' ὑγιαίνειν,
    πάντων ἥδιστον οὗ τις ἐρᾷ τὸ τυχεῖν.
12. οὔκουν γέλως ἥδιστος εἰς ἐχθροὺς γελᾶν; — Sophocles, *Ajax*
    79
13. οὐ μανθάνομεν, ἀλλὰ ἣν καλοῦμεν μάθησιν ἀνάμνησίς
    ἐστιν. — Plato, *Meno* 81e
14. τῆς γὰρ ἀρετῆς μᾶλλον τὸ εὖ ποιεῖν ἢ τὸ εὖ πάσχειν, καὶ
    τὰ καλὰ πράττειν ἢ τὰ αἰσχρὰ μὴ πράττειν. — Aristotle,
    Nicomachean Ethics
15. τοὺς μὲν παῖδας ἀστραγάλοις δεῖ ἐξαπατᾶν, τοὺς δὲ ἄνδρας
    ὅρκοις. — Plutarch

Composition

1. We used to laugh, but now our enemies are laughing.
2. Are you (plural) able to make war on each other?
3. It seemed best to us to summon our friends and band together.
4. Who was showing the laws to you?
5. It is (characteristic) of children to laugh and of men to be in love.

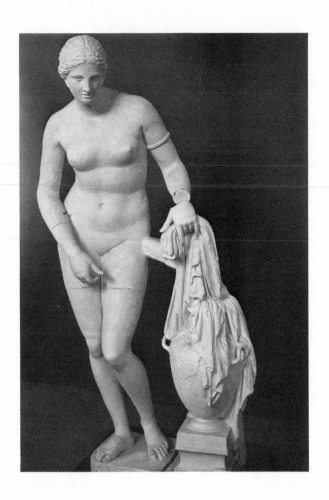

5. Praxiteles' *Cypris*.

Sculpture in the Vatican Museum; from a copy in the H. W. Sage Collection of Casts of Ancient Sculpture at Cornell University; photo by Andrew Gillis.

This statue, the original of which has been lost, is traditionally dated 364 B.C. Praxiteles was a sculptor in marble and is thought to have used his mistress, Phryne, as the model for this bold sculpture (in the fifth century, Aphrodite had always been portrayed clothed). Praxiteles' work inspired an elegiac couplet by Plato (see lesson 14) and was located in the Greek colony of Cnidos, whose principal points of interest were its medical school, its astronomical observatory, and this statue. People traveled from all over the Greek world to see it.

Lesson 14

Participles

The use of *participles* is one of the most significant features of Greek syntax. As in English, the participle is a *verbal adjective*. Its stem is formed from a verb, but its endings are declined like an adjective. As a *verb*, it can have subjects, objects, and tenses, and be modified by adverbs; as an *adjective,* it can itself modify a noun or a pronoun (expressed or understood):

The rapidly shifting breezes made the sailors dizzy. Here, the participle *shifting* is modified by an adverb (*rapidly*), and also itself modifies a noun (*breezes*).

In Greek, the uses of the participle are more numerous than in English, and the most prominent uses are listed and described below:
1. *Attributive* (pure adjective)
2. *Supplementary* (with special verbs)
3. *Circumstantial*
4. *Subordinate/coordinate*
5. *Indirect statement* (with verbs of sense perception and knowing)

1. The *attributive* participle is a simple adjective, usually accompanied by a definite article:

ὁ ἄρχων βασιλεύς *the ruling king*
ἡ παιδεύουσα μηχανή *the teaching machine*
κρυπτόμενον ὄνειδος *a disguised insult*

Often the noun is omitted, and the participle is used as a noun, sometimes with modifiers:

οἱ ἄρχοντες *those who rule*
οἱ ἐν Ἀθήναις (ὄντες ἄνθρωποι) *The (people who are) in Athens*
οἱ ἐν τέλει (ὄντες ἄνθρωποι) *Those (who are) in power*
αἱ παρὰ τῇ γεφύρᾳ (οὖσαι γυναῖκες) *The (women who are) by the bridge*

With the verb *to be,* the participle itself is often omitted, as in the last three examples.

2. A few important verbs in Greek are *supplemented,* or completed, with *supplementary* participles rather than with infinitives or separate dependent clauses. Two examples are:

   a. happen: τυγχάνω, κυρέω

       τυγχάνομεν οἰκοῦντες τὰς Ἀθήνας. *We happen to live in Athens.*

       ἀεὶ ἐκύρουν νικῶντες. *They always happened to win.*

   b. deceive, escape notice: λανθάνω

       ἐλάθομεν τὸν πατέρα διδόντες δῶρον τῇ μητρί. *We gave Mother a gift without Father's knowledge.* (literally: *We escaped Father's notice, giving Mother a gift.*)

3. The *circumstantial* participle expresses any of several circumstances which may accompany the action of the main verb, and is best translated into English by a dependent clause rather than by a single word:

   a. concession (*although, even though*):

       καίπερ ἄγροικος ὤν, βιβλία ἐφίλει. *Although he was a farmer, he loved books.* (also *without* καί *or* καίπερ)

   b. time (*when, while, after*):

       πολλὰ φαγόντες, ἀπῆλθον. *When they had eaten a great deal, they left.*

   c. cause (*because, since*):

       οὐδὲν ἔχουσα, ἀπέθανεν. *Because she had nothing, she died.*

   d. condition (*if*):

       σὲ φιλοῦσα, παράφρων ἐστίν. *If she loves you, she is crazy.*

   e. means (*by*):

       εὖ πολεμῶν, στρατηγὸς ἐγένετο. *By fighting well, he became a general.*

   f. purpose (*to, in order to; future* participle, sometimes introduced by ὡς):

       ἤλθομεν (ὡς) σώσοντες τὴν πόλιν. *We came to save the city.*

   g. genitive absolute:

       When the subject of the dependent circumstantial clause (participle) is not part of the syntax of the *main* clause of the sentence, both the participle and its subject (if expressed)

are in an *absolute* (syntactically independent) construction
in the *genitive* case:

σὲ φιλούσης, παράφρων εἰμί. *If she loves you, I am
crazy.*

καίπερ οὐ παρόντων τῶν πατέρων, δεῖ ἡμᾶς αἰσχρὰ
πράττειν; *Even though our fathers are not here, must we
act shamefully?*

4. Greek often tends to *subordinate* the action of independent verbs
   in a compound series, retaining only *one* independent verb and
   subordinating the others to the participial mood, where English tends to *coordinate* them, keeping *all* the verbs in independent moods:

   λιπόντες τὸ στρατόπεδον καὶ ἐλάσαντες οἴκαδε, οἱ
   στρατιῶται νίκην ἤγγειλαν. *The soldiers left their camp,
   marched homeward, and proclaimed a victory.* (literally:
   *Having left their camp and having marched homeward, the
   soldiers proclaimed a victory.*)

5. With certain verbs of *sense perception* and *knowing, indirect
   statement* is usually expressed with participles in Greek, in a
   construction analogous to the accusative/infinitive construction:

   νομίζω τὸν βασιλέα φεύγειν. (accusative/infinitive) *I think
   that the king is escaping.* but:
   ἀκούω τὸν βασιλέα φεύγοντα. (accusative/*participle*)
   I hear that the king is escaping.
   οἶδα τὸν βασιλέα φυγόντα. (accusative/*participle*) *I know
   that the king escaped.*

6. In English, the *verbal adjective* (participle) and the *verbal noun*
   (gerund) often have the same form and are distinguishable only
   by the context in which they occur; for example:

   Love is never having *to say you're sorry.* (gerund)
   Having *three pizzas a day is excessive.* (gerund)
   Having *too much to drink, we lost control.* (participle)

   In Greek, the *verbal adjective* and the *verbal noun* are easily
   distinguished; the verbal adjective is a *participle,* while the
   verbal noun is an *infinitive:*

καλόν ἐστι φίλους ἔχειν. (infinitive) Having *friends is good*.

φίλους ἔχων, βασιλεὺς ἐγένετο. (participle) Having *friends, he became king*.

7. Learn the following participles. Participles formed from regular verbs are similarly declined:

present active participle: νομίζω

νομίζων	νομίζουσα	νομίζον
νομίζοντος	νομιζούσης	νομίζοντος
νομίζοντι	νομιζούσῃ	νομίζοντι
νομίζοντα	νομίζουσαν	νομίζον
νομίζοντες	νομίζουσαι	νομίζοντα
νομιζόντων	νομιζουσῶν	νομιζόντων
νομίζουσι	νομιζούσαις	νομίζουσι
νομίζοντας	νομιζούσας	νομίζοντα

future active participle: οἴσω

οἴσων	οἴσουσα	οἴσον
οἴσοντος	οἰσούσης	οἴσοντος
οἴσοντι	οἰσούσῃ	οἴσοντι
οἴσοντα	οἴσουσαν	οἴσον
οἴσοντες	οἴσουσαι	οἴσοντα
οἰσόντων	οἰσουσῶν	οἰσόντων
οἴσουσι	οἰσούσαις	οἴσουσι
οἴσοντας	οἰσούσας	οἴσοντα

first aorist active participle: ἔλυσα

λύσας	λύσασα	λῦσαν
λύσαντος	λυσάσης	λύσαντος
λύσαντι	λυσάσῃ	λύσαντι
λύσαντα	λύσασαν	λῦσαν
λύσαντες	λύσασαι	λύσαντα
λυσάντων	λυσασῶν	λυσάντων
λύσασι	λυσάσαις	λύσασι
λύσαντας	λυσάσας	λύσαντα

second aorist active participle: ἔμαθον

μαθών	μαθοῦσα	μαθόν
μαθόντος	μαθούσης	μαθόντος
μαθόντι	μαθούσῃ	μαθόντι
μαθόντα	μαθοῦσαν	μαθόν
μαθόντες	μαθοῦσαι	μαθόντα
μαθόντων	μαθουσῶν	μαθόντων
μαθοῦσι	μαθούσαις	μαθοῦσι
μαθόντας	μαθούσας	μαθόντα

8. Learn the following present active participles of contract verbs:

ποιέω

ποιῶν	ποιοῦσα	ποιοῦν
ποιοῦντος	ποιούσης	ποιοῦντος
ποιοῦντι	ποιούσῃ	ποιοῦντι
ποιοῦντα	ποιοῦσαν	ποιοῦν
ποιοῦντες	ποιοῦσαι	ποιοῦντα
ποιούντων	ποιουσῶν	ποιούντων
ποιοῦσι	ποιούσαις	ποιοῦσι
ποιοῦντας	ποιούσας	ποιοῦντα

νικάω

νικῶν	νικῶσα	νικῶν
νικῶντος	νικώσης	νικῶντος
νικῶντι	νικώσῃ	νικῶντι
νικῶντα	νικῶσαν	νικῶν
νικῶντες	νικῶσαι	νικῶντα
νικώντων	νικωσῶν	νικώντων
νικῶσι	νικώσαις	νικῶσι
νικῶντας	νικώσας	νικῶντα

δηλόω

δηλῶν	δηλοῦσα	δηλοῦν
δηλοῦντος	δηλούσης	δηλοῦντος
δηλοῦντι	δηλούσῃ	δηλοῦντι
δηλοῦντα	δηλοῦσαν	δηλοῦν
δηλοῦντες	δηλοῦσαι	δηλοῦντα
δηλούντων	δηλουσῶν	δηλούντων
δηλοῦσι	δηλούσαις	δηλοῦσι
δηλοῦντας	δηλούσας	δηλοῦντα

9. Learn the following participles of -μι verbs:

present active participle: εἰμί (participle *not* enclitic)

ὤν	οὖσα	ὄν
ὄντος	οὔσης	ὄντος
ὄντι	οὔσῃ	ὄντι
ὄντα	οὖσαν	ὄν
ὄντες	οὖσαι	ὄντα
ὄντων	οὐσῶν	ὄντων
οὖσι	οὔσαις	οὖσι
ὄντας	οὔσας	ὄντα

present active participle: δίδωμι

διδούς	διδοῦσα	διδόν
διδόντος	διδούσης	διδόντος
διδόντι	διδούσῃ	διδόντι
διδόντα	διδοῦσαν	διδόν
διδόντες	διδοῦσαι	διδόντα
διδόντων	διδουσῶν	διδόντων
διδοῦσι	διδούσαις	διδοῦσι
διδόντας	διδούσας	διδόντα

future active participle: δώσω (like οἴσω)

δώσων	δώσουσα	δῶσον
κτλ	*κτλ*	*κτλ*

second aorist active participle: ἔδωκα (like δίδωμι)

δούς	δοῦσα	δόν
κτλ	*κτλ*	*κτλ*

present active participle: τίθημι

τιθείς	τιθεῖσα	τιθέν
τιθέντος	τιθείσης	τιθέντος
τιθέντι	τιθείσῃ	τιθέντι
τιθέντα	τιθεῖσαν	τιθέν
τιθέντες	τιθεῖσαι	τιθέντα
τιθέντων	τιθεισῶν	τιθέντων
τιθεῖσι	τιθείσαις	τιθεῖσι
τιθέντας	τιθείσας	τιθέντα

future active participle: θήσω (like οἴσω)

θήσων	θήσουσα	θῆσον
κτλ	κτλ	κτλ

second aorist active participle: ἔθηκα (like τίθημι)

θείς	θεῖσα	θέν
κτλ	κτλ	κτλ

present active participle: ἵημι (like τίθημι)

ἱείς	ἱεῖσα	ἱέν
κτλ	κτλ	κτλ

future active participle: ἥσω (like οἴσω)

ἥσων	ἥσουσα	ἧσον
κτλ	κτλ	κτλ

second aorist active participle: ἧκα (like τίθημι)

εἵς	εἷσα	ἕν
κτλ	κτλ	κτλ

present active participle: ἵστημι

ἱστάς	ἱστᾶσα	ἱστάν
ἱστάντος	ἱστάσης	ἱστάντος
ἱστάντι	ἱστάσῃ	ἱστάντι
ἱστάντα	ἱστᾶσαν	ἱστάν
ἱστάντες	ἱστᾶσαι	ἱστάντα
ἱστάντων	ἱστασῶν	ἱστάντων
ἱστᾶσι	ἱστάσαις	ἱστᾶσι
ἱστάντας	ἱστάσας	ἱστάντα

future active participle: στήσω (like οἴσω)

στήσων	στήσουσα	στῆσον
κτλ	κτλ	κτλ

first aorist active participle: ἔστησα (like ἔλυσα)

στήσας	στήσασα	στῆσαν
κτλ	κτλ	κτλ

second aorist active participle: ἔστην (like ἵστημι)

στάς	στᾶσα	στάν
κτλ	κτλ	κτλ

present active participle: δείκνυμι

δεικνύς	δεικνῦσα	δεικνύν
δεικνύντος	δεικνύσης	δεικνύντος
δεικνύντι	δεικνύσῃ	δεικνύντι
δεικνύντα	δεικνῦσαν	δεικνύν
δεικνύντες	δεικνῦσαι	δεικνύντα
δεικνύντων	δεικνυσῶν	δεικνύντων
δεικνῦσι	δεικνύσαις	δεικνῦσι
δεικνύντας	δεικνύσας	δεικνύντα

future active participle: δείξω (like οἴσω)

δείξων	δείξουσα	δεῖξον
κτλ	κτλ	κτλ

first aorist active participle: ἔδειξα (like ἔλυσα)

δείξας	δείξασα	δεῖξαν
κτλ	κτλ	κτλ

10. Learn the declension of πᾶς. In the *attributive* position, it means *whole:*

    τὸ πᾶν βιβλίον *the whole book*

    In the *predicate* position, it means *all:*

    πάντες οἱ στρατιῶται *all the soldiers*

    Without the article, it means *every:*

    πᾶσα γυνή *every woman*

πᾶς	πᾶσα	πᾶν
παντός	πάσης	παντός
παντί	πάσῃ	παντί
πάντα	πᾶσαν	πᾶν
πάντες	πᾶσαι	πάντα
πάντων	πασῶν	πάντων
πᾶσι	πάσαις	πᾶσι
πάντας	πάσας	πάντα

11. Learn the declension of μέγας, *large, big, great:*

μέγας	μεγάλη	μέγα
μεγάλου	μεγάλης	μεγάλου
μεγάλῳ	μεγάλῃ	μεγάλῳ
μέγαν	μεγάλην	μέγα

μεγάλοι	μεγάλαι	μεγάλα
μεγάλων	μεγάλων	μεγάλων
μεγάλοις	μεγάλαις	μεγάλοις
μεγάλους	μεγάλας	μεγάλα

12. Learn the declension of πολύς, *much* (singular), *many* (plural):

πολύς	πολλή	πολύ
πολλοῦ	πολλῆς	πολλοῦ
πολλῷ	πολλῇ	πολλῷ
πολύν	πολλήν	πολύ
πολλοί	πολλαί	πολλά
πολλῶν	πολλῶν	πολλῶν
πολλοῖς	πολλαῖς	πολλοῖς
πολλούς	πολλάς	πολλά

13. Learn the declension of ὅστις, *who, whoever; what, whatever.*
ὅστις is a combination of the relative ὅς and the indefinite
τις and is used as both the *indefinite relative* and the *indirect
interrogative* in Greek:
>   ἔστιν ὅστις οὐ νομίζει τοὺς θεούς; *Is there anyone who
>   does not believe in the gods?*
>   λέξει ἡμῖν οὕστινας ἔβλεψαν. *He will tell us whom
>   they saw.*

ὅστις	ἥτις	ὅτι
οὗτινος or ὅτου	ἧστινος	οὗτινος or ὅτου
ᾧτινι or ὅτῳ	ᾗτινι	ᾧτινι or ὅτῳ
ὅντινα	ἥντινα	ὅτι
οἵτινες	αἵτινες	ἅτινα
ὧντινων or ὅτων	ὧντινων	ὧντινων or ὅτων
οἷστισι or ὅτοις	αἷστισι	οἷστισι or ὅτοις
οὕστινας	ἅστινας	ἅτινα

Vocabulary

Ἀρταξέρξης, Ἀρταξέρξου, ὁ *Artaxerxes, brother of Cyrus; king
of Persia, 404–358 B.C.*
ἀσπίς, ἀσπίδος, ἡ *shield*

βάρβαρος, βαρβάρου, ὁ *a foreigner;* especially in the plural,
  the Persians
γῆ, γῆς, γῇ, γῆν, ἡ *earth, land; the Earth* (no plural)
δάκρυον, δακρύου, τό *tear; teardrop*
ἔγχος, ἔγχεος, τό (poetic genitive plural ἐγχέων) *spear, lance*
ἵππος, ἵππου, ὁ or ἡ *horse*
ἰχθύσιν *fish* (dative plural; see lesson 16)
κάλλος, κάλλους, τό *beauty*
κέρατα, τά *horns* (poetic accusative plural)
Κνίδος, Κνίδου, ἡ *Cnidos, Greek colony in southwest Asia Minor*
Κύπρις, Κύπρεως, ἡ *Cypris, the Cypriot goddess: Aphrodite;* also,
  a statue of Aphrodite
Κῦρος, Κύρου, ὁ *Cyrus, younger brother of Artaxerxes and son of
  the Persian king Darius; led an expedition of soldiers, including
  a large Greek mercenary force, against his brother, the fate of
  which is recorded by Xenophon in his* Anabasis; *not to be confused with Cyrus "the Great," founder of the Persian Empire*
λαγωοῖς *hares, rabbits* (poetic dative plural)
λέων, λέοντος, ὁ *lion*
νηκτόν, νηκτοῦ, τό *the skill of swimming*
ὀδούς, ὀδόντος, ὁ *tooth*
ὁπλή, ὁπλῆς, ἡ *hoof*
ὀρνέοις *birds* (poetic dative plural)
ποδωκίαν *swiftness of foot* (poetic accusative singular)
Πραξιτέλης, Πραξιτέλους, ὁ *Praxiteles, fourth-century sculptor*
σίδηρον, σιδήρου, τό *iron*
στρατόπεδον, στρατοπέδου, τό *(military) camp*
ταῦρος, ταύρου, ὁ *bull*
φρόνημα, φρονήματος, τό *spirit, pride; arrogance*
χάσμα, χάσματος, τό *yawning chasm, gulf*

αἱρέω, αἱρήσω, εἷλον (stem ἑλ-), ᾕρηκα, ᾕρημαι, ᾑρέθην
  (imperfect ᾕρουν) *take, seize;* (middle voice) *choose*
ἀσκοῦσιν *practice, exercise* (third-person plural present of ἀσκέω)
βασιλεύω, βασιλεύσω (other tenses not in common use) *be king,
  rule, reign*
δράω, δράσω, ἔδρασα, δέδρακα, δέδραμαι, ἐδράσθην *do, accomplish* (esp. *some great thing,* good or bad)
εἶπον *said* (second aorist, stem εἰπ-, sometimes used in place of
  ἔλεξα)

ἐνοικέω (+ *dative*) = οἰκέω (+ *accusative*)

θύω, θύσω, ἔθυσα, τέθυκα, τέθυμαι, ἐτύθην *offer to the gods by burning; sacrifice*

λανθάνω, λήσω, ἔλαθον, λέληθα, λέλησμαι, ἐλήσθην *deceive, escape notice of* (+ supplementary *participle*)

λείβων *pouring forth* (present participle of λείβω)

ὁράω, ὄψομαι, εἶδον (stem ἰδ-), ἑόρακα, ἑώραμαι and ὦμμαι, ὤφθην (imperfect ἑώρων) *see*

πέτασθαι *to fly* (poetic deponent infinitive; see lesson 19)

τίκτω, τέξομαι, ἔτεκον, τέτοκα, —, — *beget; give birth to* (used of both mothers and fathers)

τυγχάνω *happen* (+ supplementary *participle*; see lesson 13 for principal parts)

ὑπῆρχε *preferred* (third-person singular imperfect of ὑπάρχω + *dative*)

ἁ = ἡ (poetic)

αἴσχιστος, αἰσχίστη, αἴσχιστον (superlative of αἰσχρός)

ἄλλος, ἄλλη, ἄλλον *other, another*

ἀντάξιος, ἀνταξία, ἀντάξιον *worth as much as* (+ *genitive*)

ἁπάντων = πάντων (emphatic form)

ἁπάσων = πασῶν (emphatic form)

γυμνός, γυμνή, γυμνόν *naked, nude*

δυοῖν *two* (dative dual; see Appendix B)

ἑνός *one* (masculine genitive singular; see Appendix B)

μέγας, μεγάλη, μέγα *large, big; great*

ὅστις, ἥτις, ὅτι *who, whoever, anyone who; what, whatever, anything which*

πᾶς, πᾶσα, πᾶν *whole; all; every*

πολύς, πολλή, πολύ *much, many*

τάν = τήν (poetic)

ἀντί *instead of, in preference to* (preposition + *genitive*)

ἔνθα *there, then* (adverb of place and time)

ἐνί = ἐν (poetic)

ἐπί *upon, on* (preposition + *genitive*; see also lesson 12)

καίπερ *although, even though* (+ concessive *participle*)

κτλ = καὶ τὰ λοιπά *et cetera*

οἴκαδε *homeward, toward home* (adverb)

οὐκέτι *no longer, no more* (adverb)

οὖν *well, then, so* (postpositive narrative particle, pointing to something already mentioned or known) τί οὖν...; *what then? why then?* (used in impatient questions to ask why something desired has not already been done)

ὑπό *under, beneath; from under* (preposition + *genitive;* also with dative and accusative; see Appendix A)

φεῦ *oh; well; ah* (exclamation of astonishment or admiration)

Practice

I. Pick out the words in the following sentences that would be participles in Greek and identify the *use* of the participle (*attributive; supplementary; circumstantial*—specify the circumstance; *subordinate/coordinate;* or *indirect statement* with verb of knowing or sense perception):

1. These are the times that try men's souls.
2. That which belongs to me belongs to you.
3. If a pig had wings, he could fly.
4. They say that the British are coming.
5. But I know that they went to India.
6. By intimidating their leaders, he took command of their country.
7. When you grow up, you'll understand.
8. He gave her his horse and expected her to love him in return.
9. She's not the marrying kind.
10. I come to bury Caesar, not to praise him.
11. If you reach for that sword, you're dead where you sit.
12. Even though we are young, we have certain responsibilities.
13. I hear that your family eats no radishes.
14. We do not happen to like radishes, sir.
15. Since your mother brought you here, she must love you.
16. I see that the natives are restless tonight.
17. Those in the city will never believe your story, Miss.
18. They won't understand a talking horse.
19. He came, he saw, he conquered.
20. He who eats my flesh and drinks my blood has eternal life.
21. Loving you has given me an appreciation for music.
22. Loving you, I can never strum another lyre.

23. They slipped out of its belly, without a single Trojan's notice.

24. Most of us eat in order to live; but he lives to eat.

II. Decline the following verbs fully, in all the tenses of the participle so far presented:
1. Any three regular verbs;
2. δίδωμι, εἰμί, ἵημι, ἵστημι, τίθημι, and δείκνυμι; and
3. Three contract verbs (one from each group).

III. Compose the following sentences in Greek, using participles to express the words and phrases in italics (attributive phrases [p. 85, par. 1], supplementary verbs [par. 2], circumstantial clauses [par. 3], subordinate verbs in a series [par. 4], or indirect statement with verbs of sense perception or knowing [par. 5]):
1. I hear that a woman *is making war.*
2. She happens *to be* very brave.
3. Wise are *those who trust* her.
4. *When she saw,* she spoke.
5. *If she loses,* will she be badly off?
6. *Even though we look* (βλέπω), we do not always see (ὁράω).
7. *Because the gods are immortal,* we will sacrifice.
8. We sent a messenger *to distribute* the money.
9. *He saw, he conquered,* he died.
10. We learn well *by teaching.*

Reading

1. εἶδον τοὺς βαρβάρους τὸν ποιητὴν λύοντας.
2. χάρις χάριν γάρ ἐστιν ἡ τίκτουσ' ἀεί. — Sophocles, *Ajax* 522
3. ἔνθ' ἄλλους μὲν πάντας ἐλάνθανε δάκρυα λείβων. — Homer, *Odyssey* 8.532
4. ἁ Κύπρις τὰν Κύπριν ἐνὶ Κνίδῳ εἶπεν ἰδοῦσα,
   Φεῦ, φεῦ, ποῦ γυμνὴν εἶδέ με Πραξιτέλης; — Plato
5. πολλοὶ δρῶντες τὰ αἴσχιστα λόγους ἀρίστους ἀσκοῦσιν. — Democritus
6. πολλοὶ δοκοῦντες εἶναι φίλοι οὔκ εἰσι, καὶ οὐ δοκοῦντές εἰσιν. — Democritus
7. φίλος ἐστὶ μία ψυχὴ δυοῖν σώμασιν ἐνοικοῦσα. — Aristotle
8. πόλις γὰρ οὐκ ἔσθ' ἥτις ἀνδρός ἐσθ' ἑνός. — Sophocles, *Antigone* 737
9. πᾶς ὁ ἐπὶ γῆς καὶ ὑπὸ γῆς χρυσὸς ἀρετῆς οὐκ ἀντάξιος. — Plato, *Laws* 728a

10. τὴν πόλιν τῶν πολεμίων ἐχόντων εἷλον.
11. ἡ μήτηρ ὑπῆρχε τῷ Κύρῳ, φιλοῦσα αὐτὸν μᾶλλον ἢ τὸν
    βασιλεύοντα Ἀρταξέρξην.
12. πέμψαντες κήρυκα λέξοντα ταῦτα τοῖς Ἀθηναίοις, ἔμενον
    ἐν τῷ στρατοπέδῳ οἱ ἄρχοντες.
13. φύσις κέρατα ταύροις,
    ὁπλὰς δ᾽ ἔδωκεν ἵπποις,
    ποδωκίαν λαγωοῖς,
    λέουσι χάσμ᾽ ὀδόντων,
    τοῖς ἰχθύσιν τὸ νηκτόν,
    τοῖς ὀρνέοις πέτασθαι,
    τοῖς ἀνδράσιν φρόνημα,
    γυναιξὶν οὐκέτ᾽ εἶχεν·
    τί οὖν; δίδωσι κάλλος,
    ἀντ᾽ ἀσπίδων ἁπάσων,
    ἀντ᾽ ἐγχέων ἁπάντων·
    νικᾷ δὲ καὶ σίδηρον
    καὶ πῦρ καλή τις οὖσα. —Anacreon

Composition

1. If you write a book, you will always have problems (κακά).
2. We happen to have very good laws.
3. I see that the city is obeying us.
4. He who wishes to lead the army loves war.
5. Even though they sacrifice, the Athenians do not love their gods.
6. They sent the child into the city, led the army into the camp, and
   remained there with their friends.

Lesson 15

The Subjunctive Mood

1. Several grammatical constructions in Greek, such as indirect statement, require the verb (usually, but not always, of the *subordinate,* or *dependent,* clause) to be in a mood other than the indicative. The use of separate moods is much more extensive in Greek than it is in English and is governed by specific rules.

2. The two moods that we will study in the next few lessons are used mostly in *subordinate* clauses; they have few uses as *main* verbs of a sentence. We found this true of the infinitive and the participle, too, so it is not a new phenomenon.

3. The *subjunctive* mood is distinguished from the indicative by a different set of personal endings. There is *no future subjunctive*. As with the infinitive and the participle, there is *no augment on the aorist tense*. The augment is reserved for the indicative mood alone.

4. The endings for the subjunctive active of regular verbs (present, first aorist, and second aorist) are as follows:

-ω	-ωμεν
-ῃς	-ητε
-ῃ	-ωσι

5. Learn the following subjunctive conjugations:

present: φέρω	*first aorist:* ἔλυσα	*second aorist:* ἔμαθον
φέρω	λύσω	μάθω
φέρῃς	λύσῃς	μάθῃς
φέρῃ	λύσῃ	μάθῃ
φέρωμεν	λύσωμεν	μάθωμεν
φέρητε	λύσητε	μάθητε
φέρωσι	λύσωσι	μάθωσι

6. The tenses of the subjunctive mood rarely have a temporal significance; it is rather their *aspect* that is significant, the present being used for a *continuous or repeated* action or state, the aorist for a *single act*.

7. Learn the following paradigms for the present subjunctive active of contract verbs. Notice that there are *no* differences between indicative and subjunctive in -αω verbs, *many* in -εω verbs, and differences only in the *plural* forms of -οω verbs. Contract verbs are regular outside the present system.

(νικάω)	(ποιέω)	(δηλόω)
νικῶ	ποιῶ	δηλῶ
νικᾷς	ποιῇς	δηλοῖς
νικᾷ	ποιῇ	δηλοῖ
νικῶμεν	ποιῶμεν	δηλῶμεν
νικᾶτε	ποιῆτε	δηλῶτε
νικῶσι	ποιῶσι	δηλῶσι

8. Learn the following subjunctive conjugations of -μι verbs:

present subjunctive active

(δίδωμι)	(ἵημι)	(τίθημι)	(ἵστημι)
διδῶ	ἱῶ	τιθῶ	ἱστῶ
διδῷς	ἱῇς	τιθῇς	ἱστῇς
διδῷ	ἱῇ	τιθῇ	ἱστῇ
διδῶμεν	ἱῶμεν	τιθῶμεν	ἱστῶμεν
διδῶτε	ἱῆτε	τιθῆτε	ἱστῆτε
διδῶσι	ἱῶσι	τιθῶσι	ἱστῶσι

second aorist subjunctive active

(ἔδωκα)	(ἧκα)	(ἔθηκα)	(ἔστην)
δῶ	ὧ	θῶ	στῶ
δῷς	ἧς	θῇς	στῇς
δῷ	ἧ	θῇ	στῇ
δῶμεν	ὧμεν	θῶμεν	στῶμεν
δῶτε	ἧτε	θῆτε	στῆτε
δῶσι	ὧσι	θῶσι	στῶσι

first aorist subjunctive active (ἔστησα)

στήσω	στήσωμεν
στήσῃς	στήσητε
στήσῃ	στήσωσι

present *subjunctive active* (δείκνυμι)	*first aorist* *subjunctive active* (ἔδειξα)
δεικνύω	δείξω
δεικνύῃς	δείξῃς
δεικνύῃ	δείξῃ
δεικνύωμεν	δείξωμεν
δεικνύητε	δείξητε
δεικνύωσι	δείξωσι

present subjunctive (εἰμί), not enclitic in this mood:

ὦ	ὦμεν
ᾖς	ἦτε
ᾖ	ὦσι

9. Learn the following forms of ἔγνων, the irregular second aorist conjugation of γιγνώσκω, *know, recognize:*

INDICATIVE

ἔγνων	ἔγνωμεν
ἔγνως	ἔγνωτε
ἔγνω	ἔγνωσαν

γνῶναι (infinitive)

PARTICIPLE

γνούς	γνοῦσα	γνόν
γνόντος	γνούσης	γνόντος
γνόντι	γνούσῃ	γνόντι
γνόντα	γνοῦσαν	γνόν
γνόντες	γνοῦσαι	γνόντα
γνόντων	γνουσῶν	γνόντων
γνοῦσι	γνούσαις	γνοῦσι
γνόντας	γνούσας	γνόντα

SUBJUNCTIVE

γνῶ	γνῶμεν
γνῷς	γνῶτε
γνῷ	γνῶσι

10. One of the few *independent* or *main* uses of the subjunctive mood is called *hortatory*. The hortatory subjunctive is limited to the first-person plural (*we*) and is used to exhort or encourage a group, of which the speaker is a member:

στῶμεν καὶ πολεμῶμεν. *Let us stand and fight!*
ἀκούωμεν τῆς γυναικός. *Let's listen to the woman.*

11. The untranslatable particle ἄν accompanies the subjunctive mood in several subordinate constructions. It also combines with introductory words (conjunctions, adverbs, pronouns), *sometimes* forming new words:

εἰ (*if*) + ἄν → ἐάν or ἤν or ἄν
ὅτε (*when*) + ἄν → ὅταν
ἐπειδή (*when, since*) + ἄν → ἐπειδάν
ὅστις + ἄν → ὅστις ἄν

12. Certain conditions, more likely (than not) to come true in the future, are expressed in Greek according to a predictable formula. The syntactical formula for these conditions, called *future-more-vivid* conditions, is given below. Notice that the negative μή is used to negate the *protasis* (subordinate clause) and οὐ to negate the *apodosis* (main clause) of this conditional construction:

protasis	*apodosis*
subjunctive + ἄν	future indicative
	(or imperative)

ἐὰν ταῦτα μὴ μάθωμεν, κακῶς ἕξομεν. *If we do not learn these things, we will be badly off.*
ὅταν ἔλθῃ εἰς Ἀθήνας, λύσομεν τοὺς δούλους. *When he comes into Athens, we shall free the slaves.*

13. Conditional expressions of a general truth in present time are called *present general* conditions. The syntactical formula

for present general conditions is as follows (as with future more vivid, the protasis of this condition is negated by μή, and the apodosis by οὐ):

protasis	apodosis
subjunctive + ἄν	present indicative

ὅστις ἂν ἔχῃ παιδία ὄλβιός ἐστιν. *Whoever has children is happy.*

ἢν μὴ κακ᾽ εἴπῃς ἀνθρώπους, οὐ μῶρος εἶ. *If you don't speak evil of people, you're not a fool.*

Vocabulary

ἀγορά, ἀγορᾶς, ἡ *marketplace, shopping center*

αἴγλα, αἴγλας, ἡ *light, sunlight; glory*

αἰών, αἰῶνος, ὁ *life; period of a lifetime*

ἀργύριον, ἀργυρίου, τό *silver; money*

Καμβύσης, Καμβύσου, ὁ *Cambyses, son of Cyrus the Great and king of Persia, 529–521 B.C. He began his rule as a wise and tolerant leader, but ended a tyrannical madman. His story is told by Herodotus in* The Persian Wars, *bk. 3.*

κόλαξ, κόλακος, ὁ *flatterer, fawner, parasite*

κόραξ, κόρακος, ὁ *raven, crow*

μέτρον, μέτρου, τό *measure*

μῶρος, μώρου, ὁ *fool; dull, stupid person*

νεκρός, νεκροῦ, ὁ *corpse*

ὄναρ, τό *dream* (only nominative and accusative singular used; other cases supplied by ὄνειρος; poetic)

πλοῦς, πλοῦ, ὁ *sailing, voyage* (contract noun, declined like νοῦς)

πλοῦτος, πλούτου, ὁ *wealth, riches*

πνεῦμα, πνεύματος, τό *blast, wind; breath*

πρῷρα, πρῴρας, ἡ *prow, front end of a ship*
    πνεῦμα τοὐκ πρῴρας *a contrary wind*

σκιά, σκιᾶς, ἡ *shadow, shade*

τέχνη, τέχνης, ἡ *skill, art, craft*

φέγγος, φέγγους, τό *light, splendor; joy*

χρῆμα, χρήματος, τό *thing, matter, affair;* (often in plural) *money*

ἀκούω, ἀκούσομαι, ἤκουσα, ἀκήκοα, ἤκουσμαι, ἠκούσθην
(imperfect ἤκουον) *hear, listen to* (+ *genitive* or *accusative* of
the person heard, *accusative* of the thing heard)

ἀνίημι, *κτλ send up, let go, let loose* (transitive); *abate, slacken*
(intransitive)

ἀντιοστατεῖ *is unfavorable* (poetic for ἀνθίσταμαι, middle voice
of ἀνθίστημι; see lesson 19)

γαργαλίζει (third person singular) *tickles, is able to tickle*

γιγνώσκω, γνώσομαι, ἔγνων, ἔγνωκα, ἔγνωσμαι, ἐγνώσθην
know, recognize

δέῃ (subjunctive of δεῖ; -εω contract verbs with *monosyllabic stems*
only contract when the resultant contraction would be the syllable
ει; otherwise, they remain uncontracted)

ἐμπίπτω, *κτλ* (for parts, see πίπτω below) *fall in* or *on; fall upon,
attack; fall in with* (in all senses, either + *dative* or + prepositional phrase with ἐν or εἰς)

ἔπειμι, ἐπέσομαι *remain, last; be at hand, be present*

ἐσθίω, ἔδομαι, ἔφαγον, ἐδήδοκα, ἐδήδεσμαι, ἠδέσθην (imperfect
ἤσθιον) *eat*

ζάω, ζήσω, ἔζησα, ἔζηκα, —, — *live* (contracts into η or ῃ where
other -αω verbs contract into α or ᾳ)

ἦλθον *came, went* (stem ἐλθ-, second aorist of ἔρχομαι; see
lesson 19)

κακῶς ἔχω *be badly off; be ill*

καταβαύζω *bark at* (+ *genitive*)

λαμβάνω, λήψομαι, ἔλαβον, εἴληφα, εἴλημμαι, ἐλήφθην *take,
seize, get*

παραλαμβάνω, *κτλ call in; get control of; invite*

πίπτω, πεσοῦμαι, ἔπεσον, πέπτωκα, —, — *fall*

στελοῦμεν *we will set out, prepare to go* (contract liquid future of
στέλλω; see lesson 16)

σύνειμι, συνέσομαι *be with* (+ *dative*)

τελευτάω, τελευτήσω, ἐτελεύτησα, τετελεύτηκα, —,
ἐτελευτήθην *finish, die*

φεύγω, φεύξομαι, ἔφυγον, πέφευγα, —, — *escape, flee*

ἅπας = πᾶς

βαρύς *heavy, slow; wearisome, boring* (masculine nominative
singular; see lesson 16)

γέλοιος, γελοία, γέλοιον (also accented γελοῖος, γελοία,
   γελοῖον) *funny*
διόσδοτος, διόσδοτον *god-given; given by Zeus*
ἐπάμερος, ἐπάμερον *ephemeral, short-lived* (poetic for ἐφήμερος,
   κτλ)
ἐφικτός, ἐφικτή, ἐφικτόν *accessible, attainable*
λαμπρός, λαμπρή, λαμπρόν *shining*
μείλιχος, μειλίχα, μείλιχον *soothing, gracious*
ὄλβιος, ὀλβία, ὄλβιον *happy, blessed*

ἄν (untranslatable particle used with verbs to indicate that the action
   is limited by certain circumstances or defined by certain conditions; also = ἐάν)
ἐάν = εἰ + ἄν
ἑαυτοῦ, ἑαυτῆς, ἑαυτοῦ (sometimes contracted into αὑτοῦ, αὑτῆς,
   αὑτοῦ, *κτλ*) *himself, herself, itself, themselves* (reflexive third-
   person pronoun, only used in the genitive, dative, and accusative)
εἰ μή (ἐὰν μή, ἢν μή, ἂν μή) *if not; unless*
ἐπειδάν = ἐπειδή + ἄν
ἐπειδή *since, when, whereas* (conjunction)
ἤν = εἰ + ἄν
καθάπερ *just as, exactly as* (adverb)
κἄν = καί + ἄν
μηδείς, μηδεμία, μηδέν *no one, nothing, not one* (see Appendix B
   for declension)
ὁ μέν ... ὁ δέ *the one ... the other* (used in both singular and plural
   and all genders)
ὅταν = ὅτε + ἄν
ὅτε *when* (conjunction)
οὐδείς, οὐδεμία, οὐδέν *no one, nothing, not one* (see Appendix B
   for declension)
οὐκοῦν *very well, yes, surely*
οὔτε ... οὔτε *neither ... nor*
τοὐκ = τὸ ἐκ
ὡς *how ... !* (exclamatory adverb)

Practice

I. Pick out the verbs in the following sentences that would be subjunctive in Greek and identify the *use* (*present general, future more vivid, hortatory*):
  1. Let's call the sun "heaven's eye."
  2. When he sees us, he will bring the money.
  3. Whenever the queen is away, I am the king.
  4. Whoever wants to fly is a fool.
  5. You will find happiness wherever you go.
  6. Let us give to Caesar the things that are Caesar's.
  7. If you give him one more dime, I will leave you.
  8. Everyone is a little crazy when the moon is full.
  9. If you're going in, dear, get me a drink.
10. We never do wrong when we help a child.

II. Conjugate the following verbs fully, in the present and aorist tenses, indicative, infinitive, and subjunctive moods, and decline them fully in the present and aorist participle:
1. Any three regular verbs;
2. δίδωμι, ἵημι, τίθημι, and δείκνυμι; and
3. Three contract verbs (one from each group).

Reading

  1. γελᾷ ὁ μῶρος, κἄν τι μὴ γέλοιον ᾖ. —Menander
  2. ἂν αὐτῷ διδῷς ἀργύριον καὶ πείθῃς ἐκεῖνον, ποιήσει καί σε σοφόν. —Plato, *Protagoras* 310d
  3. τελευτήσαντος δὲ Κύρου ἦρχε Καμβύσης, Κύρου ὢν παῖς καὶ τῆς γυναικὸς αὐτοῦ.
  4. κύνες καταβαύζουσιν ὧν ἂν μὴ γιγνώσκωσιν. —Heraclitus
  5. τίς ἐστιν οὗτος;
                    ἰατρός.
               ὡς κακῶς ἔχει
     ἅπας ἰατρός, ἐὰν κακῶς μηδεὶς ἔχῃ. —Philemon
  6. οὐκ ἔστιν ἀνδρὶ ἀγαθῷ κακὸν οὐδὲν οὔτε ζῶντι οὔτε τελευτήσαντι. —Plato, *Apology of Socrates* 41d
  7. πάντα λέξει ὅταν εἰς τὴν ἀγορὰν ἔλθῃ.
  8. ὅστις ἂν ἐθέλῃ λέγειν ἀεὶ λανθάνει ἑαυτὸν τοῖς συνοῦσιν

ὢν βαρύς.
9. ἤκουσε τοὺς βαρβάρους ἐλθόντας.
10. πάντων χρημάτων μέτρον ἐστὶν ἄνθρωπος, τῶν μὲν ὄντων
    ὡς ἔστιν, τῶν δ' οὐκ ὄντων ὡς οὐκ ἔστιν. —Plato, *Cratylus*
    385e
11. ΝΕΟΠΤΟΛΕΜΟΣ
    οὐκοῦν ἐπειδὰν πνεῦμα τοὐκ πρῴρας ἀνῇ,
    τότε στελοῦμεν· νῦν γὰρ ἀντιοστατεῖ.
    ΦΙΛΟΚΤΗΤΗΣ
    ἀεὶ καλὸς πλοῦς ἐσθ' ὅταν φεύγῃς κακά. —Sophocles,
    Philoctetes 639–41
12. ὁ δὲ πλοῦτος ἡμᾶς, καθάπερ ἰατρὸς κακός,
    πάντας βλέποντας παραλαβὼν τυφλοὺς ποιεῖ. —Antiphanes
13. οὔτε τέχνη οὔτε σοφία ἐφικτόν, ἢν μὴ μάθῃ τις. —
    Democritus
14. ποιήσομεν, κἂν ἀποθανεῖν ἡμᾶς δέῃ. —Aristophanes,
    Lysistrata 123
15. κρεῖττον εἰς κόρακας ἢ εἰς κόλακας ἐμπεσεῖν· οἱ μὲν γὰρ
    νεκρούς, οἱ δὲ ζῶντας ἐσθίουσιν. —Antisthenes
16. ἐπάμεροι· τί δέ τις; τί δ' οὔ τις; σκιᾶς ὄναρ
    ἄνθρωπος. ἀλλ' ὅταν αἴγλα διόσδοτος ἔλθῃ,
    λαμπρὸν φέγγος ἔπεστιν ἀνδρῶν καὶ μείλιχος αἰών. —
    Pindar, *Pythian Ode 8*. 95–7
17. διὰ τί αὐτὸς αὑτὸν οὐδεὶς γαργαλίζει; —Aristotle, *Problems*

Composition

1. We hear that the city is badly off.
2. Even though the Persians were with us, the Athenians came into
   the marketplace.
3. Neither money nor beautiful speeches will persuade a man when
   he is in love.
4. Nothing is accessible if a man does not know himself.
5. Let's give the best gifts to our mothers and our fathers.

6. Heracles the Savior.

From the Cornell University Collection of Ancient Coins; photo by Andrew Gillis.

This silver tetradrachm from Thasos (first or second century B.C.) has the face of Dionysus on the obverse, and on the reverse (shown here), the most popular and widely worshiped Greek hero, Heracles. He holds a lion-skin in his left hand (the skin of the famous Nemean lion, which ravaged the countryside around Nemea until Heracles killed and skinned it, keeping the skin as a prize) and a club in his right hand. The monogram between the club and Heracles is made up of the first three letters of his name, HPA. The inscription reads Ἡρακλέους σωτῆρος Θασίων: (coin) of Heracles, savior of the Thasians.

Lesson 16

Contract Future, Adjectives in -υς and -ης, and υ-stem Nouns

1. Three classes of verbs in Greek have *futures* that are contracted in a manner similar to the *present* conjugations of contract verbs. These conjugations are called *Attic futures,* because they are so prominent in Attic writers.

   a. Verbs whose first principal part ends in -ιζω normally form their future with endings identical to the present endings of -εω contract verbs. Learn the future of νομίζω, νομιῶ:

νομιῶ	νομιοῦμεν
νομιεῖς	νομιεῖτε
νομιεῖ	νομιοῦσι

   νομιεῖν (infinitive)

   b. Some -εω contract verbs form their future by contracting the last stem vowel with the endings, as in the present. Learn the future of καλέω, καλῶ:

καλῶ	καλοῦμεν
καλεῖς	καλεῖτε
καλεῖ	καλοῦσι

   καλεῖν (infinitive)

   c. Some verbs whose second principal part would normally end in -ασω drop the σ and contract the last stem vowel with the endings, as -αω contract verbs do in the present. Learn the future conjugation of ἐλαύνω (*drive, march*), ἐλῶ:

ἐλῶ	ἐλῶμεν
ἐλᾷς	ἐλᾶτε
ἐλᾷ	ἐλῶσι

   ἐλᾶν (infinitive)

2. Verbs whose first-principal-part *stems* end in a *liquid* (λ, μ, ν, or ρ) regularly form their future like the present of -εω contract verbs. This conjugation is called the *liquid future*. Learn the future conjugations of κρίνω (*choose*) and ἀγγέλλω (*announce*), κρινῶ and ἀγγελῶ, respectively:

κρινῶ   κρινοῦμεν
κρινεῖς   κρινεῖτε
κρινεῖ   κρινοῦσι

κρινεῖν (infinitive)

ἀγγελῶ   ἀγγελοῦμεν
ἀγγελεῖς   ἀγγελεῖτε
ἀγγελεῖ   ἀγγελοῦσι

ἀγγελεῖν (infinitive)

3. Learn the declension of γλυκύς (*sweet, pleasant, delightful*). It is typical of an important class of adjectives in Greek:

γλυκύς   γλυκεῖα   γλυκύ
γλυκέος   γλυκείας   γλυκέος
γλυκεῖ   γλυκείᾳ   γλυκεῖ
γλυκύν   γλυκεῖαν   γλυκύ

γλυκεῖς   γλυκεῖαι   γλυκέα
γλυκέων   γλυκειῶν   γλυκέων
γλυκέσι   γλυκείαις   γλυκέσι
γλυκεῖς   γλυκείας   γλυκέα

4. Another important group of adjectives, many of which are compound adjectives, has one set of endings for the masculine and feminine, and another set for the neuter. Learn the declension of ἀληθής (*unconcealed, true, truthful, honest*), which is typical of this group:

ἀληθής   ἀληθές
ἀληθοῦς   ἀληθοῦς
ἀληθεῖ   ἀληθεῖ
ἀληθῆ   ἀληθές

ἀληθεῖς   ἀληθῆ
ἀληθῶν   ἀληθῶν
ἀληθέσι   ἀληθέσι
ἀληθεῖς   ἀληθῆ

5. Two small, but important, groups of third-declension nouns both
have -υς (masculine, feminine) or -υ (neuter) in the nominative
singular. One group, however, has -εως in the genitive singular,
while the other has -υος, and they differ in other forms as
well. Learn πέλεκυς (*battle-axe*) and ἄστυ (*town*), representative
of the first group, and ἰσχύς (*strength, power*) and μῦς (*mouse*),
representative of the other:

ὁ πέλεκυς	τὸ ἄστυ
τοῦ πελέκεως	τοῦ ἄστεως
τῷ πελέκει	τῷ ἄστει
τὸν πέλεκυν	τὸ ἄστυ
οἱ πελέκεις	τὰ ἄστη
τῶν πελέκεων	τῶν ἄστεων
τοῖς πελέκεσι	τοῖς ἄστεσι
τοὺς πελέκεις	τὰ ἄστη
ἡ ἰσχύς	ὁ μῦς
τῆς ἰσχύος	τοῦ μυός
τῇ ἰσχύϊ†	τῷ μυί [μυΐ]†
τὴν ἰσχύν	τὸν μῦν
αἱ ἰσχύες	οἱ μύες
τῶν ἰσχύων	τῶν μυῶν
ταῖς ἰσχύσι	τοῖς μυσί
τὰς ἰσχῦς or ἰσχύας	τοὺς μῦς or μύας

†The two dots (¨) above a letter are called a *mark of diaeresis*
and indicate that the vowel so marked is *not* part of a diphthong
but is to be pronounced as a separate syllable.

6. Learn the declension of ναῦς (*ship*) and of βοῦς (*bull* or *cow*):

ἡ ναῦς	ὁ (or ἡ) βοῦς
τῆς νεώς	τοῦ βοός
τῇ νηί [νηΐ]	τῷ βοί [βοΐ]
τὴν ναῦν	τὸν βοῦν
αἱ νῆες	οἱ βόες
τῶν νεῶν	τῶν βοῶν
ταῖς ναυσί	τοῖς βουσί
τὰς ναῦς	τοὺς βοῦς

7. Learn the declension of the contract adjective χρυσοῦς (*golden*):

χρυσοῦς	χρυσῆ	χρυσοῦν
χρυσοῦ	χρυσῆς	χρυσοῦ
χρυσῷ	χρυσῇ	χρυσῷ
χρυσοῦν	χρυσῆν	χρυσοῦν
χρυσοῖ	χρυσαῖ	χρυσᾶ
χρυσῶν	χρυσῶν	χρυσῶν
χρυσοῖς	χρυσαῖς	χρυσοῖς
χρυσοῦς	χρυσᾶς	χρυσᾶ

Vocabulary

Αἴας, Αἴαντος, ὁ *Ajax, the son of Telamon*
ἄστυ, ἄστεως, τό *town*
βοῦς, βοός, ὁ or ἡ *bull, ox; cow;* (plural) *cattle*
δεσπότης, δεσπότου, ὁ *master, lord; chief*
Ἰησοῦς, Ἰησοῦ, ὁ *Joshua (Old Testament); Jesus (New Testament)*
ἰσχύς, ἰσχύος, ἡ *strength, power; validity*
ἰχθύς, ἰχθύος, ὁ *fish*
ἴχνος, ἴχνους, τό *track, footstep; trace*
καιρός, καιροῦ, ὁ *exact* or *critical time, opportunity; right time,*
    season; (medical) *crisis*
κρίσις, κρίσεως, ἡ *decision, judgment*
κυβερνήτης, κυβερνήτου, ὁ *pilot, helmsman; guide*
μῦς, μυός, ὁ *mouse*
ναῦς, νεώς, ἡ *ship*
ὀμευνέτιν *sleeping partner, bedmate* (feminine accusative singular)
ὄμμα, ὄμματος, τό *eye; sight*
παιδεία, παιδείας, ἡ *training (of a child); education*
πέλεκυς, πελέκεως, ὁ *battle-axe, twin-blade axe*
πλῆθος, πλήθους, τό *great number, mass; multitude*
πούς, ποδός, ὁ *foot*
πρόσφθεγμα, προσφθέγματος, τό *greeting*
σωτήρ, σωτῆρος, ὁ *savior*
τέλος, τέλους, τό *task, duty, obligation*
τιμή, τιμῆς, ἡ *honor, esteem, dignity*
υἱός, υἱοῦ, ὁ *son*

φιλοσοφία, φιλοσοφίας, ἡ *love of knowledge, pursuit of wisdom; philosophy*

ἀγγέλλω, ἀγγελῶ, ἤγγειλα, ἤγγελκα, ἤγγελμαι, ἠγγέλθην (imperfect ἤγγελλον) *announce, report* (+ *accusative/infinitive*)

βέβηκεν *has (just) stepped* (third-person singular perfect active indicative of βαίνω; see lesson 21)

ἐκλαλέω *blurt out, blab* (for parts, see λαλέω below)

ἐλαύνω, ἐλῶ, ἤλασα, ἐλήλακα, ἐλήλαμαι, ἠλάθην (imperfect ἤλαυνον) *drive, march; push on; persecute*

ἐρίζων *quarreling, wrangling* (masculine nominative singular participle)

ἐρῶ *will say* (Attic future, conjugated like καλῶ; present supplied by λέγω or φημί; aorist supplied by εἶπον)

ἰάπτων *wounding, piercing* (masculine nominative singular participle)

ἴδετε *look at, behold!* (second-person plural imperative of εἶδον; see lesson 24)

κομίζω, κομιῶ, ἐκόμισα, κεκόμικα, κεκόμισμαι, ἐκομίσθην *take care of; carry away, carry off; convey, bring*

κρίνω, κρινῶ, ἔκρινα, κέκρικα, κέκριμαι, ἐκρίθην *separate; choose, decide, judge* (+ *accusative/infinitive*)

λαλέω, λαλήσω, ἐλάλησα, —, —, ἐλαλήθην *talk, chat, prattle;* (of insects, birds, etc.) *chirp, chatter*

μακύνων = μηκύνων *delaying, putting off* (masculine nominative singular participle, poetic spelling)

μισέω, μισήσω, ἐμίσησα, μεμίσηκα, μεμίσημαι, ἐμισήθην *hate* (+ *infinitive;* also + *accusative* of person)

σιγάω, σιγήσομαι, ἐσίγησα, σεσίγηκα, σεσίγημαι, ἐσιγήθην *be silent, be still*

ὑβρίζω, ὑβριῶ, ὕβρισα, ὕβρικα, ὕβρισμαι, ὑβρίσθην (imperfect ὕβριζον) *run riot, commit outrage, injure wantonly*

φρονέω, φρονήσω, ἐφρόνησα, πεφρόνηκα, —, — *mean, intend, have in mind; think, plan*

ἀληθής, ἀληθές *unconcealed; true, truthful, honest*
ἄφωνος, ἄφωνον *voiceless, dumb, mute*
βραδύς, βραδεῖα, βραδύ *dull, sluggish; slow*
βραχύς, βραχεῖα, βραχύ *short, small; few*
γλυκύς, γλυκεῖα, γλυκύ *sweet, pleasant, delightful*
ἡδύς, ἡδεῖα, ἡδύ *pleasant, welcome, pleasing*

λυσιτελής, λυσιτελές *paying for expenses; useful, profitable, advantageous* (as neuter noun, τὸ λυσιτελές, *profit, usefulness, advantage;* see lesson 4, par. 10)
ὅμοιος, ὁμοία, ὅμοιον *like, similar to* (+ *dative* of *equal* comparison; compare genitive of unequal comparison, lesson 10)
ὀξύς, ὀξεῖα, ὀξύ *sharp, keen, quick; shrill; urgent*
πικρός, πικρά, πικρόν *sharp, pungent, bitter*
σφαλερός, σφαλερά, σφαλερόν *slippery, perilous, dangerous*
ταχύς, ταχεῖα, ταχύ *swift, rapid, quick*
χριστός, χριστή, χριστόν *anointed;* (capitalized) *Christ (New Testament)*
χρυσοῦς, χρυσῆ, χρυσοῦν *golden*
ψευδής, ψευδές *false, lying, untrue*

ἀντία *against* (*adverb* used as *preposition* + *dative*)
πρός *in the eyes of* (preposition + *genitive*)

Practice

1. Decline three adjectives in -υς, three adjectives in -ης, and three υ-stem nouns fully.
2. Conjugate five contract-future verbs, including one of each type of Attic future and one liquid future.

Reading

1. γλῶττά σου ὁμοία ἐστὶ πελέκει ὀξεῖ.
2. τὰ δ᾽ ἄλλα σιγῶ· βοῦς ἐπὶ γλώττῃ μέγας βέβηκεν. — Aeschylus, *Agamemnon* 36–7
3. φιλοσοφία κυβερνήτης ἐστὶ τοῦ βίου.
4. φιλοσοφία βίου κυβερνήτης.
5. ἰσχύς μου ἡ ἀγάπη τοῦ λαοῦ.
6. Ἰησοῦς Χριστὸς Θεοῦ υἱὸς σωτήρ. (the words to a famous acronym)
7. ὁ βίος βραχύς, ἡ δὲ τέχνη μακρά, ὁ δὲ καιρὸς ὀξύς, ἡ δὲ πεῖρα σφαλερά, ἡ δὲ κρίσις χαλεπή. — Hippocrates
8. πάππος ἐστί, καὶ βραδὺ τὸ ἴχνος αὐτοῦ.

9. τὸ τοῦ ποδὸς μὲν βραδύ, τὸ τοῦ δὲ νοῦ ταχύ.—Euripides, *Ion* 743

10. οὐ κομιεῖς ἐξ ὀμμάτων τὴν γυναῖκα τήνδε; ἀφωνοτέρα γάρ ἐστι τῶν ἰχθύων.

11. ἐὰν ἀποθάνῃς, τί ἐροῦσί μοι οἱ δεσπόται;

12. καί τις πικρὸν πρόσφθεγμα δεσποτῶν ἐρεῖ
    λόγοις ἰάπτων, Ἴδετε τὴν ὁμευνέτιν
    Αἴαντος.—Sophocles, *Ajax* 500–02

13. ἡδύς ἐστιν οὗτος τοῖς λόγοις, ἀλλὰ φρονεῖ κακῶς.

14. ὅταν γὰρ ἡδύς τις λόγοις φρονῶν κακῶς
    πείθῃ τὸ πλῆθος, τῇ πόλει κακὸν μέγα.—Euripides, *Orestes* 907–08

15. ὅταν καλῇς θεούς, φρονῶν ψευδῇ, τίθης ψευδεῖς καὶ τοὺς θεούς.

16. οἶνος ἀληθής. (a proverb)

17. ἡ παιδεία ὁμοία ἐστὶ χρυσῷ στεφάνῳ· καὶ γὰρ τιμὴν ἔχει καὶ τὸ λυσιτελές.—Demophilus

18. ἐκεῖνος νέος ἦν ἐν τοῖς παισί, καὶ ἀνὴρ ἐν τοῖς ἀνδράσιν.

19. ἔμαθε δ' ὑβρίζοντα μισεῖν,
    οὐκ ἐρίζων ἀντία τοῖς ἀγαθοῖς,
    οὐδὲ μακύνων τέλος οὐδέν. ὁ γὰρ καιρὸς πρὸς
        ἀνθρώπων βραχὺ μέτρον ἔχει.
    εὖ ταῦτα ἔγνω.—Pindar, *Pythian Ode* 4. 284–7

20. οὐδὲν γὰρ οὕτως ἐστὶν ἀνθρώποις γλυκὺ
    ὡς τοὐκλαλεῖν τἀλλότρια.—Menander

Composition

1. My strength is the education of the town.
2. What will you say when the helmsman dies?
3. The pursuit of wisdom is often dangerous but always welcome.
4. The mind of Ajax is sharp, but the mind of the gods is sharper.
5. Will we decide that our obligations are too bitter?

Lesson 17

The Optative Mood

1. The *optative* mood is a less vivid, less distinct, and less direct form of expression than are the indicative, subjunctive, and imperative moods. It is used in constructions of the same general character as those in which the indicative, subjunctive, and imperative are used:

   φεύγωμεν. *Let's escape!* (hortatory subjunctive)
   φεύγοιμεν. *May we escape!* (optative of wish)
   πάντα ἡμῖν δώσει. *He will give us everything.* (future indicative)
   πάντα ἡμῖν ἂν διδοίη. *He might give us everything; he could give us everything.* (potential optative)

2. The two uses cited above, *wish* and *potential,* are the principal *independent* uses of the optative mood. There are also several *dependent* or *subordinate* uses of the optative mood, where the optative either expresses something *less vividly* than the subjunctive or indicative; or else it expresses something in *past time* that the subjunctive or indicative would express in present time:

   ἐὰν ἔλθω, νικήσομεν. *If I go, we will win.* (future more vivid)
   εἰ ἔλθοι, νικῷμεν ἄν. *If he should go, we would win.* (future less vivid)
   θύομεν ὅταν νείφῃ. *We sacrifice when it snows.* (present general)
   ἐθύομεν ὅτε νείφοι. *We used to sacrifice when it snowed.* (past general)

3. The particle ἄν is used with the optative only in two independent clauses: the *potential optative* and the *apodosis* (main clause) of a *future-less-vivid* condition. The *optative of wish* is never accompanied by ἄν, and ἄν is not used in subordinate clauses with the optative mood.

4. The syntactical formula for *future-less-vivid* conditions is as
   follows:

protasis	*apodosis*
optative (introduced by	optative + ἄv
εἰ, ὅτε, ὅστις, κτλ)	

5. The syntactical formula for *past general* conditions is as follows:

protasis	*apodosis*
optative (introduced by	imperfect indicative
εἰ, ὅτε, ὅστις, κτλ)	

6. The negative οὐ is used with the optative mood only in those
   constructions that also use ἄv; namely, the *potential optative* and
   the *apodosis* of the *future less vivid*. The negative μή is used
   with the optative in all other constructions, independent or
   subordinate.

7. The personal endings of the optative mood include a *mood suffix*
   (or *modal sign*), which is added between the *thematic vowel*
   and the *verb ending* (or, for those verbs that are nonthematic,
   between the verb *stem vowel* or the *tense vowel* and the *verb
   ending*). The mood suffix for *regular verbs* and -νυμι *verbs* is
   the vowel ι. The mood suffix for -μι *verbs* and *contract verbs* is
   ιη, although it is found commonly only in the *singular:* in the
   plural of -μι verbs and contracts, ι is the normal suffix. The
   thematic vowel for the optative mood is o. The optative never
   has an augment.

8. Remember that the diphthongs -αι and -οι, as the last two letters
   of a Greek word, are normally considered short for purposes
   of accent (lesson 2, par. 5c); but in the *optative mood,* they are
   considered *long*.

9. Learn the following optative forms of regular and -νυμι verbs:

present: φέρω	*future:* λύσω	*first aorist:* ἔλυσα
φέροιμι	λύσοιμι	λύσαιμι
φέροις	λύσοις	λύσειας or λύσαις
φέροι	λύσοι	λύσειε or λύσαι
φέροιμεν	λύσοιμεν	λύσαιμεν
φέροιτε	λύσοιτε	λύσαιτε
φέροιεν	λύσοιεν	λύσειαν or λύσαιεν

present: δείκνυμι	*second aorist:* ἔμαθον
δεικνύοιμι	μάθοιμι
δεικνύοις	μάθοις
δεικνύοι	μάθοι
δεικνύοιμεν	μάθοιμεν
δεικνύοιτε	μάθοιτε
δεικνύοιεν	μάθοιεν

10. Learn the following optative forms of -μι verbs and contract verbs:

present optative active

(νικάω)	(ποιέω)	(δηλόω)
νικῷην	ποιοίην	δηλοίην
νικῷης	ποιοίης	δηλοίης
νικῷη	ποιοίη	δηλοίη
νικῷμεν	ποιοῖμεν	δηλοῖμεν
νικῷτε	ποιοῖτε	δηλοῖτε
νικῷεν	ποιοῖεν	δηλοῖεν

(δίδωμι)	(ἵημι)	(τίθημι)	(ἵστημι)	(εἰμί)
διδοίην	ἱείην	τιθείην	ἱσταίην	εἴην
διδοίης	ἱείης	τιθείης	ἱσταίης	εἴης
διδοίη	ἱείη	τιθείη	ἱσταίη	εἴη
διδοῖμεν	ἱεῖμεν	τιθεῖμεν	ἱσταῖμεν	εἶμεν
διδοῖτε	ἱεῖτε	τιθεῖτε	ἱσταῖτε	εἶτε
διδοῖεν	ἱεῖεν	τιθεῖεν	ἱσταῖεν	εἶεν

second aorist optative active

(ἔδωκα)	(ἦκα)	(ἔθηκα)	(ἔστην)
δοίην	εἴην	θείην	σταίην
δοίης	εἴης	θείης	σταίης
δοίη	εἴη	θείη	σταίη
δοῖμεν	εἶμεν	θεῖμεν	σταῖμεν
δοῖτε	εἶτε	θεῖτε	σταῖτε
δοῖεν	εἶεν	θεῖεν	σταῖεν

Plural forms in ιη are also found in -μι verbs and contract verbs:

νικῷημεν	δοίημεν	εἴημεν	δηλοίημεν	
νικῷητε	δοίητε	εἴητε	δηλοίητε	κτλ
νικῷησαν	δοίησαν	εἴησαν	δηλοίησαν	

11. Learn the contract future optative of νομίζω and ἐλαύνω; other contract futures are similarly conjugated:

(νομιῶ)	(ἐλῶ)
νομιοίην	ἐλῴην
νομιοίης	ἐλῴης
νομιοίη	ἐλῴη
νομιοῖμεν	ἐλῷμεν
νομιοῖτε	ἐλῷτε
νομιοῖεν	ἐλῷεν

Vocabulary

ἀδικία, ἀδικίας, ἡ *wrongdoing, injustice*

δεῖπνον, δείπνου, τό *meal; dinner, supper*

Ζεύς, Διός, Διί, Δία, Ζεῦ, ὁ *Zeus*

κίνδυνος, κινδύνου, ὁ *danger, hazard, risk*

κόσμος, κόσμου, ὁ *order; ornament, decoration; world order, universe*

Πάν, Πανός, ὁ *Pan*

τεῖχος, τείχους, τό *wall, fortification*

ἀδικέω, ἀδικήσω, ἠδίκησα, ἠδίκηκα, ἠδίκημαι, ἠδικήθην
  (imperfect ἠδίκουν) *do wrong; harm, injure*
ἀνδάνειν *be pleasing to* (+ *dative;* present infinitive)
ἀποφεύγω, κτλ *escape, flee from* (for parts, see φεύγω)
γενέσθαι *to become* (aorist infinitive; see lesson 19)
γένοιτο *would become* (third-person singular aorist optative; see
  lesson 20)
δέοντα: τὰ δέοντα *what is necessary* (neuter plural attributive
  participle of δεῖ; see lesson 13)
ἴωμεν *Let's go* (hortatory subjunctive of εἶμι; see lesson 22)
ὄφλοις *be charged with, get a reputation for* (+ *accusative;*
  second-person singular aorist optative of ὀφλισκάνω)
συνεύχου *pray with, say a prayer for* (+ *accusative* of the prayer,
  dative of the person prayed for; second-person singular present
  imperative; see lesson 24)
τιμάω, τιμήσω, ἐτίμησα, τετίμηκα, τετίμημαι, ἐτιμήθην *honor,*
  revere

εὐσεβής, εὐσεβές *pious, righteous, holy, religious*
κοινός, κοινή, κοινόν *common, shared*
ὅσος, ὅση, ὅσον *as much as;* (plural) *as many as*
πλούσιος, πλουσία, πλούσιον *rich, wealthy*
φίλιος, φιλία, φίλιον *friendly; compatible with* (+ *dative*)
φίλος, φίλη, φίλον *dear, beloved*

ἔνδοθεν *from within, on the inside* (adverb)
ἐντός *within, inside* (adverb)
ἔξωθεν *without, on the outside* (adverb)
ἐπί *to, toward, for* (preposition + *accusative*)
ἴσως *probably, perhaps* (adverb)
μόνον *only* (adverbial accusative of μόνος)
ὁπότε *when, whenever* (less definite than ὅτε)
πρίν *before, formerly*
  ἐν τῷ πρὶν χρόνῳ *in time past, formerly*
πῶς *how?* (interrogative adverb)
τἄνδοθεν = τὰ ἔνδοθεν (ὄντα)
τῇδε *here, in this place* (adverb)
τίν = σοί (Doric dialect, used in poetry)
ὑπέρ *on behalf of, in defense of, for* (preposition + *genitive*)

ὦ *O* (particle, often left untranslated, that frequently introduces a vocative word or phrase)

Practice

Conjugate six verbs fully, in the indicative, subjunctive, and optative active, including at least one regular verb, one contract verb, and one -μι verb.

Reading

1. ταῖς μὲν πόλεσι τὰ τείχη κόσμον καὶ ἰσχὺν φέρει, ταῖς δὲ ψυχαῖς ἡ παιδεία.
2. ὁπότε ἐν τῷ πρὶν χρόνῳ παρείη, πάντα τὰ δέοντα ἐποίει.
3. εἴη, Ζεῦ, τὶν εἴη ἀνδάνειν. —Pindar, *Pythian Ode 1*. 29
4. εἰ οἱ πολέμιοι ἔλθοιεν εἰς τὴν πόλιν, πολεμοῖτε ἄν.
5. οὐκ ἔστιν οὐδεὶς ὅστις οὐκ ἂν ταῦτα καὶ μείζω τούτων ὑπὲρ τῶν παίδων ἑαυτοῦ ποιήσειε.
6. εἴ τις ἐθέλοι, πάντα ποιῶν, κίνδυνον ἀποφεύγειν, οὐκ ἂν εὐδαίμων γένοιτο.
7. δεινὸν ἂν εἴη εἰ, οὐκ ἀδικῶν, ἀδικίαν ὄφλοις.
8. οὐ μόνον ὁ ποιῶν τι, ἀλλὰ καὶ ὁ μὴ ποιῶν τι πολλάκις ἀδικεῖ.
9. εἴ με ἐπὶ δεῖπνον καλέσειας, ἴσως ἂν ἔλθοιμι.
10. πῶς ἂν κάλλιον καὶ εὐσεβέστερόν τις τοὺς θεοὺς τιμῴη, ἢ ὡς αὐτοὶ κελεύουσιν, οὕτω ποιῶν;
11. ΣΩΚΡΑΤΗΣ
    ὦ φίλε Πάν τε καὶ ἄλλοι ὅσοι τῇδε θεοί, δοίητέ μοι καλῷ γενέσθαι τἄνδοθεν· ἔξωθεν δ' ὅσα ἔχω, τοῖς ἐντὸς εἶναί μοι φίλια. πλούσιον δὲ νομίζοιμι τὸν σοφόν.
    ΦΑΙΔΡΟΣ
    καὶ ἐμοὶ ταῦτα συνεύχου· κοινὰ γὰρ τὰ τῶν φίλων.
    ΣΩΚΡΑΤΗΣ
    ἴωμεν. —Plato, *Phaedrus* 279b–c

Composition

1. If I should call you for dinner, would you come?
2. May the gods be present here!
3. Whenever they wanted to eat well, they would escape to Athens.
4. May you grant (give) me to be brave always.
5. We might be wiser than our fathers.

Lesson 18

Purpose with the Subjunctive and Optative

1. Purpose, in Greek, is expressed in several different ways:
   a. *future participle* (often introduced by ὡς):
   >αἱ γυναῖκες ἦλθον ὡς ποιήσουσαι καλά. *The women came (in order) to do good.*

   b. *genitive of the articular infinitive:*
   >λέμβον βούλομαι ὁπλίσαι τοῦ ἁρπάσαι σε νυκτός. *I want to outfit a boat (in order) to capture you during the night.*

   c. ἵνα, ὡς, or ὅπως +
   the *subjunctive* mood (*primary sequence*); or
   the *optative* mood (*secondary sequence*)
   >*Primary sequence* means "in a subordinate clause which is dependent upon a *primary* tense (*present, perfect, future, or future perfect*) main verb."
   >*Secondary sequence* means "in a subordinate clause which is dependent upon a *secondary* tense (*imperfect, aorist,* or *pluperfect*) main verb."
   >παιδεύω ἵνα μανθάνωσιν. *I teach so that they may learn.*
   >τελευτήσεις ὅπως ἄλλος τις ἄρχῃ; *Will you die so that someone else can rule?*
   >δῶρα ἐδίδουν ὡς δῶρα αἱροίην. *I used to give gifts in order to get gifts.*

   The negative of purpose clauses with the subjunctive and optative is μή.

2. Learn the participle, subjunctive conjugation, and optative conjugation of οἶδα, *know:*

εἰδώς	εἰδυῖα	εἰδός
εἰδότος	εἰδυίας	εἰδότος
εἰδότι	εἰδυίᾳ	εἰδότι
εἰδότα	εἰδυῖαν	εἰδός
εἰδότες	εἰδυῖαι	εἰδότα
εἰδότων	εἰδυιῶν	εἰδότων
εἰδόσι	εἰδυίαις	εἰδόσι
εἰδότας	εἰδυίας	εἰδότα

εἰδῶ	εἰδείην
εἰδῇς	εἰδείης
εἰδῇ	εἰδείη
εἰδῶμεν	εἰδεῖμεν
εἰδῆτε	εἰδεῖτε
εἰδῶσι	εἰδεῖεν

Vocabulary

δίκη, δίκης, ἡ *right, justice; satisfaction, penalty*
  δίδωμι δίκην *pay a penalty, give satisfaction*
λέμβος, λέμβου, ὁ *boat, fishing boat*
προφήτης, προφήτου, ὁ *interpreter, prophet*

ἁρπάσαι *to carry off, capture* (aorist infinitive)
βούλομαι *want, wish* (deponent; see lesson 19)
διώκω διώξω, ἐδίωξα, δεδίωχα, δεδίωγμαι, ἐδιώχθην *pursue,
  chase*
κατέκαυσεν *he burned completely* (third-person singular aorist of
  κατακαίω)
μηκυνοῦμεν *we will extend, prolong* (liquid future)
ὁπλίσαι *to outfit, prepare* (aorist infinitive of ὁπλίζω)

ἄδικος, ἄδικον *unjust, doing wrong*
τετρωμένος, τετρωμένη, τετρωμένον *wounded* (perfect passive
  participle of τιτρώσκω; see lesson 22)

ἵνα *in order to, so that*
ὅπως *in order to, so that*
σαφῶς *clearly, plainly, distinctly* (adverb of σαφής)
ὡς *in order to, so that*

Practice

Decline fully the present, future, and aorist active participles, and give the present, future, and aorist active infinitives, of three verbs, including at least one -μι verb and one verb with a contract future.

Reading

1. τοὺς λόγους μακροτέρους μηκυνοῦμεν, ἵνα σαφῶς πάντα δηλῶμεν.
2. γράφομεν ἵνα μάθητε.
3. ἰατροὺς καλεῖτε ὅπως μὴ ἀποθάνῃ ὁ τετρωμένος.
4. ἔφυγον οἱ ἄδικοι ὡς μὴ δοῖεν δίκην.
5. ἄξεις ἡμᾶς ἐπὶ τοὺς προφήτας ἵνα εἰδῶμεν τἀληθῆ.
6. τὰς ναῦς κατέκαυσεν, οὐχ ἵνα μείναιεν αὐτοί, ἀλλὰ μᾶλλον ἵνα μὴ διώκοι ὁ βασιλεύς.

Composition

Write the following sentences in Greek, using ἵνα, ὡς, or ὅπως and the appropriate subordinate mood. Then *rewrite* them in Greek, with the main verb in each sentence changed to a *secondary* tense:

1. We sacrifice in order to escape.
2. The children learn so that they may be good citizens.
3. We fight the barbarians to keep (*use* ἔχω) our city.
4. We (ἡμεῖς μὲν) eat in order to live, but you (ὑμεῖς δὲ) live to eat.
5. We remain here, not in order that we may die, but rather (ἀλλὰ μᾶλλον) that you may live.

EΥΡΙΠΙΔΗΣ

7. Euripides.
From a copy of a Hellenistic double herm of Sophocles and Euripides in the
H. W. Sage Collection of Casts of Ancient Sculpture at Cornell University; photo
by Andrew Gillis.

Born in Athens around 485 B.C., Euripides wrote and produced over ninety plays,
of which nineteen survive. They include seventeen tragedies, one satyr play, The
Cyclops, *and the* Alcestis, *which is not a satyr play but was presented fourth in*
the tetralogy (series of four plays), the place reserved for the satyr play, a bawdy,
burlesque treatment of a topic that might receive more serious attention in a
tragedy. In 408 B.C., he left Athens voluntarily because of political and profes-
sional controversy at home. He never returned.

Lesson 19

The Other Two Voices: Middle and Passive

1. In English, the verb can speak with one of two *voices: active* or *passive*. We distinguish passive voice from active in English by the use of auxiliary verbs, usually a form of the verb *to be:*

active	*passive*
She moved.	*She was moved.*
We drive.	*We are driven.*

2. As in English, so in Greek there are two voices, active and passive: the first denoting the subject as the *doer* of the action of the verb, the second denoting the subject as the *receiver* of the verbal action. But there are two important differences:

   a. In Greek, the passive voice is distinguished from the active, not by helping verbs, but by the use of different *personal endings:*

primary endings (present, future, perfect)		*secondary endings* (imperfect, aorist, pluperfect)	
-μαι	-μεθα	-μην	-μεθα
-σαι	-σθε	-σο	-σθε
-ται	-νται	-το	-ντο
-σθαι (infinitive)		-σθαι (infinitive)	

   b. In Greek, there is also a *third* voice, which we call *middle.* Middle-voice verbs use the personal endings of the passive, but they have meanings that are distinct from passive meanings. The middle voice is not exactly *reflexive;* that is, the subject of a middle verb is not both the subject and the direct object of the action. The subject of a middle verb *is,* however, both the *subject* and the *indirect object* of the action, and the special meanings of the middle voice can all be traced to this characteristic. For verbs in the middle voice have meanings, many of which will require the student to consult a lexicon, that

i) are *intransitive:*

> ἔχω. *I hold.* (active)
>
> ἔχομαι. *I abstain.* (middle)

ii) show the subject acting *in his own behalf, to his own advantage:*

> κομίζομεν τὰ χρήματα. *We are carrying the money.* (active)
>
> ἐκομισάμεθα τὰ χρήματα. *We recovered, got back the money (which was ours).* (middle)

iii) represent *mental,* as opposed to physical, action:

> ποίημα ποιεῖ. *He is writing a poem.* (active)
>
> συμφορὰν ποιεῖται. *He considers (it) a misfortune.* (middle)

iv) are *reciprocal:*

> ἀμείβετε. *You alter, change (something).* (active)
>
> ἀμείβεσθε. *You exchange (something with someone else).* (middle)

or v) are simply *special, unpredictable:*

> προστίθημι. *I hand over, deliver.* (active)
>
> προστίθεμαι. *I agree.* (middle)

3. The middle and passive voices share the same forms in all tenses *except* the *future* and *aorist;* in these two tenses, there are separate forms for each voice. We will learn the future and aorist *middle* forms with this lesson, as we begin to learn the shared forms (usually indicated by the abbreviation M/P) for the other tenses. We will learn the distinct future and aorist *passive* forms later, when we study the *sixth* principal part of Greek verbs (see the following chart for the forms to be derived from each principal part).

I (λύω) II (λύσω) III (ἔλυσα)

Present		Imperfect		Future		Aorist	
Act. Mid. Pass.	indic. subj. opt. ptcpl. imptv. infin.	Act. Mid. Pass.	indic.	Act. Mid.	indic. opt. ptcpl. infin.	Act. Mid.	indic. subj. opt. ptcpl. imptv. infin.

IV (λέλυκα)

Perfect		Pluperfect		Future Perfect	
Act.	indic. subj. opt. ptcpl. imptv. infin.	Act.	indic.	Act.	indic. opt. ptcpl. infin.

V (λέλυμαι)

Perfect		Pluperfect		Future Perfect	
Mid. Pass.	indic. subj. opt. ptcpl. imptv. infin.	Mid. Pass.	indic.	Mid. Pass.	indic. opt. ptcpl. infin.

VI (ἐλύθην)

Aorist		Future	
Pass.	indic. subj. opt. ptcpl. imptv. infin.	Pass.	indic. opt. ptcpl. infin.

See Appendix C for a complete synopsis of one verb (γράφω) in the third-person singular.

4. Learn the following conjugations of regular verbs:

present M/P (λύω)	*imperfect M/P* (φέρω)	*future middle* (πέμψω)
λύομαι	ἐφερόμην	πέμψομαι
λύῃ or λύει	ἐφέρου	πέμψῃ or πέμψει
λύεται	ἐφέρετο	πέμψεται
λυόμεθα	ἐφερόμεθα	πεμψόμεθα
λύεσθε	ἐφέρεσθε	πέμψεσθε
λύονται	ἐφέροντο	πέμψονται
λύεσθαι (infinitive)		πέμψεσθαι (infinitive)

first aorist middle (ἔλυσα)	*second aorist middle* (ἔμαθον)
ἐλυσάμην	ἐμαθόμην
ἐλύσω	ἐμάθου
ἐλύσατο	ἐμάθετο
ἐλυσάμεθα	ἐμαθόμεθα
ἐλύσασθε	ἐμάθεσθε
ἐλύσαντο	ἐμάθοντο
λύσασθαι (infinitive)	μαθέσθαι (infinitive; accent on second aorist middle infinitive always paroxytone)

5. Some verbs in Greek have active meanings but no active forms; they are called *deponent,* from the Latin word that means "to lay aside": these verbs have "laid aside" their active forms and use passive or middle forms in their place. Some verbs, such as those listed below, are deponent only in certain tenses; you have already learned the principal parts of several such verbs. Other verbs, such as βούλομαι, are deponent in all tenses. Each verb's peculiarities must be learned as vocabulary items.

μανθάνω, μαθήσομαι, ἔμαθον, μεμάθηκα, —, — (deponent future, like πέμψομαι above)

ἔρχομαι, ἐλεύσομαι, ἦλθον, ἐλήλυθα, —, — (deponent
   present, like λύομαι; deponent future, like πέμψομαι)
ἀποθνῄσκω, ἀποθανοῦμαι, ἀπέθανον, τέθνηκα, —, —
   (deponent contract future, like ποιοῦμαι below)

6. Learn the deponent future of εἰμί, ἔσομαι (ἔσομαι is not enclitic
   in any of its forms):

ἔσομαι	ἐσόμεθα
ἔσῃ or ἔσει	ἔσεσθε
ἔσται	ἔσονται

   ἔσεσθαι (infinitive)

7. Learn the following M/P conjugations of contract verbs:

	present M/P	
(νικάω)	(ποιέω)	(δηλόω)
νικῶμαι	ποιοῦμαι	δηλοῦμαι
νικᾷ	ποιῇ or ποιεῖ	δηλοῖ
νικᾶται	ποιεῖται	δηλοῦται
νικώμεθα	ποιούμεθα	δηλούμεθα
νικᾶσθε	ποιεῖσθε	δηλοῦσθε
νικῶνται	ποιοῦνται	δηλοῦνται
νικᾶσθαι (infinitive)	ποιεῖσθαι (infinitive)	δηλοῦσθαι (infinitive)

	imperfect M/P	
ἐνικώμην	ἐποιούμην	ἐδηλούμην
ἐνικῶ	ἐποιοῦ	ἐδηλοῦ
ἐνικᾶτο	ἐποιεῖτο	ἐδηλοῦτο
ἐνικώμεθα	ἐποιούμεθα	ἐδηλούμεθα
ἐνικᾶσθε	ἐποιεῖσθε	ἐδηλοῦσθε
ἐνικῶντο	ἐποιοῦντο	ἐδηλοῦντο

8. Learn the following middle and M/P conjugations of -μι verbs:

present M/P

(δίδωμι)	(ἵημι)	(τίθημι)	(ἵστημι)	
δίδομαι	ἵεμαι	τίθεμαι	ἵσταμαι	
δίδοσαι	ἵεσαι	τίθεσαι	ἵστασαι	
δίδοται	ἵεται	τίθεται	ἵσταται	
διδόμεθα	ἱέμεθα	τιθέμεθα	ἱστάμεθα	
δίδοσθε	ἵεσθε	τίθεσθε	ἵστασθε	
δίδονται	ἵενται	τίθενται	ἵστανται	
δίδοσθαι	ἵεσθαι	τίθεσθαι	ἵστασθαι	(infinitive)

imperfect M/P

ἐδιδόμην	ἱέμην	ἐτιθέμην	ἱστάμην
ἐδίδοσο	ἵεσο	ἐτίθεσο	ἵστασο
ἐδίδοτο	ἵετο	ἐτίθετο	ἵστατο
ἐδιδόμεθα	ἱέμεθα	ἐτιθέμεθα	ἱστάμεθα
ἐδίδοσθε	ἵεσθε	ἐτίθεσθε	ἵστασθε
ἐδίδοντο	ἵεντο	ἐτίθεντο	ἵσταντο

second aorist middle

ἐδόμην	εἵμην	ἐθέμην	(none; the
ἔδου	εἷσο	ἔθου	*first* aorist
ἔδοτο	εἷτο	ἔθετο	middle,
ἐδόμεθα	εἵμεθα	ἐθέμεθα	ἐστησάμην,
ἔδοσθε	εἷσθε	ἔθεσθε	is conjugated
ἔδοντο	εἷντο	ἔθεντο	like ἐλυσάμην
			above)
δόσθαι	ἕσθαι	θέσθαι	(infinitive)

present M/P	*imperfect M/P*
(δείκνυμι)	
δείκνυμαι	ἐδεικνύμην
δείκνυσαι	ἐδείκνυσο
δείκνυται	ἐδείκνυτο
δεικνύμεθα	ἐδεικνύμεθα
δείκνυσθε	ἐδείκνυσθε
δείκνυνται	ἐδείκνυντο
δείκνυσθαι	(infinitive)

The future middle and first aorist middle of these verbs are conjugated like the paradigms πέμψομαι and ἐλυσάμην above.

9. Middle and M/P participles also have endings that differ from their active counterparts. Learn the declensions of the following middle and M/P participles:

present M/P

λυόμενος	λυομένη	λυόμενον
λυομένου	λυομένης	λυομένου
λυομένῳ	λυομένῃ	λυομένῳ
λυόμενον	λυομένην	λυόμενον
λυόμενοι	λυόμεναι	λυόμενα
λυομένων	λυομένων	λυομένων
λυομένοις	λυομέναις	λυομένοις
λυομένους	λυομένας	λυόμενα

Other present M/P, future middle, and aorist middle participles are similarly declined:

future middle

πεμψόμενος	πεμψομένη	πεμψόμενον
κτλ	*κτλ*	*κτλ*

first aorist middle

λυσάμενος	λυσαμένη	λυσάμενον
κτλ	*κτλ*	*κτλ*

second aorist middle

μαθόμενος	μαθομένη	μαθόμενον
κτλ	*κτλ*	*κτλ*

present M/P of contract verbs

νικώμενος	νικωμένη	νικώμενον
κτλ	*κτλ*	*κτλ*
ποιούμενος	ποιουμένη	ποιούμενον
κτλ	*κτλ*	*κτλ*
δηλούμενος	δηλουμένη	δηλούμενον
κτλ	*κτλ*	*κτλ*

present M/P of -μι *verbs*

διδόμενος	διδομένη	διδόμενον
κτλ	*κτλ*	*κτλ*
ἱέμενος	ἱεμένη	ἱέμενον
κτλ	*κτλ*	*κτλ*

τιθέμενος	τιθεμένη	τιθέμενον
κτλ	κτλ	κτλ
ἱστάμενος	ἱσταμένη	ἱστάμενον
κτλ	κτλ	κτλ
δεικνύμενος	δεικνυμένη	δεικνύμενον
κτλ	κτλ	κτλ

second aorist middle of -μι *verbs*

δόμενος	δομένη	δόμενον
κτλ	κτλ	κτλ
ἕμενος	ἑμένη	ἕμενον
κτλ	κτλ	κτλ
θέμενος	θεμένη	θέμενον
κτλ	κτλ	κτλ

10. Sometimes a *general* truth may be expressed in Greek in a vivid construction that uses the *aorist indicative* rather than the present. This use is called the *gnomic* aorist and is to be translated by the present in English. It is as if the citation of a single instance in the past represented all such instances and implied that it would happen the same way in the future:

ἀπέθανε καὶ ὁ σοφὸς καὶ ὁ μῶρος. *Both the wise man and the fool come to an end* (literally, *died*).
ἐπειδάν τις μάθῃ, ἀπέδωκεν ἀργύριον. *Whenever somebody learns, he pays* (literally, *paid*) *money*.

11. When one form of ἄλλος is used in the same construction with another form of ἄλλος (or with an adverb formed from ἄλλος), a comparison is implied that does not require expression in Greek but does in English:

ἄλλος ἄλλα λέγει. *One says one thing, another says another*. (literally, *Another says other things*.)

12. The *infinitive* may be used to give a *direct command* in the second person, in an elliptical construction equivalent to the imperative mood (see lesson 24):

κατὰ τὰ πάτρια πίνειν. *Drink as your fathers did!*

Vocabulary

ἆθλον, ἄθλου, τό *contest prize*
ἀλήθεια, ἀληθείας, ἡ *truth*
 τῇ ἀληθείᾳ *in truth, really*
ἄναξ, ἄνακτος, ὁ *lord, master*
ἀρετή, ἀρετῆς, ἡ *virtue, excellence*
γέννημα, γεννήματος, τό *offspring,* (plural) *brood*
γέρων, γέροντος, ὁ *old man*
εἶδος, εἴδους, τό *form, shape; appearance*
ἔλαιον, ἐλαίου, τό *olive oil*
ἔχιδνα, ἐχίδνης, ἡ *viper*
ζημία, ζημίας, ἡ *loss, damage, expense; penalty*
κακία, κακίας, ἡ *badness;* (plural) *defects, vices*
καρδία, καρδίας, ἡ *heart*
κέρδος, κέρδους, τό *profit, advantage, gain*
κραιπάλη, κραιπάλης, ἡ *drinking party; hangover*
 ἐκ κραιπάλης either *after the hangover,* or *on account of the drinking party*
Λακεδαιμόνιος, Λακεδαιμονίου, ὁ *a Spartan, Lacedaemonian*
λόγοι (without the article) *talk, (reciprocal) words, dialogue*
ξεῖν(ε) = ξένε (poetic spelling)
ξένος, ξένου, ὁ *stranger, friend*
ὀργή, ὀργῆς, ἡ *temperament, mood, disposition*
οὖς, ὠτός, τό *ear*
ὀφθαλμός, ὀφθαλμοῦ, ὁ *eye*
περίσσευμα, περισσεύματος, τό *abundance*
πληγή, πληγῆς, ἡ *blow, stroke, impact*
πρᾶγμα, πράγματος, τό *thing, matter, affair*
ῥῆμα, ῥήματος, τό *word*
στόμα, στόματος, τό *mouth*

ἄγω (middle) *take for oneself*
 ἄγομαι γυναῖκα *take a wife, get married*
ἀποτίνω, ἀποτείσω, ἀπέτεισα, ἀποτέτεικα, ἀποτέτεισμαι,
 ἀπετείσθην (imperfect ἀπέτινον) *pay (a debt);* (middle) *take vengeance, punish*
βούλομαι, βουλήσομαι, —, —, βεβούλημαι, ἐβουλήθην *want, wish*

γίγνομαι, γενήσομαι, ἐγενόμην, γέγονα, γεγένημαι, ἐγενήθην
become, come into being

διαμείβω (for parts, see ἀμείβω) purchase; (middle) exchange
(+ accusative of the object acquired, dative of the dealer, and
genitive of price)

δύναμαι, δυνήσομαι, ἐδυνησάμην, —, δεδύνημαι, ἐδυνήθην
be able (+ infinitive)

ἐξαμαρτεῖν to fail, miss the target (second aorist infinitive)

ἐπαίρεται is lifted up, exalted (third-person singular, present
passive indicative)

ἐπισκοπέω, ἐπισκέψομαι, ἐπεσκεψάμην, —, ἐπέσκεμμαι, —
(imperfect ἐπεσκόπουν) inspect, observe; consider, reflect
(upon)

ἡγέομαι, ἡγήσομαι, ἡγησάμην, —, ἥγημαι, ἡγήθην (imperfect
ἡγούμην) think, believe, hold (+ accusative/infinitive)

ἦν = ἔφην I said (see lesson 24)

θυροκοπῆσαι breaking and entering (aorist infinitive)

κεῖμαι, κείσομαι, —, —, —, — lie, lie down

μετεωρίζεται is raised high, elevated (third-person singular, present
passive indicative)

μίγνυμι (or μείγνυμι), μίξω, ἔμιξα, —, μέμιγμαι, ἐμίχθην or
ἐμίγην join, bring together; (middle and passive) be mixed with,
come into contact with, mix with (+ dative)

ὁμοιοῦσθαι to become like (+ dative; present passive infinitive)

πατάξαι beating, assault and battery (aorist infinitive)

πείθω (middle) obey (+ dative; see lesson 11)

πένομαι (only present and imperfect) be poor; work for a living

πίνω, πίομαι, ἔπιον, πέπωκα, πέπομαι, ἐπόθην drink

πλουτέω, πλουτήσω, ἐπλούτησα, πεπλούτηκα, —, — be rich,
become rich

πρέπει (imperfect ἔπρεπε) it is fitting (impersonal verb + dative or
accusative of the person and complementary infinitive)

στεφανόω, στεφανώσω, ἐστεφάνωσα, ἐστεφάνωκα,
ἐστεφάνωμαι, ἐστεφανώθην crown, wreathe, reward with a
crown

τρέφω, θρέψω, ἔθρεψα, τέτροφα, τέθραμμαι, ἐτράφην nourish,
support, raise

φαίνω, φανῶ, ἔφηνα, πέφηνα, πέφασμαι, ἐφάνην show, reveal,
set forth; (middle and passive) appear

φασίν (enclitic) they say (see lesson 24)

ἀγαθός, ἀγαθή, ἀγαθόν *wellborn; aristocratic*
ἄξιος, ἀξία, ἄξιον *worthy* (+ *genitive* or *infinitive*)
δρομικός, δρομική, δρομικόν *good at running; swift*
ἔμπεδος, ἔμπεδον *fixed, firm, secure*
κακοδαίμων, κακόδαιμον *unfortunate, unhappy*
κακός, κακή, κακόν *lowborn; lower-class*
κείνων = ἐκείνων (poetic spelling)
ὅσος, ὅση, ὅσον *how much! how many!* (exclamatory adjective)
πλεῖστος, πλείστη, πλεῖστον *most, greatest, largest*
πολλοῖσι = πολλοῖς (poetic)
ταὐτόν = τὸ αὐτόν (i.e., τὸ αὐτό)

αἰεί = ἀεί (poetic)
ἄλλοτε *at another time* (adverb)
ἀπό *from* (preposition + *genitive*)
δήπου *I presume, I would hope, surely* (particle used to add a
   touch of irony to an obvious statement)
δίς *twice* (adverb)
ἐγγύθεν *from close at hand; near* (adverb)
ἔπειτα *next, then, afterward* (adverb)
κἄπειτ' = καὶ ἔπειτ(α)
οἴμοι *oh! ah! woe is me!* (exclamation of pain, fear, pity, anger,
   grief, or surprise)
πρόσωθεν *from afar* (adverb)
τρίς *thrice, three times* (adverb)
ὑπό *by* (preposition with passive voice + *genitive* of agent)

Practice

1. Conjugate six verbs in the present and imperfect M/P and the
   future and aorist middle indicative (+ infinitive).
2. Decline any two middle or M/P participles fully: all three genders, present, future, and aorist.

Reading

1. ὁ πλεῖστα δυνάμενος φαγεῖν τε καὶ πίνειν ἀνήρ ἐστιν.
2. οἱ βάρβαροι γὰρ ἄνδρας ἡγοῦνται μόνους
   τοὺς πλεῖστα δυναμένους φαγεῖν τε καὶ πίνειν. —
   Aristophanes, *Acharnians* 77–8
3. ὑπὸ γὰρ λόγων ὁ νοῦς μετεωρίζεται
   ἐπαίρεταί τ᾽ ἄνθρωπος. —Aristophanes, *Birds* 1447–8
4. Τρέφεται δέ, ὦ Σώκρατες, ψυχὴ τίνι;
   Μαθήμασι δήπου, ἦν δ᾽ ἐγώ. —Plato, *Protagoras* 313c
5. ὕδωρ οὐ μίγνυται ἐλαίῳ, οὐδὲ τῷ ψευδεῖ τὸ ἀληθές.
6. βούλομαι δ᾽, ἄναξ, καλῶς
   δρῶν ἐξαμαρτεῖν μᾶλλον ἢ νικᾶν κακῶς. —Sophocles,
   Philoctetes 94–5
7. πολλοῖσι γὰρ
   κέρδη πονηρὰ ζημίαν ἠμείψατο. —Euripides, *Cyclops* 311–12
8. οὐ ταὐτὸν εἶδος φαίνεται τῶν πραγμάτων
   πρόσωθεν ὄντων, ἐγγύθεν δ᾽ ὁρωμένων. —Euripides, *Ion* 585–6
9. γεννήματα ἐχιδνῶν, πῶς δύνασθε ἀγαθὰ λαλεῖν πονηροὶ
   ὄντες; ἐκ γὰρ τοῦ περισσεύματος τῆς καρδίας τὸ στόμα
   λαλεῖ. —Saint Matthew xii.34
10. οἱ δὲ τῇ ἀληθείᾳ δρομικοὶ εἰς τέλος ἐλθόντες τά τε ἆθλα
    λαμβάνουσι καὶ στεφανοῦνται. —Plato, *Republic* 613c2
11. πολλὰ μὲν βασιλέως ὦτα, πολλοὶ δ᾽ ὀφθαλμοὶ
    νομίζονται. —Xenophon, *Cyropaedia*
12. πολλοί τοι πλουτοῦσι κακοί, ἀγαθοὶ δὲ πένονται·
    ἀλλ᾽ ἡμεῖς τούτοις οὐ διαμειψόμεθα
    τῆς ἀρετῆς τὸν πλοῦτον, ἐπεὶ τὸ μὲν ἔμπεδον αἰεί,
    χρήματα δ᾽ ἀνθρώπων ἄλλοτε ἄλλος ἔχει. —Solon
13. τὰς μὲν ἀρετὰς ἡμῶν ἡ πενία, τὰς δὲ κακίας ὁ πλοῦτος
    ἐδήλωσεν.
14. ὀργὰς πρέπει θεοὺς οὐχ ὁμοιοῦσθαι βροτοῖς. —Euripides,
    Bacchae 1348
15. οἴμοι κακοδαίμων, ὅτι γέρων ὢν ἠγόμην
    γυναῖχ᾽· ὅσας εἰμὶ ἄξιος πληγὰς λαβεῖν. —Aristophanes,
    Ecclesiazusae 323–4
16. ὦ ξεῖν᾽, ἀγγέλλειν Λακεδαιμονίοις ὅτι τῇδε
    κείμεθα, τοῖς κείνων ῥήμασι πειθόμενοι. —Simonides
17. καὶ δὶς καὶ τρίς φασιν καλὸν εἶναι τὰ καλὰ λέγειν τε καὶ
    ἐπισκοπεῖσθαι. —Plato, *Gorgias* 498e11

18. κακὸν τὸ πίνειν· ἀπὸ γὰρ οἴνου γίγνεται
    καὶ θυροκοπῆσαι καὶ πατάξαι καὶ βαλεῖν,
    κἄπειτ' ἀποτίνειν ἀργύριον ἐκ κραιπάλης. — Aristophanes,
    Wasps 1253–5

Composition

1. By what are our minds nourished, Socrates?
2. "You are able, I presume, both to see and to observe for yourselves," said I.
3. We always obey the words of our master.
4. Drinking often mixes well with speaking.
5. But the advantages do not appear to be compatible with our virtue.

Lesson 20

Subjunctive and Optative M/P, Contrary-to-Fact Conditions, Review of Conditions

1. Conditions *contrary to fact* use the *indicative* mood and follow the formulas below:

   a. *present contrary-to-fact condition*

protasis (negative μή)	*apodosis* (negative οὐ)
imperfect indicative	imperfect indicative + ἄν

   b. *past contrary-to-fact condition*

protasis (negative μή)	*apodosis* (negative οὐ)
aorist indicative	aorist indicative + ἄν

   present:

   εἰ πλούσιος ἦν, οὐκ ἂν εἴχομεν κακά. *If I were a rich man, we would not have troubles.*

   past:

   εἰ πλούσιος ἐγενόμην, εἰς Ἀθήνας ἂν ἦλθον. *If I had become rich, I would have gone to Athens.*

   mixed:

   εἰ νέος ἔγημας, ἤδη πάππος ἂν ἦσθα. *If you had married young, you would be a grandfather already.*

2. The subjunctive mood is used in primary sequence in many subordinate constructions, and in the middle and passive voices, it also uses *primary endings,* even in secondary tenses. Learn the following M/P subjunctive forms:

present M/P subjunctive

(λύω)	(νικάω)	(ποιέω)	(δηλόω)
λύωμαι	νικῶμαι	ποιῶμαι	δηλῶμαι
λύῃ	νικᾷ	ποιῇ	δηλοῖ
λύηται	νικᾶται	ποιῆται	δηλῶται
λυώμεθα	νικώμεθα	ποιώμεθα	δηλώμεθα
λύησθε	νικᾶσθε	ποιῆσθε	δηλῶσθε
λύωνται	νικῶνται	ποιῶνται	δηλῶνται

(δίδωμι)	(ἵημι)	(τίθημι)	(ἵστημι)
διδῶμαι	ἱῶμαι	τιθῶμαι	ἱστῶμαι
διδῷ	ἱῇ	τιθῇ	ἱστῇ
διδῶται	ἱῆται	τιθῆται	ἱστῆται
διδώμεθα	ἱώμεθα	τιθώμεθα	ἱστώμεθα
διδῶσθε	ἱῆσθε	τιθῆσθε	ἱστῆσθε
διδῶνται	ἱῶνται	τιθῶνται	ἱστῶνται

(δείκνυμι)
δεικνύωμαι
δεικνύῃ
δεικνύηται

δεικνυώμεθα
δεικνύησθε
δεικνύωνται

Notice that in the M/P subjunctive, present reduplicating class -μι verbs (except δίδωμι) and -νυμι verbs are *thematic*.

3. Learn the following middle subjunctive forms:

first aorist middle subjunctive
(ἔλυσα)

λύσωμαι	λυσώμεθα
λύσῃ	λύσησθε
λύσηται	λύσωνται

second aorist middle subjunctive

(ἔμαθον)	(ἔδωκα)	(ἧκα)	(ἔθηκα)	(ἔστην)
μάθωμαι	δῶμαι	ὦμαι	θῶμαι	[none]
μάθῃ	δῷ	ᾗ	θῇ	
μάθηται	δῶται	ἧται	θῆται	
μαθώμεθα	δώμεθα	ὤμεθα	θώμεθα	
μάθησθε	δῶσθε	ἧσθε	θῆσθε	
μάθωνται	δῶνται	ὦνται	θῶνται	

Notice the remarkable similarities between the present M/P and aorist middle subjunctive conjugations of each -μι verb.

4. The optative mood is used in secondary sequence in many subordinate constructions, and in the middle and passive voices, it also uses *secondary endings,* even in primary tenses. Learn the following M/P optative forms:

present M/P optative

(λύω)	(νικάω)	(ποιέω)	(δηλόω)
λυοίμην	νικῴμην	ποιοίμην	δηλοίμην
λύοιο	νικῷο	ποιοῖο	δηλοῖο
λύοιτο	νικῷτο	ποιοῖτο	δηλοῖτο
λυοίμεθα	νικῴμεθα	ποιοίμεθα	δηλοίμεθα
λύοισθε	νικῷσθε	ποιοῖσθε	δηλοῖσθε
λύοιντο	νικῷντο	ποιοῖντο	δηλοῖντο

(δίδωμι)	(ἵημι)	(τίθημι)	(ἵστημι)
διδοίμην	ἱείμην	τιθείμην	ἱσταίμην
διδοῖο	ἱεῖο	τιθεῖο	ἱσταῖο
διδοῖτο	ἱεῖτο	τιθεῖτο	ἱσταῖτο
διδοίμεθα	ἱείμεθα	τιθείμεθα	ἱσταίμεθα
διδοῖσθε	ἱεῖσθε	τιθεῖσθε	ἱσταῖσθε
διδοῖντο	ἱεῖντο	τιθεῖντο	ἱσταῖντο

(δείκνυμι)
δεικνυοίμην
δεικνύοιο
δεικνύοιτο
δεικνυοίμεθα
δεικνύοισθε
δεικνύοιντο

5. Learn the following middle optative forms:

future middle optative		*first aorist middle optative*	
(πέμψω)		(ἔλυσα)	
πεμψοίμην	πεμψοίμεθα	λυσαίμην	λυσαίμεθα
πέμψοιο	πέμψοισθε	λύσαιο	λύσαισθε
πέμψοιτο	πέμψοιντο	λύσαιτο	λύσαιντο

second aorist middle optative

(ἔμαθον)	(ἔδωκα)	(ἧκα)	(ἔθηκα)	(ἔστην)
μαθοίμην	δοίμην	εἵμην	θείμην	[none]
μάθοιο	δοῖο	εἷο	θεῖο	
μάθοιτο	δοῖτο	εἷτο	θεῖτο	
μαθοίμεθα	δοίμεθα	εἵμεθα	θείμεθα	
μάθοισθε	δοῖσθε	εἷσθε	θεῖσθε	
μάθοιντο	δοῖντο	εἷντο	θεῖντο	

6. We have now learned eight of the nine most common conditional formulas and have used them in one or more contexts. The ninth, which uses the *future indicative* in both protasis and apodosis, is called *future most vivid,* or *emotional future,* and is restricted to situations that call for a dramatic, emotionally charged statement about the future or, often, one that is expressed by a god. It is equivalent to the future-more-vivid construction, except that it is more emphatic.

In the review that follows, the formula for each of the nine common conditions is given (three each in present, past, and future time), and following the formulas are examples of each condition in Greek, numbered to correspond with the formula. Remember that these so-called conditional sentences may have subordinate clauses (protases) introduced by εἰ or ἐάν, in which case they are really *conditional;* but they may also have subordinate clauses introduced by relative pronouns, adverbs, and other subordinating conjunctions (ὅστις, ὅτε, ἐπεί, ὅπου, etc.). A fuller treatment of these conditions can be found in a *reference* grammar, such as the one written by H. W. Smyth (*Greek Grammar,* rev. ed. Gordon M. Messing, [Cambridge: Harvard University Press, 1956], pars. 2297ff.).

condition	protasis	apodosis
1. *present simple*	present indicative	present indicative
2. *present general*	subjunctive + ἄν	present indicative
3. *present contrary-to-fact*	imperfect indicative	imperfect indicative + ἄν
4. *past simple*	imperfect, aorist, or pluperfect indicative	imperfect, aorist, or pluperfect indicative
5. *past general*	optative	imperfect indicative
6. *past contrary-to-fact*	aorist indicative	aorist indicative + ἄν
7. *future less vivid*	optative	optative + ἄν
8. *future more vivid*	subjunctive + ἄν	future indicative
9. *future most vivid*	future indicative	future indicative

1. εὐτυχεῖς ἐσμεν εἰ ἡ στρατιὰ ἐν τῇ πόλει ἐστίν. *We are in luck if the army is in the city.*
2. γελᾷ ὁ μῶρος, κἄν τι μὴ γέλοιον ᾖ. *The fool laughs, even if something isn't funny.* —Menander
3. εἰ μὴ ἐτύγχανεν αὐτοῖς ἐπιστήμη ἐνοῦσα, οὐκ ἂν οἷοί τ' ἦσαν τοῦτο ποιήσειν. *If they didn't happen to have any knowledge, they wouldn't be able to do this.* —Plato, *Phaedo*
4. εἰ μὲν θεοῦ ἦν, οὐκ ἦν αἰσχροκερδής· εἰ δ' αἰσχροκερδής, οὐκ ἦν θεοῦ. *If he was divine, then he wasn't greedy; and if he was greedy, he wasn't divine.* —Plato, *Republic*
5. εἴ του φίλων βλέψειεν οἰκετῶν δέμας, ἔκλαιεν. *If she saw the form of any of her beloved household slaves, she would weep.* —Sophocles, *Women of Trachis*
6. εἰ τοίνυν ὁ Φίλιππος τότε ταύτην ἔσχε τὴν γνώμην, οὐδὲν ὧν νυνὶ πεποίηκεν ἔπραξεν ἄν. *The thing is, if Philip had held this opinion then, he wouldn't have done any of the things which he has just now done.* —Demosthenes
7. εἰ ἀναγκαῖον εἴη ἀδικεῖν ἢ ἀδικεῖσθαι, ἑλοίμην ἂν μᾶλλον ἀδικεῖσθαι ἢ ἀδικεῖν. *If one should be forced either to do harm or to be harmed, I would prefer to be harmed rather than do harm.* —Plato, *Gorgias*
8. ἐάντε νῦν ἐάντε αὖθις ζητήσητε ταῦτα, οὕτως εὑρήσετε. *Whether you investigate these matters now or later, you will find them to be so.* —Plato, *Apology of Socrates*
9. εἰ ταῦτα λέξεις, ἐχθαρῇ μὲν ἐξ ἐμοῦ. *If you shall say this, you shall be hated by me!* —Sophocles, *Antigone*

7. In Plato, the *present subjunctive* with μή is used to express a *doubtful assertion;* that is, a statement that the speaker expresses uncertainty about. It is often ironic in Plato, being used to express a truth of which the speaker is, in fact, perfectly certain. The negative of this construction is the present subjunctive introduced by μὴ οὐ:

μὴ ἀγροικότερον ᾖ τὸ ἀληθὲς εἰπεῖν. *I wonder if it is (I suspect that it is, it may be) rather rude to tell the truth.* μὴ οὐχ οὕτως ἔχῃ. *Perhaps it may not be so.*

Vocabulary

Ἀγάθων, Ἀγάθωνος, ὁ *Agathon, the tragedian*
ἔριον, ἐρίου, τό *wool* (a length of wool fiber was sometimes used as a siphon to transfer liquids from one container to another)
κόρος, κόρου, ὁ *one's fill; abundance, satiety*
κύλιξ, κύλικος, ἡ *cup, wine-cup; kylix*
νόος = νοῦς (poetic)
ὄλβος, ὄλβου, ὁ *happiness; wealth*
πονηρία, πονηρίας, ἡ *wickedness, evil, cowardice*
πρόνοια, προνοίας, ἡ *foreknowledge; foresight, forethought*
ὕβρις, ὕβρεως, ἡ *wanton insolence; hubris*
φυά, φυᾶς, ἡ *inborn nature* (poetic word, used by Pindar and others, for φύσις; in Attic, this word is spelled φυή)

ἀδυνατεῖ *is unable* (third-person singular, present indicative of ἀδυνατέω; + *infinitive*)
αἰάζειν *to cry* αἰαῖ, *to lament* (present infinitive)
ἀπεργάσασθαι *to complete, to finish* (deponent aorist infinitive of ἀπεργάζομαι)
ἅπτω, ἅψω, ἧψα, —, ἧμμαι, ἥφθην (imperfect ἧπτον) *bind, join;* (middle) *grasp, fasten oneself to, touch*
βουλεύω, βουλεύσω, ἐβούλευσα, βεβούλευκα, βεβούλευμαι, ἐβουλεύθην *deliberate, plan, determine*
ἐκφεύγω, κτλ (for parts, see φεύγω) *escape; be acquitted* (on charges of + *accusative* of the charge)
ἐντυγχάνω, κτλ (for parts, see τυγχάνω) *fall in with, meet with* (+ *dative*)
ἐπιτελεῖ *finishes, completes* (third-person singular, present indicative of ἐπιτελέω)

ἕπομαι, ἕψομαι, ἑσπόμην, —, —, — (imperfect εἱπόμην) *come after, follow* (+ *dative*)

ἔχει (+ adverb) *it is* (so and so):
εὖ ἔχει or καλῶς ἔχει *it is well*
οὕτως ἔχει *it is so*

θέω, θεύσομαι, ἔθευσα, —, —, — (other tenses supplied by τρέχω) *run*

κρατέω, κρατήσω, ἐκράτησα, κεκράτηκα, κεκράτημαι, ἐκρατήθην *be strong; rule, hold sway*

μάρνασθαι *to fight* (deponent present infinitive):
μάρνασθαι φυᾷ *to fight with all one's natural powers*

μεθύω (present and imperfect only) *be drunk*

μιμέομαι, μιμήσομαι, ἐμιμησάμην, —, μεμίμημαι, ἐμιμήθην *imitate; represent*

οἶμαι (or οἴομαι), οἰήσομαι, —, —, —, ᾠήθην (imperfect ᾠόμην) *think* (+ *accusative/infinitive*)

πάρεστι *it is possible* (impersonal verb, + *dative/infinitive*)

ῥέω, ῥυήσομαι, —, ἐρρύηκα, —, ἐρρύην *flow, stream, gush, run*

στείχοντα *walking* (present participle masculine accusative singular, modifies the subject of μάρνασθαι, i.e., [ἄνθρωπον])

συμφέρω, κτλ (for parts, see φέρω) *bring* (one thing) *together* (with another) (+ *accusative* and *dative*)

φοβέομαι, φοβήσομαι, —, —, πεφόβημαι, ἐφοβήθην (properly, the middle and passive of φοβέω, *terrify*) *be frightened, seized with fear*

ἄρτιος, ἀρτία, ἄρτιον *complete*

ἐμός, ἐμή, ἐμόν *my, mine*

ἐπώνυμος, ἐπώνυμον *significant, given as a significant name* (that is, a name that reveals something about the character or destiny of the person)

εὐθύς, εὐθεῖα, εὐθύ *straight, direct; straightforward*

θάττων, θᾶττον *swifter, faster* (comparative of ταχύς)

κενός, κενή, κενόν *empty*

πλήρης, πλῆρες *full*

σαφής, σαφές *clear, plain, distinct*

τοιοῦτος, τοιαύτη, τοιοῦτο (declined like οὗτος; see lesson 11) *such, such a; so* (demonstrative)

τοὐμόν = τὸ ἐμόν

αἰαῖ (exclamation of grief)
εἰκῇ *without purpose or plan, at random* (adverb)
ὅλως *in short, generally* (adverb)
ὅπως *in whatever way, however* (relative conjunction)
οὐδενός *of nothing* (here, objective genitive with πρόνοια)
ποτέ *at any time, ever;* (in questions, it is intensive: τίς ποτε . . . ;
   who in the world . . . ?; postpositive enclitic adverb)
ὧδε *in this way, thus* (demonstrative adverb of ὅδε)
ὥστε *so as, so that* (conjunction, introducing a result clause;
   + *indicative* [actual result] or *infinitive* [potential result])

Practice

Conjugate ten verbs, including some contracts, some -μι verbs, and
some regular verbs, in the following:

1. present active subjunctive
2. aorist active subjunctive
3. present M/P subjunctive
4. aorist middle subjunctive
5. present active optative
6. future active optative
7. aorist active optative
8. present M/P optative
9. future middle optative
10. aorist middle optative

Reading

1. ὅλως ἡ τέχνη τὰ μὲν ἐπιτελεῖ ἃ ἡ φύσις ἀδυνατεῖ
   ἀπεργάσασθσι, τὰ δὲ μιμεῖται. — Aristotle, *Physics* 199a15
2. ἄλλος ἄλλην τέχνην ἔχει.
3. ἕτερος ἑτέραν τέχνην ἔχει.
4. τέχναι ἑτέρων ἕτεραί εἰσιν.
5. τέχναι δ' ἑτέρων ἕτεραι· χρὴ δ' ἐν εὐθείαις ὁδοῖς στείχοντα
   μάρνασθαι φυᾷ. — Pindar, *Nemean Ode 1*. 25
6. πῶς ἂν μεθύων χρηστόν τι βουλεύσαιτ' ἀνήρ; —
   Aristophanes, *Knights* 88

7. ἀνθρώπῳ τὰ τῆς τύχης κρατεῖ, καὶ οὐκ ἔχει αὐτὸς πρόνοιαν
   οὐδενός.
8. τί δ᾽ ἂν φοβοῖτ᾽ ἄνθρωπος ᾧ τὰ τῆς τύχης
   κρατεῖ, πρόνοια δ᾽ ἐστὶν οὐδενὸς σαφής;
   εἰκῇ κράτιστον ζῆν, ὅπως δύναιτό τις. — Sophocles, *Oedipus
   the King* 977–9
9. τίκτει τοι κόρος ὕβριν ὅταν κακῷ ὄλβος ἔπηται
      ἀνθρώπῳ καὶ ὅτῳ μὴ νόος ἄρτιος ᾖ. — Theognis
10. μὴ οὐ τοῦτ᾽ ᾖ χαλεπόν, ὦ ἄνδρες, θάνατον ἐκφυγεῖν, ἀλλὰ
    πολὺ χαλεπώτερον πονηρίαν· θᾶττον γὰρ θανάτου θεῖ. —
    Plato, *Apology of Socrates* 39a
11. οὐκ ἂν τοῖς χρηστοῖς οἱ πονηροί ποτε φίλοι γένοιντο· πῶς
    γὰρ οἱ τὰ πονηρὰ ποιοῦντες τοῖς τὰ τοιαῦτα μισοῦσι φίλοι
    γένοιντ᾽ ἄν;
12. εὖ ἂν ἔχοι, ὦ Ἀγάθων, εἰ τοιοῦτο εἴη ἡ σοφία ὥστ᾽ ἐκ τοῦ
    πληρεστέρου εἰς τὸ κενώτερον ῥεῖν ἡμῶν, ἐὰν ἁπτώμεθα
    ἀλλήλων, ὥσπερ τὸ ἐν ταῖς κύλιξιν ὕδωρ τὸ διὰ τοῦ ἐρίου
    ῥέον ἐκ τῆς πληρεστέρας εἰς τὴν κενωτέραν. — Plato,
    Symposium 175d
13. ΑΙΑΣ
    αἰαῖ· τίς ἄν ποτ᾽ ᾤεθ᾽ ὧδ᾽ ἐπώνυμον
    τοὐμὸν συνοίσειν ὄνομα τοῖς ἐμοῖς κακοῖς;
    νῦν γὰρ πάρεστι καὶ δὶς αἰάζειν ἐμοὶ
    καὶ τρίς· τοιούτοις γὰρ κακοῖς ἐντυγχάνω. — Sophocles,
    Ajax 430–3

Composition

1. It would be well if we should all become wise.
2. Who in the world would think that our children are imitating us?
3. Different people have different opinions.
4. If we had been able to run more swiftly, we would have
   escaped.
5. If we were brave, we would not be frightened.

Lesson 21

The Fourth Principal Part

1. The *perfect* tense in Greek is analogous to the present perfect in English: it denotes an action *completed* (Latin *perfectum,* hence the name) *recently* enough that its effect is still felt in the present:

πάντα ἐδηδόκαμεν. *We have eaten everything* (and there is *now* nothing left in the house).

2. The perfect may also emphasize the *absolute* or *utter* degree of a present state or action:

πεφόβηνται. *They are sore afraid.*

3. The endings for the perfect indicative active are as follows:

$$
\begin{array}{ll}
-\alpha & -\alpha\mu\epsilon\nu \\
-\alpha\varsigma & -\alpha\tau\epsilon \\
-\epsilon & -\alpha\sigma\iota
\end{array}
$$

-έναι (infinitive)

The perfect active indicative, first-person singular, is the *fourth principal part* of Greek verbs and must be learned for each verb. It normally uses a so-called reduplicated stem, consisting of the first consonant, the vowel -ε-, and a recognizable stem, to which is added the perfect active *tense sign* (the letter -κ-), followed by the personal endings:

λ + ε + λυ + κ + α → λέλυκα
μ + ε + μαθη + κ + ας → μεμάθηκας
ν + ε + νομι + κ + ατε → νενομίκατε

Verbs whose *stems* end in a consonant or a liquid, however, normally omit the tense sign -κ-:

π + ε + πομφ + αμεν → πεπόμφαμεν (πέμπω)
γ + ε + γον + ασι → γεγόνασι (γίγνομαι)

And verbs that begin with a *vowel* normally use a stem that is indistinguishable from an augmented stem:

ἦρχα (from ἄρχω)
ἦχα (from ἄγω)
εἴληφα (from λαμβάνω)

Keep in mind that these are reduplicated stems, however, and *not* augmented stems: they belong to the *entire* tense, and not only to the indicative mood. Nonindicative forms (participle, infinitive, etc.) do not shorten the lengthened vowel:

ἠχέναι
εἰληφότες

4. Learn the following perfect active indicative conjugations:

λέλυκα *I have set free, etc.*
λέλυκας
λέλυκε
                     λελυκέναι (infinitive)
λελύκαμεν
λελύκατε
λελύκασι

πέπομφα *I have sent, etc.*
πέπομφας
πέπομφε
                     πεπομφέναι (infinitive)
πεπόμφαμεν
πεπόμφατε
πεπόμφασι

ἕστηκα *I stand, etc.* (the perfect of ἵστημι = intransitive
ἕστηκας   *present)*
ἕστηκε
                     ἑστάναι (infinitive)
ἕσταμεν
ἕστατε
ἑστᾶσι

ἦχα *I have led, etc.*
ἦχας
ἦχε
                     ἠχέναι (infinitive)
ἤχαμεν
ἤχατε
ἤχασι

γέγονα *I have become, come to be, etc.*
γέγονας
γέγονε
γεγονέναι (infinitive)
γεγόναμεν
γεγόνατε
γεγόνασι

ἐλήλυθα *I have come, gone, etc.*
ἐλήλυθας
ἐλήλυθε
ἐληλυθέναι (infinitive)
ἐληλύθαμεν
ἐληλύθατε
ἐληλύθασι

5. The *pluperfect* active is also formed from the fourth principal part. It is analogous to the past perfect in English, and it only
exists in the indicative mood. To express the same tense in other
moods, Greek uses either the perfect or the aorist.

   The pluperfect is formed by *augmenting* the fourth principal
part stem (where possible: verbs that begin with a vowel, such as
ἦχα and εἴρηκα, and use temporal augment rather than syllabic
augment, cannot be augmented) and adding the separate pluperfect endings. Learn the following pluperfect active indicative
conjugations:

(λέλυκα)
ἐλελύκη *I had set free, etc.*
ἐλελύκης
ἐλελύκει(ν)

ἐλελύκεμεν
ἐλελύκετε
ἐλελύκεσαν

(πέπομφα)
ἐπεπόμφη *I had sent, etc.*
ἐπεπόμφης
ἐπεπόμφει(ν)

ἐπεπόμφεμεν
ἐπεπόμφετε
ἐπεπόμφεσαν

(ἕστηκα)
εἱστήκη *I stood, etc.*
εἱστήκης
εἱστήκει(ν)

ἕσταμεν
ἕστατε
ἕστασαν

(ἦχα)
ἤχη *I had led, etc.*
ἤχης
ἤχει(ν)

ἤχεμεν
ἤχετε
ἤχεσαν

(γέγονα)
ἐγεγόνη *I had become, come to be, etc.*
ἐγεγόνης
ἐγεγόνει(ν)

ἐγεγόνεμεν
ἐγεγόνετε
ἐγεγόνεσαν

(ἐλήλυθα)
ἐληλύθη *I had come, gone, etc.*
ἐληλύθης
ἐληλύθει(ν)

ἐληλύθεμεν
ἐληλύθετε
ἐληλύθεσαν

6. The *future perfect* active is also formed from the fourth principal part, but it is very rarely seen in classical Greek literature. It is usually a *periphrastic* conjugation, formed from the perfect active *participle* and the future indicative of εἰμί:

πεπομφὼς ἔσομαι *I shall have sent*
πεπαιδευκυῖαι ἔσονται *they will have taught*

7. The *perfect active participle* is formed by adding the particular participial endings of the perfect tense to the stem of the fourth principal part: λελυκώς, πεπομφυῖα, ἠχός, and so on. Learn the declension of the perfect active participle of λύω:

λελυκώς	λελυκυῖα	λελυκός
λελυκότος	λελυκυίας	λελυκότος
λελυκότι	λελυκυίᾳ	λελυκότι
λελυκότα	λελυκυῖαν	λελυκός
λελυκότες	λελυκυῖαι	λελυκότα
λελυκότων	λελυκυιῶν	λελυκότων
λελυκόσι	λελυκυίαις	λελυκόσι
λελυκότας	λελυκυίας	λελυκότα

8. Learn the irregular perfect active participle of ἵστημι:

ἑστώς	ἑστῶσα	ἑστός
ἑστῶτος	ἑστώσης	ἑστῶτος
ἑστῶτι	ἑστώσῃ	ἑστῶτι
ἑστῶτα	ἑστῶσαν	ἑστός
ἑστῶτες	ἑστῶσαι	ἑστῶτα
ἑστώτων	ἑστωσῶν	ἑστώτων
ἑστῶσι	ἑστώσαις	ἑστῶσι
ἑστῶτας	ἑστώσας	ἑστῶτα

9. The perfect *subjunctive* active in Greek is *periphrastic:* that is, it is not a new inflection but a combination of the *perfect active participle* and the auxiliary *subjunctive* conjugation of εἰμί. Learn the perfect subjunctive active of γράφω (masculine subject):

γεγραφὼς ὦ	γεγραφότες ὦμεν
γεγραφὼς ᾖς	γεγραφότες ἦτε
γεγραφὼς ᾖ	γεγραφότες ὦσι

10. The perfect *optative* active in Greek is also periphrastic, using the participle and the optative conjugation of εἰμί. Learn the perfect optative active of τίθημι (feminine subject):

τεθηκυῖα εἴην	τεθηκυῖαι εἶμεν
τεθηκυῖα εἴης	τεθηκυῖαι εἶτε
τεθηκυῖα εἴη	τεθηκυῖαι εἶεν

11. Periphrastic conjugations of the perfect and pluperfect indicative
are also found, with the perfect active participle of the main
verb combined with the indicative conjugation of εἰμί (for
perfect) or ἦν (for pluperfect):
λελυκώς εἰμι = λέλυκα
πεπομφότες ἦσαν = ἐπεπόμφεσαν

12. Sometimes the *pluperfect* may be used in a contrary-to-fact
condition, to emphasize the effect of the verbal action in the
present:
εἰ ἀπεκρίνω τὸ κεφάλαιον, ἱκανῶς ἂν ἤδη παρὰ σοῦ
τὴν ὁσιότητα ἐμεμαθήκη. *If you had answered the main
point, I would already have learned from you* (and would
now know) *sufficiently what piety is.* — Plato, *Euthyphro*

Vocabulary

ἀριθμός, ἀριθμοῦ, ὁ *number*
δύναμις, δυνάμεως, ἡ *strength; power, influence*
ὑποθήκη, ὑποθήκης, ἡ *suggestion*
ψῆφος, ψήφου, ἡ *pebble; ballot*

ἀγανακτεῖν *showing outward signs of grief* (articular infinitive,
direct object of συμβάλλεται)
ἀποφεύγω, κτλ (for parts, see φεύγω) *be acquitted*
βλάπτω, βλάψω, ἔβλαψα, βέβλαφα, βέβλαμμαι, ἐβλάφθην and
ἐβλάβην *distract, mislead; damage, hurt*
βοηθέω, βοηθήσω, ἐβοήθησα, βεβοήθηκα, βεβοήθημαι,
ἐβοήθην *run to help* (+ *dative*)
δακρύειν *to cry for, lament* (present infinitive)
ἔοικε *it seems* (impersonal)
ἐπεγγελάω, κτλ (for parts, see γελάω) *laugh, laugh at*
θνήσκη = ἀποθνήσκη
καταλείπω, κτλ (for parts, see λείπω) *leave behind*
καταψηφίζομαι, κτλ (for parts, see ψηφίζομαι) *vote against, vote
to condemn* (+ *genitive*)
λείπω, λείψω, ἔλιπον, λέλοιπα, λέλειμμαι, ἐλείφθην *leave*
μεταπίπτω, κτλ (for parts, see πίπτω) *fall differently; change, be
changed*

μνημονεύω, μνημονεύσω, ἐμνημόνευσα, ἐμνημόνευκα,
ἐμνημόνευμαι, ἐμνημονεύθην *call to mind; remember*
πέφυκα *be; be inbred; be* so and so *by nature* (perfect of φύω,
beget)
ποθέω, ποθήσω or ποθέσομαι, ἐπόθησα or ἐπόθεσα, —, —, —
long for; yearn to, need to (+ *infinitive*)
συμβάλλεται *contribute to* (third-person singular present middle;
the subject is ἄλλα . . . πολλά)
τολμάω, τολμήσω, ἐτόλμησα, τετόλμηκα, —, — *have the
courage to, dare to* (+ *infinitive*)
ψηφίζομαι, ψηφιοῦμαι, ἐψηφισάμην, —, ἐψήφισμαι, — *vote*

ἀνέλπιστος, ἀνέλπιστον *unexpected*
γεγονώς, γεγονυῖα, γεγονός *total* (with ἀριθμός and sums of
numbers; perfect participle of γίγνομαι)
ἑκάτερος, ἑκατέρα, ἑκάτερον *each (of two)*
ἑκών, ἑκοῦσα, ἑκόν *readily; willing, willingly*
οἰκτρός, οἰκτρά, οἰκτρόν *pitiable, lamentable*
πολιτικός, πολιτική, πολιτικόν *pertaining to the* πόλις; *political*
προσήκων, προσήκουσα, προσῆκον *one's own*
πρότερος, προτέρα, πρότερον *before, former, preceding, earlier*
(comparative formed from preposition πρό; superlative is
πρῶτος)
τριάκοντα *thirty* (indeclinable; see Appendix B)

γε (emphatic particle, postpositive and enclitic, implying *at least,
anyway, indeed;* it indicates agreement, concession, scorn, irony,
or any of several other moods and is often best rendered by vo-
cal intonation in English rather than by a separate word or
phrase)
δίκῃ = δικαίως
ἔγωγε = ἐγώ + γε
παρά *by* (preposition + *accusative*)
τἄν = τοι + ἄν
τοὔνομα = τὸ ὄνομα
χὠ = καὶ ὁ

Practice

Conjugate ten verbs from Appendix C that you have already been introduced to in earlier lessons, in the perfect active indicative, subjunctive, optative, and infinitive, and in the pluperfect active indicative. Decline the perfect active participles from the same verbs fully.

Reading

1. τῶν ποιητῶν τινες ὑποθήκας ὡς χρὴ ζῆν καταλελοίπασιν.
   —Isocrates
2. ἀκήκοα μὲν τοὔνομα, μνημονεύω δ' οὔ.—Plato, *Theaetetus* 144b
3. πολλοὶ διὰ δόξαν καὶ πολιτικὴν δύναμιν μεγάλα κακὰ πεπόνθασιν.—Xenophon, *Memorabilia*
4. ἐτόλμα λέγειν ὡς ἐγὼ τὸ πρᾶγμ' εἰμὶ τοῦτο πεπραχώς.—Demosthenes
5. πῶς οὐκ ἂν οἰκτρότατα πάντων ἐγὼ πεπονθὼς εἴην, εἰ ἐμὲ ψηφίσαιντο εἶναι ξένον;—Demosthenes
6. καὶ γὰρ πέφυκε τοῦτ' ἐν ἀνθρώπου φύσει·
   ἢν καὶ δίκῃ θνῄσκῃ τις, οὐχ ἧττον ποθεῖ
   πᾶς τις δακρύειν τοὺς προσήκοντας φίλους.—Euripides
7. χρὴ νόμον θήσειν μηδενὶ τῶν Ἑλλήνων ὑμᾶς βοηθεῖν ὃς ἂν μὴ πρότερος βεβοηθηκὼς ὑμῖν ᾖ.—Demosthenes
8. ἄλλα πολλὰ συμβάλλεται τὸ μὴ ἀγανακτεῖν ἐπὶ τούτῳ.
9. τὸ μὲν μὴ ἀγανακτεῖν, ὦ ἄνδρες Ἀθηναῖοι, ἐπὶ τούτῳ τῷ γεγονότι, ὅτι μου κατεψηφίσασθε, ἄλλα τέ μοι πολλὰ συμβάλλεται, καὶ οὐκ ἀνέλπιστόν μοι γέγονεν τὸ γεγονὸς τοῦτο, ἀλλὰ πολὺ μᾶλλον θαυμάζω ἑκατέρων τῶν ψήφων τὸν γεγονότα ἀριθμόν. οὐ γὰρ ᾠόμην ἔγωγε οὕτω παρ' ὀλίγον ἔσεσθαι, ἀλλὰ παρὰ πολύ· νῦν δέ, ὡς ἔοικεν, εἰ τριάκοντα μόναι μετέπεσον τῶν ψήφων, ἀπεπεφεύγη ἄν.—Plato, *Apology of Socrates* 35e–36a
10. κεῖνοι δ' ἐπεγγελῶσιν ἐκπεφευγότες,
    ἐμοῦ μὲν οὐχ ἑκόντος· εἰ δέ τις θεῶν
    βλάπτοι, φύγοι τἂν χὠ κακὸς τὸν κρείττονα.—Sophocles, *Ajax* 454–6

Composition

1. I have seen the face, but I don't remember the name.
2. Whoever has not run to help us is not worthy to be called a friend.
3. If they should vote to condemn me, would you dare to lament?
4. We had sent the soldiers home, but they did not report to the commander.
5. If we had not sent them home, they would be with us now.

Review of Conditions

present simple	*past simple*	*future less vivid*
present general	*past general*	*future more vivid*
present contrary-to-fact	*past contrary-to-fact*	*future most vivid*

Identify the following conditional sentences in English and explain how they would be constructed in Greek:

1. If today is Tuesday, we must be in Belgium.
2. If I were a rich man, I would live in a palace.
3. When I win the lottery, I'll build a palace *for* you.
4. Anyone who thinks he can win the lottery is living in a dream world.
5. You never used to come when we invited you.
6. If you had invited me to anything interesting, I would have considered it.
7. Smile when you say that, partner.
8. When he smiled at me, I wanted to cry.
9. When he smiled at me last night, I wanted to cry.
10. When he smiled at me at work every day, I wanted to cry.
11. Every time you start to cry, I want to laugh.
12. If we should ever cry together, it would be a miracle.
13. If we had ever laughed together, I would not be crying now.
14. Verily, I say unto thee, if thou shalt not end this pursuit, I shall end it for thee!
15. Would you think I was crazy if I told you I just heard the voice of a goddess?
16. Nobody hears goddesses unless he has been drinking too much.
17. If I'm lying to you, may lightning strike me down!
18. Just get us out of here, if you please!

8. Sophocles.

From a copy of a Hellenistic sculpture in the H. W. Sage Collection of Casts of Ancient Sculpture at Cornell University; photo by Andrew Gillis.

Born in the Athenian suburb of Colonus around 496 B.C., Sophocles won his first victory in a dramatic competition by beating Aeschylus at the festival of Dionysus in 468 B.C. He may have written over thirty tetralogies (one hundred twenty plays) and never won less than second prize. Only seven of his plays survive complete, and yet they are enough to show that he was not only a master of dramatic craftsmanship but also more subtle than his contemporaries in his treatment of serious moral complexities onstage. He died in 406 B.C., just a few months after the death of his chief competitor, Euripides.

Lesson 22

The Fifth Principal Part

1. The *fifth principal part* of Greek verbs is not a new tense but rather a different voice (or more accurately, different *voices*) of a tense you have already studied. It is the *middle and passive* (*M/P*) voices of the *perfect* tense, and there are not separate forms for these two voices in the perfect.

   In fact, the *stem* of the perfect M/P is often identical to the perfect *active* stem (without the tense sign -κ-), but not often enough: it is listed as a separate principal part because the stem undergoes euphonic and other changes in enough verbs to make the fifth principal part unpredictable.

2. Learn the following perfect M/P conjugations, formed by adding the *primary M/P endings* directly to the *perfect M/P stem* (the perfect M/P conjugation is nonthematic):

λέλυμαι *I have been set free,*	ἐνήνεγμαι *I have been*
λέλυσαι *etc.*	ἐνήνεξαι *carried, etc.*
λέλυται	ἐνήνεκται
λελύμεθα	ἐνηνέγμεθα
λέλυσθε	ἐνήνεχθε
λέλυνται	ἐνηνεγμένοι εἰσί
λελύσθαι (infinitive)	ἐνηνέχθαι (infinitive)
νενόμισμαι *I have been thought,*	ἤμειμμαι *I have been*
νενόμισαι *etc.*	ἤμειψαι *changed, etc.*
νενόμισται	ἤμειπται
νενομίσμεθα	ἠμείμμεθα
νενόμισθε	ἤμειφθε
νενομισμένοι εἰσί	ἠμειμμένοι εἰσί
νενομίσθαι (infinitive)	ἠμεῖφθαι (infinitive)

Notice the periphrastic forms of the third-person plural of verbs whose perfect M/P stem ends in a *mute* (π, β, φ, κ, γ, χ, τ, δ, θ) or in ζ. The perfect M/P infinitive is always accented on the penult.

3. There are several spelling changes in the so-called mute-stem perfect M/P conjugations. These are not random changes but follow regular patterns for all mute-stem verbs:
   a. before σ, a *labial mute* (π, β, φ) blends with the σ to form ψ: ἤμειψαι;
   a *palatal mute* (κ, γ, χ) blends with the σ to form ξ: ἐνήνεξαι;
   a *dental mute* (τ, δ, θ) or ζ disappears: νενόμισαι;
   b. before μ, a labial becomes μ: ἡμείμμεθα;
   a palatal becomes γ: ἐνηνέγμεθα;
   a dental becomes σ: νενόμισμαι;
   c. before τ, a labial becomes π: ἤμειπται;
   a palatal becomes κ: ἐνήνεκται;
   a dental becomes σ: νενόμισται;
   d. before θ, a labial becomes φ: ἤμειφθαι;
   a palatal becomes χ: ἐνήνεχθε;
   a dental becomes σ: νενομίσθαι;
   e. between consonants, σ disappears (that is, the σ of the *second-person plural* ending -σθε and of the *infinitive* ending -σθαι disappear): ἤμειφθε, ἠμεῖφθαι, ἐνηνέχθαι, νενόμισθε (i.e., νενόμισ-θε).

   The patterns in (*d*) above will also be significant in working with the *sixth* principal part (see lesson 23).

4. The *future perfect M/P* is extremely rare. It was formed, apparently, by adding the future middle tense sign and endings to the perfect M/P stem: λελύσομαι, *κτλ.* You will not be required to learn it this year.

5. The *pluperfect M/P* occurs only in the indicative mood and uses an augmented perfect M/P stem (where possible) and secondary endings. Mute-stem verbs use a periphrastic form in the third-person plural:

(λέλυμαι)	(ἐνήνεγμαι)
ἐλελύμην *I had been set free,*	ἐνηνέγμην *I had been*
ἐλέλυσο *etc.*	ἐνήνεξο *carried, etc.*
ἐλέλυτο	ἐνήνεκτο
ἐλελύμεθα	ἐνηνέγμεθα
ἐλέλυσθε	ἐνήνεχθε
ἐλέλυντο	ἐνηνεγμένοι ἦσαν

(νενόμισμαι)	(ἤμειμμαι)
ἐνενομίσμην *I had been thought,*	ἠμείμμην *I had been*
ἐνενόμισο *etc.*	ἤμειψο *changed, etc.*
ἐνενόμιστο	ἤμειπτο
ἐνενομίσμεθα	ἠμείμμεθα
ἐνενόμισθε	ἤμειφθε
νενομισμένοι ἦσαν	ἠμειμμένοι ἦσαν

6. The perfect M/P *participle* is declined much like the present and future middle participles: it uses the perfect M/P stem and the middle participial endings, but notice that the accent is *always paroxytone*. Learn the declension of the perfect M/P participle of λύω:

λελυμένος	λελυμένη	λελυμένον
λελυμένου	λελυμένης	λελυμένου
λελυμένῳ	λελυμένῃ	λελυμένῳ
λελυμένον	λελυμένην	λελυμένον
λελυμένοι	λελυμέναι	λελυμένα
λελυμένων	λελυμένων	λελυμένων
λελυμένοις	λελυμέναις	λελυμένοις
λελυμένους	λελυμένας	λελυμένα

7. The perfect M/P *subjunctive* and *optative* both use periphrastic conjugations with the participle and the subjunctive and optative of εἰμί:

ἐνηνεγμένος ὦ	ἐνηνεγμένοι ὦμεν
ἐνηνεγμένος ᾖς	ἐνηνεγμένοι ἦτε
ἐνηνεγμένος ᾖ	ἐνηνεγμένοι ὦσι
λελυμένη εἴην	λελυμέναι εἶμεν
λελυμένη εἴης	λελυμέναι εἶτε
λελυμένη εἴη	λελυμέναι εἶεν

8. *Personal agency* with the passive voice is normally expressed in Greek by the preposition ὑπό and the *genitive* of personal agent:

παιδευόμεθα ὑπὸ τῶν διδασκάλων. *We are instructed by our teachers.*

With the *perfect passive*, however, the *dative of personal agency* may be used alone, without a preposition, when the subject of the passive verb is not a person:

τὰ ἐδάφη λέλυται τῷ βασιλεῖ. *The foundations have been destroyed by the king.*

9. Learn the following forms of εἶμι, *go,* commonly used as a substitute for the *future* of ἔρχομαι:

present indicative		*present subjunctive*	
εἶμι	ἴμεν	ἴω	ἴωμεν
εἶ	ἴτε	ἴῃς	ἴητε
εἶσι	ἴασι	ἴῃ	ἴωσι

present optative		*present infinitive*
ἴοιμι	ἴοιμεν	ἰέναι
ἴοις	ἴοιτε	
ἴοι	ἴοιεν	

present participle

ἰών	ἰοῦσα	ἰόν
ἰόντος	ἰούσης	ἰόντος
ἰόντι	ἰούσῃ	ἰόντι
ἰόντα	ἰοῦσαν	ἰόν
ἰόντες	ἰοῦσαι	ἰόντα
ἰόντων	ἰουσῶν	ἰόντων
ἰοῦσι	ἰούσαις	ἰοῦσι
ἰόντας	ἰούσας	ἰόντα

Vocabulary

αἶσα, αἴσης, ἡ *one's lot, destiny*
ἀνάγκη, ἀνάγκης, ἡ *necessity*
ἄναυρος, ἀναύρου, ὁ *river, mountain torrent*
ἄστρον, ἄστρου, τό *star*

ἀσχολία, ἀσχολίας, ἡ *business, being busy*
βοτόν, βοτοῦ, τό *beast*
δένδρος, δένδρους, τό *tree*
   δένδρεα = δένδρη
εἰρήνη, εἰρήνης, ἡ *peace*
ἔργον, ἔργου, τό *work, deed*
ἑταῖρος, ἑταίρου, ὁ *comrade, companion*
ἥλιος, ἡλίου, ὁ *sun*
θάλασσα = θάλαττα
θεά, θεᾶς, ἡ *goddess*
   θεὰ Διός *divine daughter of Zeus*, i.e., *Athena*
Ἴλιος, Ἰλίου, ἡ *Ilios (Troy)*
λήθη, λήθης, ἡ *forgetfulness*
νῆσος, νήσου, ἡ *island*
νόσος, νόσου, ὁ *sickness*
οὐρανός, οὐρανοῦ, ὁ *heaven, sky*
πάθημα, παθήματος, τό *suffering, misfortune*
πέλαγος, πελάγους, τό *sea*
σελήνη, σελήνης, ἡ *moon*
σθένος, σθένους, τό *strength, power*
στρατός, στρατοῦ, ὁ *army*
σχολή, σχολῆς, ἡ *leisure, rest*
Τροία, Τροίας, ἡ *Troy*
χείρ, χειρός, ἡ (genitive plural χερῶν, dative plural χερσί) *hand*
ὥρα, ὥρας, ἡ *hour, season; time*
   ὥρα (ἐστί) *it is time* (to do such and such) (+ *infinitive*)

αἱμάξαι *to bloody, stain with blood* (aorist infinitive)
δέδοικα *fear* (perfect of δείδω, used as a present; the aorist is
   ἔδεισα; + subordinate clause introduced by μή [*that, lest*] or μὴ
   οὐ [*that . . . not*] and the *subjunctive* [primary sequence] or
   optative [secondary sequence])
εἶμι *will go, will come* (present used as future of ἔρχομαι)
εἴρηται *has been said* (third-person singular, perfect passive of
   εἴρω, for which Attic Greek uses λέγω or φημί)
ἐμβάλλω, κτλ *inflict, lay on, impose*
ἔπειμι *come upon, approach; come after, follow* (from εἶμι, not
   εἰμί)
ἐπεντύνοντα *preparing, setting, arming* (present participle, masculine accusative singular; modifies με)

μ᾽ ἐπ᾽ αὐτοῖς χεῖρ᾽ ἐπεντύνοντ᾽ ἐμὴν *as I was setting my hand*
against them (i.e., Agamemnon, Menelaus, and Odysseus)
ἐχθαίρομαι *I am hated* (present passive of ἐχθαίρω)
ἔχθω (imperfect ἤχθον) *hate* (only in present and imperfect)
θέλω = ἐθέλω
κατθανεῖν = ἀποθανεῖν
κέκρανται *has been cast* (third-person singular, perfect passive of
κραίνω; subject is ψῆφος)
κοσμέω, κοσμήσω, ἐκόσμησα, κεκόσμηκα, κεκόσμημαι,
ἐκοσμήθην *order, arrange; adorn, embellish, honor*
μάχομαι, μαχοῦμαι, ἐμαχεσάμην, —, μεμάχημαι, ἐμαχέσθην
fight, do battle against (+ dative)
ὀφείλεται *is required (of us), is (our) destiny* (third-person singular, present passive of ὀφείλω; subject is κατθανεῖν)
παύω, παύσω, ἔπαυσα, πέπαυκα, πέπαυμαι, ἐπαύθην *put an
end to, stop;* (middle) *cease, rest from* (+ genitive)
παῦσαι (aorist middle imperative, second-person singular; see
lesson 24)
πεπορθηκέναι *to have sacked, plundered* (perfect active infinitive
of πορθέω)
προαιρέω, κτλ *choose beforehand; plan, undertake*
σκοπέω (only present and imperfect) *consider, look closely*
σφάλλω, σφαλῶ, ἔσφηλα, —, ἔσφαλμαι, ἐσφάλην *trip up, throw*
(in wrestling); *overthrow; baffle, foil*

ἀδάματος, ἀδάματον *unconquered; unwedded*
ἀδήριτος, ἀδήριτον *unconquerable, not to be challenged*
Αἰγαῖος, Αἰγαία, Αἰγαῖον *Aegean*
ἀρχαῖος, ἀρχαία, ἀρχαῖον *ancient, former, old*
ἀχάριτα *unpleasant, disagreeable* (neuter nominative plural of
ἄχαρις)
γοργῶπις *fierce-eyed, terrible-eyed* (feminine nominative singular)
εὐγενής, εὐγενές *wellborn, highborn, noble*
λυσσώδης, λυσσῶδες *stark-raving*
μέλαινα *black, dark* (feminine nominative singular)
πεπρωμένος, πεπρωμένη, πεπρωμένον *fated* (properly, a perfect
passive participle)
προαιρετός, προαιρετή, προαιρετόν *deliberately chosen, planned*
τοιόσδε, τοιάδε, τοιόνδε (τοῖος + -δε, κτλ) *such as this; such*

αὖ *on the other hand; in turn; again, moreover* (adverb)
ἐμφανῶς *openly, visibly; undoubtedly* (adverb)
ἔτι *yet, still;* (with a negative) *(no) longer*
ἤδη *already, by this time* (adverb)
καὐτῷ = καὶ αὐτῷ
οἷον *as for example* (adverbial accusative of οἷος)
ὅμως *all the same, nevertheless* (conjunction)
τί; *why? what? how?*
ὕπερ = ὑπέρ (when it *follows* its object; other disyllabic oxytone
    prepositions are also accented recessively when they come
    after the words they govern)

Practice

Conjugate (and decline the participles of) five verbs in the perfect
M/P fully: indicative, infinitive, subjunctive, optative, and participle, including at least one regular verb and one of each type of
mute-stem (see par. 3 above). Then conjugate each verb in the
pluperfect M/P indicative.

Reading

1. τὸ χρόνον γεγενῆσθαι πολὺν δέδοικα μή τινα λήθην ὑμῖν
   πεποιηκὸς ᾖ.
2. οὐδὲ βουλεύεσθαι ἔτι ὥρα, ἀλλὰ βεβουλεῦσθαι· τῆς γὰρ
   ἐπιούσης νυκτὸς πάντα ταῦτα δεῖ πεπρᾶχθαι. — Plato, *Crito*
   46a
3. οὐκ ἔστι δὲ προαιρετὸν οὐδὲν γεγονός, οἷον οὐδεὶς
   προαιρεῖται Ἴλιον πεπορθηκέναι. — Aristotle, *Nicomachean
   Ethics*
4. τὰ δέ μοι παθήματα ὄντα ἀχάριτα μαθήματα γέγονε. —
   Herodotus
5. παῦσαι δὲ λύπης τῶν τεθνηκότων ὕπερ,
   πᾶσιν γὰρ ἀνθρώποισιν ἥδε πρὸς θεῶν
   ψῆφος κέκρανται κατθανεῖν τ᾿ ὀφείλεται. — Euripides,
   Andromache 1270–2
6. ἡ γῆ μέλαινα πίνει,
   πίνει δὲ δένδρε᾿ αὖ γῆν·
   πίνει θάλασσ᾿ ἀναύρους,

ὁ δ' ἥλιος θάλασσαν,
τὸν δ' ἥλιον σελήνη.
τί μοι μάχεσθ', ἑταῖροι,
καὐτῷ θέλοντι πίνειν; — Anacreon

7. τέλος γάρ, ὥσπερ εἴρηται πολλάκις, εἰρήνη μὲν πολέμου,
σχολὴ δ' ἀσχολίας. — Aristotle

8. κρίνουσιν οἱ ἄνθρωποι τὸν πόλεμον ἐν ᾧ ἂν πολεμῶσι τὸν
μέγιστον πόλεμον εἶναι.

9. ἐπειδὰν παύσωνται, θαυμάζουσι μᾶλλον τοὺς ἀρχαίους
πολέμους.

10. οὗτος ὁ πόλεμος φανεῖται μείζων τοῖς σκοποῦσιν.

11. ὁ πόλεμος οὗτος, καίπερ τῶν ἀνθρώπων ἐν ᾧ μὲν ἂν
πολεμῶσι τὸν παρόντα ἀεὶ μέγιστον κρινόντων,
παυσαμένων δὲ τὰ ἀρχαῖα μᾶλλον θαυμαζόντων, ἀπ' αὐτῶν
τῶν ἔργων σκοποῦσι δηλώσει ὅμως μείζων γεγενημένος
αὐτῶν. — Thucydides 1.21

12. ὥσπερ ὁ οὐρανὸς τοῖς ἄστροις κεκόσμηται, οὕτω καὶ τὸ
Αἰγαῖον πέλαγος ταῖς νήσοις κεκόσμηται.

13. τὴν πεπρωμένην δὲ χρὴ
αἶσαν φέρειν ὡς ῥᾷστα, γιγνώσκονθ' ὅτι
τὸ τῆς ἀνάγκης ἐστ' ἀδήριτον σθένος. — Aeschylus,
Prometheus Bound 103–5

14. ΑΙΑΣ
αἰαῖ· τίς ἄν ποτ' ᾤεθ' ὧδ' ἐπώνυμον
τοὐμὸν συνοίσειν ὄνομα τοῖς ἐμοῖς κακοῖς;
νῦν γὰρ πάρεστι καὶ δὶς αἰάζειν ἐμοὶ
καὶ τρίς· τοιούτοις γὰρ κακοῖς ἐντυγχάνω.
νῦν δ' ἡ Διὸς γοργῶπις ἀδάματος θεὰ
ἤδη μ' ἐπ' αὐτοῖς χεῖρ' ἐπεντύνοντ' ἐμὴν
ἔσφηλεν ἐμβαλοῦσα λυσσώδη νόσον,
ὥστ' ἐν τοιοῖσδε χεῖρας αἱμάξαι βοτοῖς·
κεῖνοι δ' ἐπεγγελῶσιν ἐκπεφευγότες,
ἐμοῦ μὲν οὐχ ἑκόντος· εἰ δέ τις θεῶν
βλάπτοι, φύγοι τἂν χὡ κακὸς τὸν κρείττονα.
καὶ νῦν τί χρὴ δρᾶν; ὅστις ἐμφανῶς θεοῖς
ἐχθαίρομαι, μισεῖ δέ μ' Ἑλλήνων στρατός,
ἔχθει δὲ Τροία πᾶσα καὶ πεδία τάδε.
ἀλλ' ἢ καλῶς ζῆν ἢ καλῶς τεθνηκέναι
τὸν εὐγενῆ χρή. πάντ' ἀκήκοας λόγον. — Sophocles, *Ajax*
430–3, 450–9, 479–80

Composition

1. It is now no longer time to fight, but to have fought.
2. I fear that the passage of time has put an end to our strength.
3. Is it not true that peace is the goal of war?
4. All the beasts have been destroyed by Ajax.
5. Even though he was wellborn, he has been tripped up by the goddess.

Lesson 23

The Sixth Principal Part
and Verbals

1. The *sixth principal part* of Greek verbs is the first-person singular, *aorist passive indicative*. It is built on a stem that normally has the so-called aorist passive sign, -θη- (in the indicative, infinitive, and imperative) or -θε- (in the subjunctive, optative, participle, and imperative), *between* the actual verb stem and the endings:

   ἐλύθημεν *we were set free*
   δοθεῖεν *they be given*

   Mutes and ζ undergo the same changes in the aorist passive as in the perfect M/P (see lesson 22), when they immediately precede θ:

   ἐδείχθη *it was shown*
   ἐπέμφθην *I was sent*
   ἐπείσθημεν *we were persuaded*

   Often, however, particularly with consonant-stem verbs, the θ of the aorist passive sign is omitted:

   ἐγράφη *it was written*
   τραπείς *having been turned*

2. Learn the aorist passive of λύω:

	indicative	subjunctive	infinitive
	ἐλύθην *I was set free,*	λυθῶ	λυθῆναι
	ἐλύθης *etc.*	λυθῇς	
	ἐλύθη	λυθῇ	
	ἐλύθημεν	λυθῶμεν	
	ἐλύθητε	λυθῆτε	
	ἐλύθησαν	λυθῶσι	

optative

λυθείην
λυθείης
λυθείη

λυθεῖμεν or λυθείημεν
λυθεῖτε or λυθείητε
λυθεῖεν or λυθείησαν

participle

λυθείς	λυθεῖσα	λυθέν
λυθέντος	λυθείσης	λυθέντος
λυθέντι	λυθείσῃ	λυθέντι
λυθέντα	λυθεῖσαν	λυθέν
λυθέντες	λυθεῖσαι	λυθέντα
λυθέντων	λυθεισῶν	λυθέντων
λυθεῖσι	λυθείσαις	λυθεῖσι
λυθέντας	λυθείσας	λυθέντα

3. The *future passive* is also built on the sixth principal part, using the *unaugmented* stem, the future tense sign -σ-, the thematic vowel, the modal sign (in the optative mood only), and the regular M/P endings:

ἐλύθην → λυθη + σ + ο + μαι → λυθήσομαι

Learn the future passive of λύω:

indicative	*optative*	*infinitive*
λυθήσομαι	λυθησοίμην	λυθήσεσθαι
λυθήσῃ or λυθήσει	λυθήσοιο	
λυθήσεται	λυθήσοιτο	
λυθησόμεθα	λυθησοίμεθα	
λυθήσεσθε	λυθήσοισθε	
λυθήσονται	λυθήσοιντο	

participle

λυθησόμενος	λυθησομένη	λυθησόμενον
κτλ	κτλ	κτλ

(accent and endings like λυόμενος, lesson 19, par. 9)

4. Learn the following forms of φημί, *say, speak, tell*. Like εἰμί, φημί is enclitic in the present active *indicative*, in all forms except the second-person singular:

present indicative	subjunctive	optative	infinitive
φημί	φῶ	φαίην	φάναι
φής	φῇς	φαίης	
φησί	φῇ	φαίη	
φαμέν	φῶμεν	φαῖμεν	
φατέ	φῆτε	φαῖτε	
φασί	φῶσι	φαῖεν	

second aorist indicative

ἔφην	ἔφαμεν
ἔφης or ἔφησθα	ἔφατε
ἔφη	ἔφασαν

5. Some deponent verbs, such as ἕπομαι, *follow,* have an aorist middle but no aorist passive. These verbs are called *middle deponents*. Others, such as βούλομαι, *want, wish,* use only an aorist passive; they are known as *passive deponents*. Still others use both an aorist passive and an aorist middle and make little or no distinction between them. Such distinctions as are made must be learned from experience with each verb.

6. In addition to participles, Greek has two other classes of verbal adjectives (usually called simply *verbals*). Most verbals, though not all, are formed from the *unaugmented* sixth principal part stem *without* the tense sign -θη- and add the endings -τος, -τη, -τον, *κτλ,* or -τέος, -τέα, -τέον, *κτλ,* to the stem. Those ending in -τος either are equivalent in meaning to a perfect passive participle:

προαιρετός *deliberately chosen*
ἀνέλπιστον *unexpected*

or denote possibility:

ἀδήριτος *unconquerable*

Those ending in -τέος, however, indicate *necessity:*

λεκτέος *must be said*
ποιητέον *must be done*

As with the perfect passive system, so with verbals the dative of personal agency expresses the person in whose interest something has been (or must be) done (this use of the dative is really a dative of interest):

ἄλλοι στρατιῶται μεταπεμπτέοι ἡμῖν. *We must send for additional troops* (literally, they *must be sent for by us*). τοῦτο ἀνέλπιστόν μοι. *This was unexpected by me*.

Vocabulary

δαιμόνιον, δαιμονίου, τό *divine power, divinity*
Δημοσθένης, Δημοσθένους, ὁ *Demosthenes*
ἔλαιον, ἐλαίου, τό *olive oil*
μῖσος, μίσους, τό *hatred; object of hate*
πόρος, πόρου, ὁ *path, opening, way*

δαπανάω, δαπανήσω, ἐδαπάνησα, —, δεδαπάνημαι,
  ἐδαπανήθην *consume, use up*
δεῖν = infinitive of δεῖ
διαπτυχθέντες *when they are opened up, spread out, unfolded*
  (aorist passive participle of διαπτύττω; modifies the subject of
  ὤφθησαν)
εἰδῇς (second-person singular subjunctive of οἶδα)
ἐξανευρίσκω, κτλ (for parts, see εὑρίσκω) *invent*
ἐρωτάω, ἐρωτήσω, ἠρώτησα, ἠρώτηκα, ἠρώτημαι, ἠρωτήθην
  (imperfect ἠρώτων) *ask, question*
εὑρίσκω, εὑρήσω, εὗρον or ηὗρον, εὕρηκα, εὕρημαι or
  ηὕρημαι, εὑρέθην or ηὑρέθην (imperfect εὕρισκον or
  ηὕρισκον) *find, discover*
κραίνω, κρανῶ, ἔκρανα, —, κέκραμαι, ἐκράνθην *accomplish,
  fulfill, bring to pass* (poetic word)
κρατέω (see lesson 20) *be lord or master of, rule over* (+ *genitive*)
μέλλω, μελλήσω, ἐμέλλησα or ἠμέλλησα, —, —, — *be destined
  to, be likely to, be about to* (+ *infinitive*)
παρέχομαι, παρέξομαι or παρασχήσομαι, παρεσχόμην, —,
  παρέσχημαι, — (middle of παρέχω) *furnish* (from one's own
  resources), *supply, present, display*
περιγίγνομαι, κτλ *be superior, become superior* (to someone in
  something; + *genitive* of the person, *dative* of the thing)
προτείνω, κτλ *hold out, offer* (often as a pretext or excuse)
τείνω, τενῶ, ἔτεινα, τέτακα, τέταμαι, ἐτάθην *stretch, stretch out,
  hold out, present*
τελέω, τελῶ, ἐτέλεσα, τετέλεκα, τετέλεσμαι, ἐτελέσθην
  perform, accomplish, bring to an end; do

ὑπηρετῶ *I am (his) minister, (his) servant* (present indicative)
φημί, φήσω, ἔφησα and ἔφην, —, —, — *say, speak, tell; say*
  (something is) *so*
ὤφθησαν (third-person plural aorist passive of ὁράω)

ἀδόκητος, ἀδόκητον *unexpected*
ληπτέος, ληπτέα, ληπτέον *must be taken, must be chosen*
οἷος, οἵα, οἷον *such...! such a...!* (exclamatory adjective)
πειστέον *one must obey* (impersonal verbal)
πιθανός, πιθανή, πιθανόν *persuasive, plausible, credible*
ποιητέος, ποιητέα, ποιητέον *must be done; must be considered*
  περὶ πολλοῦ ποιητέον *one must consider important*
  περὶ πλέονος ποιητέον *one must consider more important*
  περὶ πλείστου ποιητέον *one must consider most important*
πορευτέος, πορευτέα, πορευτέον *must be traversed, must be taken*
ῥητορικός, ῥητορική, ῥητορικόν *oratorical*
  ἡ ῥητορική (τέχνη) *rhetoric*
τάλας (εἰμί) *(I am) wretched, miserable!*

ἀέλπτως *beyond all hope* (adverb)
ἄρα *then, so then, it seems* (indeclinable postpositive particle)
περί *about, around; above, beyond, of* (preposition + *genitive*)
πρῶτον *first* (adverbial accusative)

Practice

Study the synopsis of γράφω in Appendix C. Then make a synopsis
for six verbs (some regular, some -μι verbs, and so on), one in
each person and number, listing every tense, voice, and mood you
have studied (i.e., everything except the imperative).

Reading

  1. οὐ μόνον ἄρ’, ὡς ἔοικεν, ὁ γέρων δὶς παῖς γίγνοιτ’ ἄν, ἀλλὰ
    καὶ ὁ μεθυσθείς.—Plato, *Laws*
  2. Δημοσθένης ἐρωτηθείς, Πῶς τῇ ῥητορικῇ περιεγένου;
    Πλέον, ἔφη, ἔλαιον οἴνου δαπανήσας.
  3. τὰ γὰρ ἔργα οἶμαί σοι πιθανώτερα παρεσχῆσθαι τῶν νῦν
    λεχθέντων λόγων.—Xenophon, *Cyropaedia*

4. τὰ ἐλάχιστα ληπτέον τῶν κακῶν. — Aristotle, *Nicomachean Ethics*

5. τὸν μέλλοντα καλῶς ἄρχειν, ἀρχθῆναί φασι δεῖν πρῶτον. — Aristotle, *Politics* 1333a

6. οὐ τὸ ζῆν περὶ πλείστου ποιητέον, ἀλλὰ τὸ εὖ ζῆν. — Plato, *Crito* 48a

7. νομίζουσιν αὐτοὶ ἔχειν ψυχήν, ἣν ἄλλοι οὐκ ἔχουσιν.

8. ὅστις γὰρ αὐτὸς ἢ φρονεῖν μόνος δοκεῖ
ἢ γλῶτταν, ἣν οὐκ ἄλλος, ἢ ψυχὴν ἔχειν,
οὗτοι διαπτυχθέντες ὤφθησαν κενοί. — Sophocles, *Antigone* 707–9

9. ΟΔΥΣΣΕΥΣ
Ζεὺς ἔσθ᾽, ἵν᾽ εἰδῇς, Ζεύς, ὁ τῆσδε γῆς κρατῶν,
Ζεύς, ᾧ δέδοκται ταῦθ᾽· ὑπηρετῶ δ᾽ ἐγώ.
ΦΙΛΟΚΤΗΤΗΣ
ὦ μῖσος, οἷα κἀξανευρίσκεις λέγειν·
θεοὺς προτείνων τοὺς θεοὺς ψευδεῖς τίθης.
ΟΔ.
οὔκ, ἀλλ᾽ ἀληθεῖς. ἡ δ᾽ ὁδὸς πορευτέα.
ΦΙ.
οὔ φημ᾽.
    ΟΔ.
    ἐγὼ δέ φημι. πειστέον τάδε.
ΦΙ.
οἴμοι τάλας. — Sophocles, *Philoctetes* 989–95

10. πολλαὶ μορφαὶ τῶν δαιμονίων,
πολλὰ δ᾽ ἀέλπτως κραίνουσι θεοί.
καὶ τὰ δοκηθέντ᾽ οὐκ ἐτελέσθη,
τῶν δ᾽ ἀδοκήτων πόρον ηὗρε θεός. — Euripides, the closing choral lines of *Alcestis, Andromache, Bacchae,* and *Helen* (and, except for the first line, also of *Medea*)

Composition

1. We must choose (*use verbal*) the true, not the false.
2. When mother comes home, a way will be found.
3. All the unexpected (things) were brought to an end during the night.
4. Rhetoric, it seems, must be considered more important than wisdom; or what do you say?
5. The play was written in Athens, but it was not seen by the Athenians.

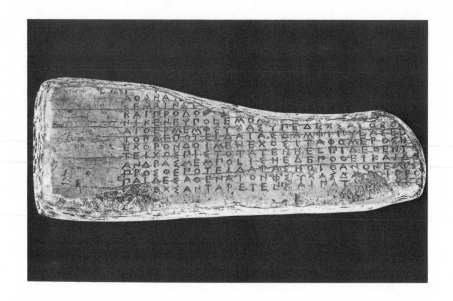

9. A Greek Inscription, 432 B.C.

Supplementum Epigraphicum Graecum, *vol. 10, p. 143, no. 414; from a copy in the H. W. Sage Collection of Casts of Ancient Sculpture at Cornell University; photo by Andrew Gillis.*

This inscription is a fragment of a memorial set up to honor the Athenians who died during the siege of Potidaea at the beginning of the Peloponnesian War. It is written in an epigraphic style called στοιχηδόν, *which means that all the letters occupy the same amount of space, and that the vertical rows of letters are as perfectly ordered as the horizontal lines. Notice that it is written in the "old Attic" alphabet, which did not use* ω, ξ, ψ, *or* η *(as a letter; H was used as a rough breathing). The fifth and sixth lines (right margin restored by epigraphers) read:*

ΑΙΘΕΡΜΕΜΦΣΥΧΑΣΥΠΕΔΕΧΣΑΤΟΣΟ[ΜΑΤΑΔΕΧΘΟΝ
ΤΟΝΔ .... *That is:*

αἰθὲρ μὲμ φσυχὰς ὑπεδέχσατο, σό[ματα δὲ χθὸν
τõνδ' .... *That is:*

αἰθὴρ μὲν ψυχὰς ὑπεδέξατο σώ[ματα δὲ χθὼν
τῶνδ' ....

Air received the souls, and earth the bodies
of these men . . . .

Lesson 24

The Imperative Mood

1. *Direct commands* in Greek may be given in the subjunctive and infinitive moods:

   ἀκούωμεν τῆς γυναικός. *Let's hear the woman.*
   τὸν Ἴωνα χαίρειν. *Farewell, Ion!*

2. But there is a separate mood in Greek, the *imperative,* with distinct personal endings, that is used *only* to give direct commands, in the second and third person:

   ἢ λέγε τι σιγῆς κρεῖττον, ἢ σιγὴν ἔχε. *Either say something better than silence, or keep quiet.*
   λαμψάτω τὸ φῶς ὑμῶν. *Let your light shine* (or *May your light shine*).

3. *Prohibitions,* or negative direct commands in the second and third person, use μή + either the *present imperative* or the *aorist subjunctive* but usually *not* the aorist imperative. The difference in tense denotes aspect, as often outside the indicative mood, rather than time, since the time reference of the imperative is always future. The present imperative stresses duration or continuance, while the aorist imperative (or aorist subjunctive in prohibitions) stresses a simple occurrence:

   μὴ λέγε ταῦτα. *Don't go on saying this, don't keep saying this; stop saying this.*
   μὴ λέξῃς ταῦτα. *Don't say this.*

4. In addition to the present and aorist imperative, Greek has a *perfect* imperative, which you will be required to learn this year only for a few verbs. The perfect imperative is usually found in the third-person singular, passive, and is common in the language of mathematics to express a proof or assumption:

   εἰλήφθω ἐπὶ τῆς ΑΒ τυχὸν σημεῖον τὸ Γ... *Let any point Γ be chosen on a line AB...* —Euclid

It is the regular imperative (instead of the present), however, for verbs whose perfect is equivalent to a present. Learn the perfect imperative of οἶδα, *know,* and ἕστηκα, *stand:*

2 sg.	ἴσθι	ἔσταθι
3 sg.	ἴστω	ἑστάτω
2 pl.	ἴστε	ἔστατε
3 pl.	ἴστων	ἑστάντων

5. The imperative endings are added to the unaugmented stem of the tense and voice to which they correspond (see lesson 19, par. 3):

    I: present (active, middle, passive)
    III: aorist (active, middle)
    VI: aorist (passive)

The imperative endings are as follows. The present endings include the thematic vowel (ε or o), which must be removed for nonthematic verbs (-μι verbs). The first aorist endings include the tense sign vowel (active and middle, -α-; passive, -η- or -ε-):

PRESENT

	active	*M/P*
2 sg.	-ε	-ου (-μι verbs, -σο)
3 sg.	-έτω	-έσθω
2 pl.	-ετε	-εσθε
3 pl.	-όντων	-έσθων

FIRST AORIST

	active	*middle*	*passive*
2 sg.	-ον	-αι	-ητι (*after* θ; -ηθι *elsewhere*)
3 sg.	-άτω	-άσθω	-ήτω
2 pl.	-ατε	-ασθε	-ητε
3 pl.	-άντων	-άσθων	-έντων

SECOND AORIST

active	*middle*	*passive*
(exactly like the *present* endings, except for the five verbs below)	2 sg. -οῦ (otherwise, like *present*)	(exactly like the *first aorist* passive endings)

Five second-aorist imperatives have accents that fall *after* the stem (on the ending) in their uncompounded forms of the second person. The *third*-person imperatives of these verbs and all imperatives of *compounds* of these verbs are regular. Learn the second-person active imperatives of εἶπον, ἦλθον, ηὗρον, εἶδον, and ἔλαβον:

sg.	εἰπέ	ἐλθέ	εὑρέ	ἰδέ	λαβέ
pl.	εἴπετε	ἐλθέτε	εὑρέτε	ἰδέτε	λαβέτε

6. Learn the following imperative forms of λύω:

PRESENT

	active	M/P
2 sg.	λῦε	λύου
3 sg.	λυέτω	λυέσθω
2 pl.	λύετε	λύεσθε
3 pl.	λυόντων	λυέσθων

FIRST AORIST

	active	middle	passive
2 sg.	λῦσον	λῦσαι	λύθητι
3 sg.	λυσάτω	λυσάσθω	λυθήτω
2 pl.	λύσατε	λύσασθε	λύθητε
3 pl.	λυσάντων	λυσάσθων	λυθέντων

7. Learn the second aorist imperative of ἔβαλον:

	active	middle	passive
2 sg.	βάλε	βαλοῦ	βλήθητι
3 sg.	βαλέτω	βαλέσθω	βληθήτω
2 pl.	βάλετε	βάλεσθε	βλήθητε
3 pl.	βαλόντων	βαλέσθων	βληθέντων

8. Learn the following present imperatives of contract verbs:

	active	M/P
2 sg.	νίκα	νικῶ
3 sg.	νικάτω	νικάσθω
2 pl.	νικᾶτε	νικᾶσθε
3 pl.	νικώντων	νικάσθων

2 sg.	ποίει	ποιοῦ
3 sg.	ποιείτω	ποιείσθω
2 pl.	ποιεῖτε	ποιεῖσθε
3 pl.	ποιούντων	ποιείσθων
2 sg.	δήλου	δηλοῦ
3 sg.	δηλούτω	δηλούσθω
2 pl.	δηλοῦτε	δηλοῦσθε
3 pl.	δηλούντων	δηλούσθων

9. Learn the following imperatives of -μι verbs:

PRESENT

active	M/P
δίδου	δίδοσο
διδότω	διδόσθω
δίδοτε	δίδοσθε
διδόντων	διδόσθων
ἵει	ἵεσο
ἱέτω	ἱέσθω
ἵετε	ἵεσθε
ἱέντων	ἱέσθων
τίθει	τίθεσο
τιθέτω	τιθέσθω
τίθετε	τίθεσθε
τιθέντων	τιθέσθων
ἵστη	ἵστασο
ἱστάτω	ἱστάσθω
ἵστατε	ἵστασθε
ἱστάντων	ἱστάσθων
δείκνυ	δείκνυσο
δεικνύτω	δεικνύσθω
δείκνυτε	δείκνυσθε
δεικνύντων	δεικνύσθων

AORIST

active	middle	passive
δός	δοῦ	δόθητι
δότω	δόσθω	δοθήτω
δότε	δόσθε	δόθητε
δόντων	δόσθων	δοθέντων
ἕς	οὗ	ἕθητι
ἕτω	ἕσθω	ἑθήτω
ἕτε	ἕσθε	ἕθητε
ἕντων	ἕσθων	ἑθέντων
θές	θοῦ	τέθητι
θέτω	θέσθω	τεθήτω
θέτε	θέσθε	τέθητε
θέντων	θέσθων	τεθέντων
στῆθι	(no	στάθητι
στήτω	second	σταθήτω
στῆτε	aorist	στάθητε
στάντων	middle)	σταθέντων
δεῖξον	δεῖξαι	δείχθητι
δειξάτω	δειξάσθω	δειχθήτω
δείξατε	δείξασθε	δείχθητε
δειξάντων	δειξάσθων	δειχθέντων

present imperatives

	(εἰμί)	(εἶμι)	(φημί)
2 sg.	ἴσθι	ἴθι	φαθί
3 sg.	ἔστω	ἴτω	φάτω
2 pl.	ἔστε	ἴτε	φάτε
3 pl.	ἔστων	ἰόντων	φάντων

Vocabulary

ἀνόμημα, ἀνομήματος, τό *sin, transgression*
βασιλεία, βασιλείας, ἡ *kingdom*
γονεύς, γονέως, ὁ *father, begetter;* (plural) *parents*
δηνάριον, δηναρίου, τό = Latin *denarius,* a Roman silver coin

worth about one Greek δραχμή

δυσπραξία, δυσπραξίας, ἡ *bad luck*

εἰκών, εἰκόνος, ἡ *image, likeness; picture*

ἐπιγραφή, ἐπιγραφῆς, ἡ *inscription, name*

Καῖσαρ, Καίσαρος, ὁ *Caesar*

κῆνσος, κήνσου, ὁ = Latin *census*, a registration of citizens that included a taxation; the *tax* itself

νόμισμα, νομίσματος, τό *coin*

ῥήτωρ, ῥήτορος, ὁ *public speaker, orator*

ὑποκριτής, ὑποκριτοῦ, ὁ *actor; pretender, hypocrite*

ἀντιλέγω, κτλ *say in response, reply; say in opposition, answer*

ἀπέρχομαι, κτλ *go away*

ἀποδίδωμι, κτλ *give back, return; pay* (debts, etc.)

ἀρθήσεται *shall be lifted and taken away, removed* (future passive of αἴρω)

γνῶθι (second-person singular aorist imperative of γιγνώσκω)

ἔξεστι *it is allowed, it is possible* (impersonal verb + complementary *infinitive*)

ἐπιδείκνυμι, κτλ *show, point out; give a specimen of*

εὔχομαι, εὔξομαι, εὐξάμην or ηὐξάμην, ηὖγμαι, —, — (imperfect ηὐχόμην) *pray; pray for, long for; profess pride that* (+ *accusative/infinitive*)

κωλύω, κωλύσω, ἐκώλυσα, κεκώλυκα, κεκώλυμαι, ἐκωλύθην *hinder, prevent* (+ *accusative/infinitive*)

μέμνησο *remember* (second-person singular perfect imperative of μιμνήσκω)

νίζω, νίψομαι, ἔνιψα, —, νένιμμαι, — *wash, purge, cleanse*

πειράζω (only present and imperfect) *try, tempt, put to the test*

προσέχω, κτλ *apply, direct, turn toward*
  προσέχω τὸν νοῦν *turn one's mind, pay attention*

προσφέρω, κτλ *bring* (something) *to* (someone) (+ *dative* of the person, *accusative* of the thing)
  προσήνεγκαν = προσήνεγκον

σημαίνω, σημανῶ, ἐσήμηνα, —, σεσήμασμαι, ἐσημάνθην *give signs, give signals*

σιγάω, σιγήσομαι, ἐσίγησα, σεσίγηκα, σεσίγημαι, ἐσιγήθην *be silent, be still*

σιωπάω, σιωπήσομαι, ἐσιώπησα, σεσιώπηκα, —, ἐσιωπήθην *keep silent, be still*

σωφρονοῦντος *of one who is sound of mind* (masculine genitive
  singular present participle of σωφρονέω; genitive of
  characteristic)
ταρασσέσθω *let* (so and so) *be troubled, may* (it) *be disturbed*
  (third-person singular present passive imperative)
χρέμπτεται *she is clearing her throat* (in preparation for delivering
  a speech) (third-person singular indicative deponent)

ἀνθρώπειος, ἀνθρωπεία, ἀνθρώπειον *human, fit for mankind*
  τὰ ἀνθρώπεια *human affairs*
δόκιμος, δόκιμον *trustworthy; of proven character*
εὐήθης, εὔηθες *simple; foolish, absurd*
ὅπερ *the very thing which*

πανταχοῦ *everywhere* (adverb)
περί *concerning, with regard to* (preposition + *accusative*)
πρός *toward* (preposition + *accusative*)
σαυτοῦ, σαυτῆς, σαυτοῦ (uncontracted form σεαυτοῦ, *κτλ*)
  yourself (reflexive pronoun; no nominative)
σιγῇ *in silence, silently*
τὰ μέν . . . τὰ δέ *some things . . . other things*

Practice

Give a complete synopsis of ten verbs from the list in Appendix C.

Reading

1. μὴ πάντ᾽ ἄκουε, μηδὲ πάντα μάνθανε.
2. πράττων καλῶς μέμνησο τὴν δυσπραξίαν. —Menander
3. νίψον ἀνομήματα μὴ μόναν ὄψιν. (a palindrome, reading the
   same from right to left as from left to right)
4. μὴ πᾶσιν, ἀλλὰ τοῖς δοκίμοις πίστευε· τὸ μὲν γὰρ εὔηθες,
   τὸ δὲ σωφρονοῦντος. —Democritus
5. μὴ ταρασσέσθω ὑμῶν ἡ καρδία. —Saint John xiv. 1
6. γνῶθι σαυτόν.
7. ἁ δὲ χεὶρ τὰν χεῖρα νίζει· δός τι καί τι λάμβανε. —
   Epicharmus
8. περὶ πλείονος ποιοῦ δόξαν καλὴν ἢ πλοῦτον μέγαν τοῖς

παισὶ καταλιπεῖν. — Isocrates

9. ΧΟΡΟΣ ΓΥΝΑΙΚΩΝ

σίγα, σιώπα, πρόσεχε τὸν νοῦν, χρέμπτεται γὰρ ἤδη
ὅπερ ποιοῦσ᾽ οἱ ῥήτορες· μακρὰν ἔοικε λέξειν. —
Aristophanes, *Thesmophoriazusae* 381–2

10. Εἰπὲ οὖν ἡμῖν, τί σοι δοκεῖ; ἔξεστι δοῦναι κῆνσον
Καίσαρι; ἢ οὔ; γνοὺς δὲ ὁ Ἰησοῦς τὴν πονηρίαν αὐτῶν
εἶπε, Τί με πειράζετε, ὑποκριταί; ἐπιδείξατέ μοι τὸ νόμισμα
τοῦ κήνσου. οἱ δὲ προσήνεγκαν αὐτῷ δηνάριον. καὶ λέγει
αὐτοῖς, Τίνος ἡ εἰκὼν αὕτη καὶ ἡ ἐπιγραφή; λέγουσιν
αὐτῷ, Καίσαρος. τότε λέγει αὐτοῖς, Ἀπόδοτε οὖν τὰ
Καίσαρος Καίσαρι, καὶ τὰ τοῦ Θεοῦ τῷ Θεῷ. καὶ
ἀκούσαντες ἐθαύμασαν, καὶ ἀφέντες αὐτὸν ἀπῆλθον. — Saint
Matthew xxii.17–22

11. τοιοῦτος γίγνου περὶ τοὺς γονεῖς, οἵους ἂν εὔξαιο περὶ
σαυτὸν γενέσθαι τοὺς σαυτοῦ παῖδας. — Isocrates

12. Ἄφετε τὰ παιδία καὶ μὴ κωλύετε αὐτὰ ἐλθεῖν πρός με· τῶν
γὰρ τοιούτων ἐστὶν ἡ βασιλεία τῶν οὐρανῶν. — Saint
Matthew xix.14

13. οὗτοι μὲν γὰρ οἴονται τοὺς θεοὺς τὰ μὲν εἰδέναι, τὰ δ᾽ οὐκ
εἰδέναι· Σωκράτης δὲ πάντα μὲν ἡγεῖτο θεοὺς εἰδέναι, τά
τε λεγόμενα καὶ πραττόμενα καὶ τὰ σιγῇ βουλευόμενα,
πανταχοῦ δὲ παρεῖναι καὶ σημαίνειν τοῖς ἀνθρώποις περὶ
τῶν ἀνθρωπείων πάντων.

14. εἴ τι ἔχεις ἀντιλέγειν, ἀντίλεγε· εἰ δὲ μή, παῦσαι ἤδη
πολλάκις μοι λέγων τὸν αὐτὸν λόγον.

15. λέγω ὑμῖν ὅτι παντὶ τῷ ἔχοντι δοθήσεται· ἀπὸ δὲ τοῦ μὴ
ἔχοντος, καὶ ὃ ἔχει ἀρθήσεται ἀπ᾽ αὐτοῦ. — Saint Luke xix.26

Composition

1. Give us the money, but don't give us a speech.
2. Be still and pay attention; learn what he tells you.
3. So tell us, what do you think? Will a crown be given to
   everyone?
4. If you have something to say, say it; but if not, go away in
   silence.
5. Honor thy father and thy mother.

Supplementary Readings
Appendixes
Vocabularies
Indexes

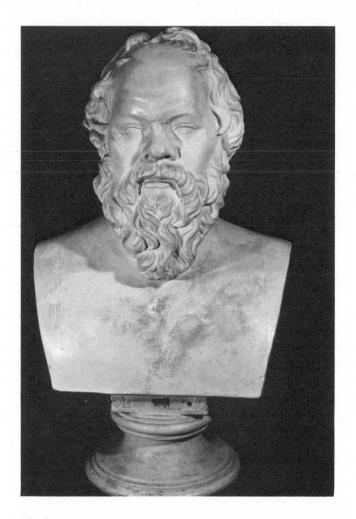

10. Socrates.

Reproduction of a portrait of Socrates by the fourth-century sculptor Lysippus, in the Vatican Museum; from a copy in the H. W. Sage Collection of Casts of Ancient Sculpture at Cornell University; photo by Andrew Gillis.

The philosopher who claimed to be merely an intellectual midwife, helping others give birth to their thoughts while being barren himself, spent most of his seventy years in the pursuit of knowledge and wisdom. He started life as a sculptor, apprenticed to his father, but soon devoted himself completely to philosophical inquiry. He is the principal character in the dialogues of Plato and is featured prominently in a typically comic exaggeration as the head of the φροντιστήριον in Aristophanes' Clouds. He was put to death in 399 B.C. after a public trial at which he made little effort to defend himself against charges of corrupting the young men of Athens.

Supplementary Readings

The two basic tools for the student of Greek literature are a lexicon and a thorough reference grammar. Notes to the following readings are keyed to H. G. Liddell and Robert Scott, *An Abridged Greek-English Lexicon* (Oxford University Press, 1957), and to H. W. Smyth: *Greek Grammar,* revised by Gordon M. Messing (Cambridge: Harvard University Press, 1956), cited as *LS* and *Smyth,* respectively. The numbers in *Smyth* are paragraph numbers, unless otherwise specified.

1. The first passage is the opening of Plato's dialogue entitled *Ion.* Plato was born around 428 B.C., was a student of Socrates, and wrote and taught philosophy until he died at an advanced age. Many of his philosophical writings are in the form of a dialogue, with the character Socrates as the protagonist, and a multitude of well-known and not so well known characters as "interlocutors." The advantages of the dialogue over the essay or straightforward treatise are many, but it has its drawbacks as well. Among its advantages are its liveliness (when it is well written), its immediate accessibility to nonprofessional philosophers, and its humor. Among its disadvantages is the problem that technical terms that are not in the current vernacular must always be defined anew, as they would have to be in real conversation.

The subject of the *Ion* is the interpretation and criticism of art, specifically, the art of poetry. Ion is a "rhapsodist," a man who makes his living by reciting poems—particularly the poems of Homer. Of course, in order to recite the *Iliad* and the *Odyssey* properly, it is not enough for the rhapsodist to memorize the poems: he must also *understand* them. Socrates marvels at Ion's performing skills and at his costume, but it is the issue of understanding Homer that he ultimately wants to discuss with Ion.

We have the first scenes of the dialogue, which include the meeting of Socrates and Ion, occasional small talk, and the beginning of the conversation that leads naturally into an investigation of Ion's profession.

ΤΑ ΤΟΥ ΔΙΑΛΟΓΟΥ ΠΡΟΣΩΠΑ
ΣΩΚΡΑΤΗΣ
ΙΩΝ

¹ Σ. Τὸν Ἴωνα χαίρειν. πόθεν τὰ νῦν ἡμῖν ἐπιδεδήμηκας;
ἢ οἴκοθεν ἐξ Ἐφέσου;
Ι. οὐδαμῶς, ὦ Σώκρατες, ἀλλ' ἐξ Ἐπιδαύρου ἐκ τῶν
Ἀσκληπιείων.
⁵ Σ. μῶν καὶ ῥαψῳδῶν ἀγῶνα τιθέασι τῷ θεῷ οἱ
Ἐπιδαύριοι;
Ι. πάνυ γε, καὶ τῆς ἄλλης γε μουσικῆς.
Σ. τί οὖν; ἠγωνίζου τι ἡμῖν; καὶ πῶς τι ἠγωνίσω;
Ι. τὰ πρῶτα τῶν ἄθλων ἠνεγκάμεθα, ὦ Σώκρατες.
¹⁰ Σ. εὖ λέγεις· ἄγε δὴ ὅπως καὶ τὰ Παναθήναια
νικήσομεν.
Ι. ἀλλ' ἔσται ταῦτα, ἐὰν θεὸς ἐθέλῃ.
Σ. καὶ μὴν πολλάκις γε ἐζήλωσα ὑμᾶς τοὺς ῥαψῳδούς, ὦ
Ἴων, τῆς τέχνης· τὸ γὰρ ἅμα μὲν τὸ σῶμα κεκοσμῆσθαι
¹⁵ ἀεὶ πρέπον ὑμῶν εἶναι τῇ τέχνῃ καὶ ὡς καλλίστοις
φαίνεσθαι, ἅμα δὲ ἀναγκαῖον εἶναι ἔν τε ἄλλοις ποιηταῖς
διατρίβειν πολλοῖς καὶ ἀγαθοῖς καὶ δὴ καὶ μάλιστα ἐν
Ὁμήρῳ, τῷ ἀρίστῳ καὶ θειοτάτῳ τῶν ποιητῶν, καὶ τὴν
τούτου διάνοιαν ἐκμανθάνειν, μὴ μόνον τὰ ἔπη, ζηλωτὸν
²⁰ ἐστιν. οὐ γὰρ ἂν γένοιτό ποτε ῥαψῳδός, εἰ μὴ συνείη
τὰ λεγόμενα ὑπὸ τοῦ ποιητοῦ. τὸν γὰρ ῥαψῳδὸν ἑρμηνέα δεῖ
τοῦ ποιητοῦ τῆς διανοίας γίγνεσθαι τοῖς ἀκούουσι· τοῦτο
δὲ καλῶς ποιεῖν μὴ γιγνώσκοντα ὅτι λέγει ὁ ποιητὴς
ἀδύνατον. ταῦτα οὖν πάντα ἄξια ζηλοῦσθαι.
²⁵ Ι. ἀληθῆ λέγεις, ὦ Σώκρατες· ἐμοὶ γοῦν τοῦτο
πλεῖστον ἔργον παρέσχε τῆς τέχνης, καὶ οἶμαι κάλλιστα
ἀνθρώπων λέγειν περὶ Ὁμήρου, ὡς οὔτε Μητρόδωρος ὁ
Λαμψακηνὸς οὔτε Στησίμβροτος ὁ Θάσιος οὔτε Γλαύκων οὔτε
ἄλλος οὐδεὶς τῶν πώποτε γενομένων ἔσχεν εἰπεῖν οὕτω
³⁰ πολλὰς καὶ καλὰς διανοίας περὶ Ὁμήρου, ὅσας ἐγώ.
Σ. εὖ λέγεις, ὦ Ἴων· δῆλον γὰρ ὅτι οὐ φθονήσεις μοι
ἐπιδεῖξαι.
Ι. καὶ μὴν ἄξιόν γε ἀκοῦσαι, ὦ Σώκρατες, ὡς εὖ κεκόσμηκα
τὸν Ὅμηρον· ὥστε οἶμαι ὑπὸ Ὁμηριδῶν ἄξιος εἶναι χρυσῷ
³⁵ στεφάνῳ στεφανωθῆναι.
Σ. καὶ μὴν ἐγὼ ἔτι ποιήσομαι σχολὴν ἀκροᾶσθαί σου· νῦν
δέ μοι τοσόνδε ἀπόκριναι· πότερον περὶ Ὁμήρου μόνον
δεινὸς εἶ ἢ καὶ περὶ Ἡσιόδου καὶ Ἀρχιλόχου;
Ι. οὐδαμῶς, ἀλλὰ περὶ Ὁμήρου μόνον· ἱκανὸν γάρ μοι

⁴⁰ δοκεῖ εἶναι.

Σ. ἔστι δὲ περὶ ὅτου Ὅμηρός τε καὶ Ἡσίοδος ταὐτὰ
λέγετον;

Ι. οἶμαι ἔγωγε καὶ πολλά.

Σ. πότερον οὖν περὶ τούτων κάλλιον ἂν ἐξηγήσαιο ἃ
⁴⁵ Ὅμηρος λέγει ἢ ἃ Ἡσίοδος;

Ι. ὁμοίως ἂν περί γε τούτων, ὦ Σώκρατες, περὶ ὧν ταὐτὰ
λέγουσιν.

Σ. τί δέ; ὧν πέρι μὴ ταὐτὰ λέγουσιν; οἷον περὶ μαντικῆς
λέγει τι Ὅμηρός τε καὶ Ἡσίοδος;

⁵⁰ Ι. πάνυ γε.

Σ. τί οὖν; ὅσα τε ὁμοίως καὶ ὅσα διαφόρως περὶ μαντικῆς
λέγετον τὼ ποιητὰ τούτω, πότερον σὺ κάλλιον ἂν ἐξηγήσαιο
ἢ τῶν μάντεών τις τῶν ἀγαθῶν;

Ι. τῶν μάντεων.

⁵⁵ Σ. εἰ δὲ σὺ ἦσθα μάντις, οὐκ, εἴπερ περὶ τῶν ὁμοίως
λεγομένων οἷός τ᾽ ἦσθα ἐξηγήσασθαι, καὶ περὶ τῶν
διαφόρως λεγομένων ἠπίστω ἂν ἐξηγεῖσθαι;

Ι. δῆλον ὅτι.

Σ. τί οὖν ποτε περὶ μὲν Ὁμήρου δεινὸς εἶ, περὶ δὲ
⁶⁰ Ἡσιόδου οὔ;

NOTES

1. χαίρειν: *LS* s.v. χαίρω IV.1.
   τὰ νῦν: *LS* s.v. νῦν I.2.
   ἡμῖν: ethic dative; *Smyth* 1486.
   ἐπιδεδήμηκας: perfect of ἐπιδημέω.

2. Ἔφεσος, Ἐφέσου, ἡ: *Ephesus, a Greek city in Asia Minor.*

3. Ἐπίδαυρος, Ἐπιδαύρου, ἡ: *Epidaurus, famous for its temple to Asclepius.*

4. Ἀσκληπιεῖα, Ἀσκληπιείων, τά (sc. ἱερά): *festival of Asclepius.*

5. μῶν: introduces questions that normally expect a negative reply; *Smyth* 2651.

7. πάνυ: *LS* s.v. 2.
   γε: *Smyth* 2821.

8. τί οὖν: *Smyth* 2962.
   ἠγωνίζου . . . ἠγωνίσω: notice the different tenses, the imperfect pointing to the duration of the contest and the aorist emphasizing the outcome.

10. ἄγε: *Smyth* 1836; *LS* s.v.
    ὅπως: *Smyth* 1920, 2213.

τὰ Παναθήναια: internal object (cognate accusative); *Smyth* 1554a, N.1 and N.2; 1570d.

13.   καὶ μὴν...γε: *Smyth* 2921.

14.   τέχνης: ζηλόω and other verbs of emotion take a *genitive of cause; Smyth* 1405.

14–20. τὸ γὰρ...πρέπον...εἶναι and ἀναγκαῖον εἶναι: articular infinitives, subjects of ζηλωτόν ἐστιν. κεκοσμῆσθαι and φαίνεσθαι are complementary infinitives explaining πρέπον. διατρίβειν and ἐκμανθάνειν are complementary to ἀναγκαῖον.

14.   σῶμα: retained accusative with κεκοσμῆσθαι; *Smyth* 1748.

15.   καλλίστοις: modifies an understood ὑμῖν.

23.   μὴ γιγνώσκοντα: circumstantial participle of condition.

24.   ἀδύνατον (ἐστι): predicate modifier of ποιεῖν.
      οὖν: confirmatory; *Smyth* 2955, 2956.

25.   γοῦν: *Smyth* 2830.

27.   λέγειν: subject ἐγώ implied.

33.   καὶ μὴν...γε: *Smyth* 2921.
      ὡς: *how.*

36.   καὶ μὴν: *Smyth* 2921.

37–38. πότερον...ἢ: *Smyth* 2656.

38.   Ἡσίοδος, Ἡσιόδου, ὁ: *Hesiod, author of* Theogony, Works and Days.
      Ἀρχίλοχος, Ἀρχιλόχου, ὁ: *Archilochus, seventh-century* B.C. *iambic poet.*

42.   λέγετον: third-person *dual,* present indicative active; *Smyth* 383.

46.   γε: modifies the whole prepositional phrase; *Smyth* 2821.

48.   πέρι: anastrophic; *Smyth* 175a, 1665.
      μὴ: the indefinite antecedent of ὧν causes the clause to be negated with μή rather than with οὐ; *Smyth* 2506, 2507.
      οἷον: *LS* s.v. οἷος V.3.

52.   τὼ ποιητὰ τούτω: nominative dual; *Smyth* 222, 332, 333.

55.   εἴπερ: *Smyth* 2965.

56.   οἷός τ᾽ ἦσθα: *LS* s.v. οἷος III.1.

57.   ἠπίστω: second-person singular imperfect of ἐπίσταμαι.

2. Saint Paul apparently took the occasion of internal dissension among the early Christians at Corinth to write his famous sermon against such bickering and in favor of ἀγάπη. (It will serve the student of the New Testament well, incidentally, to trace the origins of the word ἀγάπη in *LS,* in order to appreciate the full range of its meanings.)

At the beginning of this sermon, which he wrote as the first of two "letters" to the Corinthians, Paul mentions the rumors of squabbling at Corinth among this and that self-proclaimed sect of Christians and scolds them all, asking, μεμέρισται ὁ Χριστός; (*Has Christ been divided up into pieces and distributed [among you]?*) He reasons, pleads, and prays throughout the letter for Christian unity, and near the end, he composes this simple and compelling description of love. It is the thirteenth chapter of his first letter to the Corinthians, and it is reproduced here in its entirety.

ΠΡΟΣ ΚΟΡΙΝΘΙΟΥΣ Α′

1 Ἐὰν ταῖς γλώσσαις τῶν ἀνθρώπων λαλῶ καὶ τῶν ἀγγέλων, ἀγάπην δὲ μὴ ἔχω, γέγονα χαλκὸς ἠχῶν ἢ κύμβαλον ἀλαλάζον. καὶ ἐὰν ἔχω προφητείαν καὶ εἰδῶ τὰ μυστήρια πάντα καὶ πᾶσαν τὴν γνῶσιν, καὶ ἐὰν ἔχω πᾶσαν τὴν πίστιν ὥστε ὄρη
5 μεθιστάνειν, ἀγάπην δὲ μὴ ἔχω, οὐθέν εἰμι. καὶ ἐὰν ψωμίσω πάντα τὰ ὑπάρχοντά μου, καὶ ἐὰν παραδῶ τὸ σῶμά μου ἵνα καυθήσωμαι, ἀγάπην δὲ μὴ ἔχω, οὐδὲν ὠφελοῦμαι. ἡ ἀγάπη μακροθυμεῖ, χρηστεύεται· ἡ ἀγάπη οὐ ζηλοῖ· ἡ ἀγάπη οὐ περπερεύεται, οὐ φυσιοῦται, οὐκ ἀσχημονεῖ, οὐ
10 ζητεῖ τὰ ἑαυτῆς, οὐ παροξύνεται, οὐ λογίζεται τὸ κακόν, οὐ χαίρει ἐπὶ τῇ ἀδικίᾳ, συγχαίρει δὲ τῇ ἀληθείᾳ, πάντα στέγει, πάντα πιστεύει, πάντα ἐλπίζει, πάντα ὑπομένει. ἡ ἀγάπη οὐδέποτε πίπτει· εἴτε δὲ προφητεῖαι, καταργηθήσονται· εἴτε γλῶσσαι, παύσονται· εἴτε γνῶσις,
15 καταργηθήσεται. ἐκ μέρους γὰρ γινώσκομεν, καὶ ἐκ μέρους προφητεύομεν· ὅταν δὲ ἔλθῃ τὸ τέλειον, τὸ ἐκ μέρους καταργηθήσεται. ὅτε ἤμην νήπιος, ἐλάλουν ὡς νήπιος, ἐφρόνουν ὡς νήπιος, ἐλογιζόμην ὡς νήπιος· ὅτε γέγονα ἀνήρ, κατήργηκα τὰ τοῦ νηπίου. βλέπομεν γὰρ ἄρτι
20 δι᾽ ἐσόπτρου ἐν αἰνίγματι, τότε δὲ πρόσωπον πρὸς πρόσωπον· ἄρτι γινώσκω ἐκ μέρους, τότε δὲ ἐπιγνώσομαι καθὼς καὶ ἐπεγνώσθην. νυνὶ δὲ μένει πίστις, ἐλπίς, ἀγάπη, τὰ τρία ταῦτα· μείζων δὲ τούτων ἡ ἀγάπη.

NOTES

2. ἠχῶν: present participle of ἠχέω.

4–5. ὥστε . . . μεθιστάνειν: natural result (capacity); *Smyth* 2250, 2251, 2257–59.

5. οὐθέν: *LS* s.v. οὐθείς.

6. ψωμίσω: aorist subjunctive active of ψωμίζω, *give away bit by bit.*
    τὰ ὑπάρχοντα: *LS* s.v. ὑπάρχω IV.2.

7. καυθήσωμαι: first aorist passive subjunctive of καίω.
    ὠφελοῦμαι: passive; *LS* s.v. ὠφελέω II.

11. ἐπὶ: classical Greek would omit the preposition; *LS* s.v. χαίρω I.2.
13. προφητεῖαι (ἔσονται): future most vivid; *Smyth* 2328.
15. γινώσκομεν: κοινή (New Testament Greek) for γιγνώσκομεν.
17. ἤμην: = ἦν, *I was* (imperfect of εἰμί).
19. κατήργηκα: perfect active of καταργέω (cf. καταργηθήσεται, καταργηθήσονται above).
23. μείζων: comparative for the superlative μεγίστη, a common use in the New Testament.

3. Plato's Πολιτεία (commonly translated *Republic*) is one of his most discussed and least understood works. πολιτεία is not merely "republic," or the political sovereignty of the state; it is also the relation of a citizen *to* the republic, the condition and rights of a citizen, citizenship, the life of a citizen. And it is the citizen who captures Plato's interest in this work, much more than the state itself.

Unlike the *Ion,* the *Republic* is not exactly a dialogue; it is more like a narrative, with extensive dialogue in it. The narrator is the character Socrates, and he narrates the long, ten-book work as if it had taken place yesterday (χθές). This selection, from book 2, makes it clear that it is the life of the citizen that animates the work, and that Socrates (or rather, Plato) is using the πόλις chiefly as a metaphorical enlargement of the individual.

During their discussion of the nature and value of δικαιοσύνη, Socrates and his friends find themselves looking for an instructive analogy—a good metaphor to help them discover the truth.

ΠΟΛΙΤΕΙΑΣ Β′

¹ Ὅ τε οὖν Γλαύκων καὶ οἱ ἄλλοι ἐδέοντο παντὶ τρόπῳ
βοηθῆσαι καὶ μὴ ἀνεῖναι τὸν λόγον, ἀλλὰ διερευνήσασθαι
τί τέ ἐστιν ἑκάτερον καὶ περὶ τῆς ὠφελίας αὐτοῖν
τἀληθὲς ποτέρως ἔχει.
⁵ εἶπον οὖν ὅπερ ἐμοὶ ἔδοξεν, ὅτι Τὸ ζήτημα ᾧ ἐπι-
χειροῦμεν οὐ φαῦλον ἀλλ’ ὀξὺ βλέποντος, ὡς ἐμοὶ
φαίνεται. ἐπειδὴ οὖν ἡμεῖς οὐ δεινοί, δοκῶ μοι, ἦν δ’
ἐγώ, τοιαύτην ποιήσασθαι ζήτησιν αὐτοῦ, οἵανπερ ἂν εἰ
προσέταξέ τις γράμματα σμικρὰ πόρρωθεν ἀναγνῶναι μὴ
¹⁰ πάνυ ὀξὺ βλέπουσιν, ἔπειτά τις ἐνενόησεν, ὅτι τὰ
αὐτὰ γράμματα ἔστι που καὶ ἄλλοθι μείζω τε καὶ ἐν
μείζονι, ἕρμαιον ἂν ἐφάνη, οἶμαι, ἐκεῖνα πρῶτον ἀναγνόντας οὕτως ἐπισκοπεῖν τὰ ἐλάττω, εἰ τὰ αὐτὰ ὄντα
τυγχάνει.
¹⁵ Πάνυ μὲν οὖν, ἔφη ὁ Ἀδείμαντος· ἀλλὰ τί τοιοῦτον,

ὦ Σώκρατες, ἐν τῇ περὶ τὸ δίκαιον ζητήσει καθορᾷς;
Ἐγώ σοι, ἔφην, ἐρῶ. δικαιοσύνη, φαμέν, ἔστι μὲν
ἀνδρὸς ἑνός, ἔστι δέ που καὶ ὅλης πόλεως;
Πάνυ γε, ἦ δ' ὅς.
20   Οὐκοῦν μεῖζον πόλις ἑνὸς ἀνδρός;
Μεῖζον, ἔφη.
Ἴσως τοίνυν πλείων ἂν δικαιοσύνη ἐν τῷ μείζονι
ἐνείη καὶ ῥᾴων καταμαθεῖν. εἰ οὖν βούλεσθε, πρῶτον ἐν
ταῖς πόλεσι ζητήσωμεν ποῖόν τί ἐστιν· ἔπειτα οὕτως ἐπι-
25   σκεψώμεθα καὶ ἐν ἑνὶ ἑκάστῳ, τὴν τοῦ μείζονος ὁμοιό-
τητα ἐν τῇ τοῦ ἐλάττονος ἰδέᾳ ἐπισκοποῦντες.
Ἀλλά μοι δοκεῖς, ἔφη, καλῶς λέγειν.
Ἆρ' οὖν, ἦν δ' ἐγώ, εἰ γιγνομένην πόλιν θεασαίμεθα
λόγῳ, καὶ τὴν δικαιοσύνην αὐτῆς ἴδοιμεν ἂν γιγνομένην
30   καὶ τὴν ἀδικίαν;
Τάχ' ἄν, ἦ δ' ὅς.
Οὐκοῦν γενομένου αὐτοῦ ἐλπὶς εὐπετέστερον ἰδεῖν ὃ
ζητοῦμεν;
Πολύ γε.
35   Δοκεῖ οὖν χρῆναι ἐπιχειρῆσαι περαίνειν; οἶμαι μὲν
γὰρ οὐκ ὀλίγον ἔργον αὐτὸ εἶναι· σκοπεῖτε οὖν.
Ἔσκεπται, ἔφη ὁ Ἀδείμαντος· ἀλλὰ μὴ ἄλλως ποίει.

NOTES

1.   ἐδέοντο: imperfect of δέομαι, *ask for, beg for;* LS s.v. δέω (B) III.
2.   βοηθῆσαι . . . ἀνεῖναι: complementary infinitives with ἐδέοντο.
     ἀνεῖναι: aorist infinitive of ἀνίημι.
3.   ἑκάτερον: *each of the two (concepts being discussed):* δικαιοσύνη
     and its opposite, ἀδικία.
     ὠφελίας: *usefulness, advantage.*
     αὐτοῖν: i.e., justice and injustice; genitive dual; Smyth 327.
4.   τἀληθὲς ποτέρως ἔχει: *which way the truth prevailed;* for the in-
     transitive sense, see LS s.v. ἔχω B.
5.   ὅπερ: neuter of ὅσπερ: *exactly what, the very thing which;* LS s.v.
     πέρ and Smyth 2965.
     ὅτι: what follows is a *direct* quotation, but it is common in colloquial
     or familiar writing for direct quotations to be introduced by ὅτι;
     Smyth 2590a.
     ᾧ: ἐπιχειρέω takes its objects in the *dative* case.
6.   ὀξὺ βλέποντος: the participle modifies ἀνθρώπου (understood):
     genitive of characteristic; Smyth 1305; ὀξὺ is adverbial accusative
     modifying the verbal force of the participle.

7. δεινοί: *LS* s.v. δεινός III.
   δοκῶ μοι: *I am determined* (+ complementary *infinitive*).
7–8. ἦν δ᾽ ἐγώ: *said I;* ἦν = ἔφην.
8. αὐτοῦ: sc. τοῦ ζητήματος (line 5).
   οἷανπερ: answers τοιαύτην; translate *just as, for example.*
   ἄν: proleptic, with ἐφάνη, and repeated below.
9. προσέταξε: protasis, past contrary-to-fact condition.
10. βλέπουσιν: the indirect object of προστάττω (i.e., the recipient of the command) is in the *dative* case.
    ἐνενόησεν: second protasis, parallel with προσέταξε.
12. ἂν ἐφάνη: apodosis.
12–13. ἀναγνόντας: the same group as βλέπουσιν (line 10); it is accusative because these hypothetical persons are now the subject of the infinitive ἐπισκοπεῖν.
14. τυγχάνει: the subject is τὰ ἐλάττω.
17–18. ἔστι μὲν... ἔστι δέ: notice the accent; *Smyth* 187b.
18. ἀνδρὸς... πόλεως: genitives of characteristic.
19. ἦ δ᾽ ὅς: *said he;* ἦ = ἔφη; ὅς = οὗτος; *Smyth* 1113.
20. οὐκοῦν: *Smyth* 2951.
21. μεῖζον: *Smyth* 1048.
22. ἴσως: *LS* s.v. III.
24. ζητήσωμεν: why subjunctive?
25. ἑνὶ ἑκάστῳ: i.e., each person.
28. ἆρ᾽: *Smyth* 2650.
29. λόγῳ: *in (our make-believe) story; in (our) conversation.*
31. τάχ᾽ ἄν: *LS* s.v. τάχα II.
32. οὐκοῦν: *Smyth* 2951.
    γενομένου αὐτοῦ: genitive absolute.
35. δοκεῖ... περαίνειν: each of the first three verbs in this sentence governs the one that follows it.
37. ἔσκεπται: perfect passive of σκοπέω.
    ποίει: what mood?

4. Aristophanes was a writer of comedy in Athens in the last half of the fifth century B.C. We have fragments (scattered lines quoted by other writers) from several comic playwrights, but of his era, only Aristophanes has survived the accidents of transmitting Greek literature from generation to generation, as a representative of the art of Attic Old Comedy. We have nearly a dozen of his plays complete, more than for any Greek dramatist (tragedy or comedy) except Euripides.

The action in Aristophanes' comedy Νεφέλαι (*The Clouds*) really begins with the second scene, when an old farmer named Strepsiades applies for admission to the school operated by the philosopher Socrates, in the hope of acquiring the skills necessary to outwit and outargue his creditors in court.

ΤΑ ΤΟΥ ΔΡΑΜΑΤΟΣ ΠΡΟΣΩΠΑ
ΣΤΡΕΨΙΑΔΗΣ
ΜΑΘΗΤΗΣ ΣΩΚΡΑΤΟΥΣ
ΣΩΚΡΑΤΗΣ

¹   Στ. Ἀλλ' οὐχὶ κόπτω τὴν θύραν; παῖ, παιδίον.

Μ. βάλλ' ἐς κόρακας· τίς ἐσθ' ὁ κόψας τὴν θύραν;

Στ. Φείδωνος υἱὸς Στρεψιάδης Κικυννόθεν.

Μ. ἀμαθής γε νὴ Δί' ὅστις οὑτωσὶ σφόδρα

5   ἀπεριμερίμνως τὴν θύραν λελάκτικας
καὶ φροντίδ' ἐξήμβλωκας ἐξηυρημένην.

Στ. σύγγνωθί μοι· τηλοῦ γὰρ οἰκῶ τῶν ἀγρῶν.
ἀλλ' εἰπέ μοι τὸ πρᾶγμα τοὐξημβλωμένον.

Μ. ἀλλ' οὐ θέμις πλὴν τοῖς μαθηταῖσιν λέγειν.

10   Στ. λέγε νυν ἐμοὶ θαρρῶν· ἐγὼ γὰρ οὑτοσὶ
ἥκω μαθητὴς ἐς τὸ φροντιστήριον.

Μ. λέξω. νομίσαι δὲ ταῦτα χρὴ μυστήρια.
ἀνήρετ' ἄρτι Χαιρεφῶντα Σωκράτης
ψύλλαν ὁπόσους ἄλλοιτο τοὺς αὑτῆς πόδας·

15   δακοῦσα γὰρ τοῦ Χαιρεφῶντος τὴν ὀφρῦν
ἐπὶ τὴν κεφαλὴν τὴν Σωκράτους ἀφήλατο.

Στ. πῶς δῆτα διεμέτρησε;

                Μ. δεξιώτατα.
κηρὸν διατήξας, εἶτα τὴν ψύλλαν λαβὼν
ἐνέβαψεν ἐς τὸν κηρὸν αὐτῆς τὼ πόδε,

20   κᾆτα ψυχείσῃ περιέφυσαν Περσικαί.
ταύτας ὑπολύσας ἀνεμέτρει τὸ χωρίον.

Στ. τί δῆτ' ἐκεῖνον τὸν Θαλῆν θαυμάζομεν;
ἄνοιγ' ἄνοιγ' ἀνύσας τὸ φροντιστήριον,
καὶ δεῖξον ὡς τάχιστά μοι τὸν Σωκράτη.

25   μαθητιῶ γάρ· ἀλλ' ἄνοιγε τὴν θύραν.
πρὸς τῶν θεῶν τί γὰρ τάδ' ἐστίν; εἰπέ μοι.

Μ. ἀστρονομία μὲν αὑτηί.

              Στ. τουτὶ δὲ τί;

Μ. γεωμετρία.

          Στ. τοῦτ' οὖν τί ἐστι χρήσιμον;

Μ. γῆν ἀναμετρῆσαι.

        Στ. πότερα τὴν κληρουχικήν;

30   Μ. οὔκ, ἀλλὰ τὴν σύμπασαν.

                Στ. ἀστεῖον λέγεις.
τὸ γὰρ σόφισμα δημοτικὸν καὶ χρήσιμον.

Μ. αὕτη δέ σοι γῆς περίοδος πάσης. ὁρᾷς;

αἵδε μὲν Ἀθῆναι.

     Στ. τί σὺ λέγεις; οὐ πείθομαι,
ἐπεὶ δικαστὰς οὐχ ὁρῶ καθημένους.
35 Μ. ὡς τοῦτ᾽ ἀληθῶς Ἀττικὸν τὸ χωρίον.
Στ. καὶ ποῦ Κικυννῆς εἰσιν οὑμοὶ δημόται;
Μ. ἐνταῦθ᾽ ἔνεισιν. ἡ δέ γ᾽ Εὔβοι᾽, ὡς ὁρᾷς,
ἡδὶ παρατέταται μακρὰ πόρρω πάνυ.
Στ. οἶδ᾽· ὑπὸ γὰρ ἡμῶν παρετάθη καὶ Περικλέους.
40 ἀλλ᾽ ἡ Λακεδαίμων ποῦ ᾽σθ᾽;

        Μ. ὅπου ᾽στίν; αὑτηί.
Στ. ὡς ἐγγὺς ἡμῶν. τοῦτο πάνυ φροντίζετε,
ταύτην ἀφ᾽ ἡμῶν ἀπαγαγεῖν πόρρω πάνυ.
Μ. ἀλλ᾽ οὐχ οἷόν τε.

     Στ. νὴ Δί᾽ οἰμώξεσθ᾽ ἄρα.
φέρε τίς γὰρ οὗτος οὑπὶ τῆς κρεμάθρας ἀνήρ;
45 Μ. αὐτός.

    Στ. τίς αὐτός;

      Μ. Σωκράτης.

         Στ. ὦ Σώκρατες.
ἴθ᾽ οὗτος, ἀναβόησον αὐτόν μοι μέγα.
Μ. αὐτὸς μὲν οὖν σὺ κάλεσον· οὐ γάρ μοι σχολή.
Στ. ὦ Σώκρατες·
ὦ Σωκρατίδιον.

     Σω. τί με καλεῖς ὦφήμερε;
50 Στ. πρῶτον μὲν ὅτι δρᾷς ἀντιβολῶ κάτειπέ μοι.
Σω. ἀεροβατῶ καὶ περιφρονῶ τὸν ἥλιον.
Στ. ἔπειτ᾽ ἀπὸ ταρροῦ τοὺς θεοὺς ὑπερφρονεῖς,
ἀλλ᾽ οὐκ ἀπὸ τῆς γῆς, εἴπερ;

       Σω. οὐ γὰρ ἄν ποτε
ἐξηῦρον ὀρθῶς τὰ μετέωρα πράγματα,
55 εἰ μὴ κρεμάσας τὸ νόημα καὶ τὴν φροντίδα
λεπτὴν καταμείξας ἐς τὸν ὅμοιον ἀέρα.
εἰ δ᾽ ὢν χαμαὶ τἄνω κάτωθεν ἐσκόπουν,
οὐκ ἄν ποθ᾽ ηὗρον· οὐ γὰρ ἀλλ᾽ ἡ γῆ βίᾳ
ἕλκει πρὸς αὑτὴν τὴν ἰκμάδα τῆς φροντίδος.
60 πάσχει δὲ ταὐτὸ τοῦτο καὶ τὰ κάρδαμα.
Στ. τί φής;
ἡ φροντὶς ἕλκει τὴν ἰκμάδ᾽ ἐς τὰ κάρδαμα;
ἴθι νυν κατάβηθ᾽ ὦ Σωκρατίδιον ὡς ἐμέ,
ἵνα με διδάξῃς ὧνπερ οὕνεκ᾽ ἐλήλυθα.

NOTES

2. βάλλ᾽ ἐς κόρακας: *LS* s.v. κόραξ I.

3. Κικυννόθεν: *from Kikynna (County);* Kikynna was a demotic (political) suburb of Athens.

4. οὑτωσί: particularly in the plays of Aristophanes, the one-letter suffix known as the *deictic,* or *pointing, iota* is added to demonstratives for emphasis; *Smyth* 333g.

6. ἐξηυρημένην: *which was (in the process of) being discovered.*

7. σύγγνωθι: *LS* s.v. συγγιγνώσκω IV.
   τῶν ἀγρῶν: from ἀγρός; genitive of place; *Smyth* 1448.

9. θέμις (ἐστί): *LS* s.v. θέμις I.
   μαθηταῖσιν: *(Registered) Students.*

10. θαρρῶν: from θαρσέω (Attic θαρρέω); subordinate/coordinate with λέγε: *Don't be afraid; you can tell* me!
    οὑτοσί: deictic iota; *Smyth* 333g.

11. μαθητὴς: appositive, in agreement with the subject of ἥκω; *Smyth* 976.
    ἐς: = εἰς.

12. νομίσαι: infinitive, dependent upon χρή; the subject of the infinitive is σε (understood).

13. Χαιρεφῶντα: *Chaerephon,* an enthusiastic student of Socrates; third-declension name.

14. ψύλλαν: the apparent object of ἀνήρετο, but really the subject of ἅλλοιτο (indirect question); *Smyth* 2182.
    ἅλλοιτο: Aristophanes uses the optative here: why? (*Smyth* 2677).

15. δακοῦσα: aorist participle of δάκνω.

16. ἀφήλατο: aorist of ἀφάλλομαι.

17. When a line of dramatic poetry is divided between two speakers (or more), it is conventional to print it on separate lines on the page; cf. also lines 27–30, 33, 45, etc.
    δῆτα: *Smyth* 2851 (b).

19. ἐνέβαψεν: aorist of ἐμβάπτω.
    αὐτῆς: i.e., τῆς ψύλλης.
    τὼ πόδε: accusative dual of ὁ πούς.

20. κᾆτα: = καὶ εἶτα.
    ψυχείσῃ: feminine dative singular participle, aorist passive of ψύχω; why dative? (*LS* s.v. περιφύω); why feminine?
    Περσικαί: *LS* s.v. Περσικός 1.

22. Θαλῆν: *Thales,* the pre-Socratic philosopher from Miletus, one of the Seven Sages of ancient Greece.

23. ἀνύσας: idiomatic use of the circumstantial participle of manner; *Smyth* 2062a.

26. πρὸς τῶν θεῶν: *LS* s.v. πρός (with genitive) I.3.

    τάδ': The door to the φροντιστήριον is opened, revealing all sorts of mysterious (comic) pseudoscientific equipment. Strepsiades is overwhelmed and with childlike innocence points at the devices, asking the Registered Student to explain them, one by one.

29. κληρουχικήν: Strepsiades' experience of "measuring the earth" is strictly limited to acreage allotments, although he fully understands the *politics* of land distribution.

31. σόφισμα δημοτικὸν καὶ χρήσιμον: a useful device (χρήσιμον) that also has political (δημοτικὸν) applications, especially for the Athenians, who seemed to many people in the late fifth century B.C. to be interested in gaining control over the entire world (τὴν σύμπασαν γῆν). Aristophanes takes a well-aimed jab at his audience with this line.

32. περίοδος: *LS* s.v. III.

33. τί σὺ λέγεις: *What do you mean?* Strepsiades, of course, has never seen a map, and he confuses the symbols with reality.

34. δικαστάς: Strepsiades' confusion provides Aristophanes with another comic barb for his audience, directed this time at the Athenian fondness for serving on juries: a fondness that was multiplied when Pericles instituted a juror's honorarium of three obols a day.

35. ὡς: (sc. λέγω) ὡς.

37. Εὔβοι': *Euboea,* the long narrow island strategically located off the north coast of Boeotia.

38. παρατέταται: perfect passive of παρατείνω. The island stretches out from the Gulf of Pagasae to the island of Andros.

39. παρετάθη: Strepsiades, true to form, misinterprets what the Student says (*LS* s.v. παρατείνω I.3), and in so doing, he provides Aristophanes with a political one-liner: in 446 B.C. (twenty-three years before *The Clouds* was produced), Euboea had revolted from Athenian control. Not long after, Pericles reconquered it, apportioning the land among Athenian citizens (*LS* s.v. κληρουχία, and cf. lines 29–31 above).

40. Λακεδαίμων: *Sparta* (or *Lacedaemon*), the leading force opposing Athens in the Peloponnesian War.

41. ὡς: exclamatory: *how close . . . !*

43. οἷόν τε: *LS* s.v. οἷος III.1 (end).

44. φέρε: *LS* s.v. φέρω IX; it is equivalent to *hey!* Something has just happened onstage, or at least Strepsiades has just noticed it: the character Socrates has appeared, standing in a "basket" (κρεμάθρα) that is suspended from a large crane and dangling immediately overhead.

    οὑπὶ: = ὁ ἐπὶ.

45. αὐτός: Again, a misunderstanding by Strepsiades. The Student means *Himself, the Master* when he says αὐτός, but all that Strepsiades hears is the intensive adjective: *Himself? Himself who?* *Smyth* 1209d.

46. ἴθ' οὗτος: *LS* s. vv. ἴθι and οὗτος III.

47. With this line, the Student goes back inside the φροντιστήριον, leaving the stage to Strepsiades and the suspended Socrates.

48. ὦ Σώκρατες: obviously not a complete line of poetry. An interjection, a cry of joy or grief, or as here, a name, is often inserted *ametrically* (without having to fit the metrical rules of dramatic poetry).

49. ὦ Σωκρατίδιον: diminutive of Σωκράτης, used by Strepsiades to express familiarity, not contempt; *Smyth* 856.
     ὦφήμερε: = ὦ ἐφήμερε.

52. ταρροῦ: = ταρσοῦ.
     ὑπερφρονεῖς: Strepsiades misunderstands again, perfectly.

53. εἴπερ: here, elliptical: *if you must.*

55. εἰ μὴ: *Smyth* 2346a.

56. καταμείξας: aorist participle of καταμίγνυμι.
     ὅμοιον: The air and Socrates' thought-process are similarly λεπτός; for the joke here, read the entire *LS* article at λεπτός.

57. τἄνω: τὰ ἄνω = both τὰ μετέωρα πράγματα (line 54) and *lofty matters* (the comic attitude toward philosophy generally).

58. οὐ γὰρ ἀλλ': *no, for indeed . . . ; Smyth* 2767.

61. τί φής;: cf. note to line 48.

62–64. Strepsiades completely misunderstands the pseudophilosophical jargon of the Master and gives up his attempts at polite small talk, demanding admission as a full-time Registered Student. He even tries to demonstrate his own erudition, by using both ὡς ἐμέ and ἵνα με: *in order that to me, so that to myself (you might give instruction).*

Appendix A

Prepositions

ἀμφί (+ *accusative*) *around, about, by*
ἀνά (+ *accusative*) *up, up to, along, throughout*
ἄνευ (+ *genitive*) *without, away from, except*
ἀντί (+ *genitive*) *opposite, against, instead of, in place of*
ἀπό (+ *genitive*) *from, away from, by means of*
διά (+ *genitive*) *through*
    (+ *accusative*) *because of, thanks to*
εἰς (+ *accusative*) *into, to, toward, up to*
ἐκ (ἐξ before vowels) (+ *genitive*) *out of, from, beyond, by*
ἐν (+ *dative*) *in, among, on*
ἕνεκα or ἕνεκεν (+ *genitive;* usually *follows* its object) *on account of,*
    because of, as far as . . . is concerned
ἐπί (+ *genitive*) *upon, on, in the presence of, at, concerning*
    (+ *dative*) *upon, in addition to, for*
    (+ *accusative*) *upon, to, toward, for, according to, by*
κατά (+ *genitive*) *down from, down upon, against, down into*
    (+ *accusative*) *down, over, throughout, in relation to, like*
μετά (+ *genitive*) *among, between, with*
    (+ *accusative*) *into the middle of, after*
παρά (+ *genitive*) *from, from beside*
    (+ *dative*) *beside, in the presence of*
    (+ *accusative*) *near, along, beyond*
περί (+ *genitive*) *around, about, concerning*
    (+ *accusative*) *around, about, concerning, in the case of, in*
πλήν (+ *genitive*) *except, besides*
πρό (+ *genitive*) *before, in front of, rather than*
πρός (+ *genitive*) *from, toward, in the name of, like*
    (+ *dative*) *near, at, close to, besides*
    (+ *accusative*) *toward, upon, against, in reference to*
σύν (+ *dative*) *with*
ὑπέρ (+ *genitive*) *over, above, beyond, instead of, for*
    (+ *accusative*) *over, above, beyond, in violation of*
ὑπό (+ *genitive*) *from under, beneath, by*
    (+ *dative*) *under, behind, by*
    (+ *accusative*) *toward and under, into, during, about*

Appendix B

Numbers

Below is a list of the cardinal numbers in Greek, together with the symbol for each number. Any standard reference grammar will contain the ordinal adjectives and numeral adverbs (e.g., H. W. Smyth, *Greek Grammar,* rev. ed. G. M. Messing [Cambridge, Harvard University Press, 1956], pars. 347–54). Notice that the numbers from 1 through 4 (and the single-digit portion of numbers 13 and 14, 21 through 24, 31 through 34, etc.) are declined, while the other numbers from 5 through 199 are indeclinable. The numbers from 200 up are declined like the plural of ἄριστος.

The symbols for the numbers are letters of the alphabet (including three symbols that are not found in most Greek alphabets: ϛ [or occasionally Ϲ or Ϝ], called *digamma* and pronounced *wow,* for the number 6; Ϙ, called *koppa,* for the number 90; and ϡ, called *sanpi,* for the number 900). ϛ must not be confused with ς, the final form of the letter *sigma.* A mark similar to an acute accent is placed above and to the right of numbers from 1 to 999, and below and to the left of numbers over 1,000. Compound numbers below 1,000 have only one such mark, while compounds over 1,000 usually have both:

$\gamma' = 3$
$\lambda\gamma' = 33$
$\tau\lambda\gamma' = 333$
$,\gamma\tau\lambda\gamma' = 3,333$

number	symbol	cardinal name
1	α′	εἷς, μία, ἕν
2	β′	δύο
3	γ′	τρεῖς, τρία
4	δ′	τέτταρες, τέτταρα
5	ε′	πέντε
6	ϛ′	ἕξ
7	ζ′	ἑπτά
8	η′	ὀκτώ
9	θ′	ἐννέα
10	ι′	δέκα
11	ια′	ἕνδεκα
12	ιβ′	δώδεκα
13	ιγ′	τρεῖς καὶ δέκα

14	ιδ′	τέτταρες καὶ δέκα
15	ιε′	πεντεκαίδεκα
16	ιϛ′	ἑκκαίδεκα
17	ιζ′	ἑπτακαίδεκα
18	ιη′	ὀκτωκαίδεκα
19	ιθ′	ἐννεακαίδεκα
20	κ′	εἴκοσι
21	κα′	εἴκοσιν εἷς,
		εἴκοσι καὶ εἷς, or
		εἷς καὶ εἴκοσι
30	λ′	τριάκοντα
40	μ′	τετταράκοντα
50	ν′	πεντήκοντα
60	ξ′	ἑξήκοντα
70	ο′	ἑβδομήκοντα
80	π′	ὀγδοήκοντα
90	ϟ′	ἐνενήκοντα
100	ρ′	ἑκατόν
200	σ′	διακόσιοι, -αι, -α
300	τ′	τριακόσιοι, κτλ
400	υ′	τετρακόσιοι, κτλ
500	φ′	πεντακόσιοι, κτλ
600	χ′	ἑξακόσιοι, κτλ
700	ψ′	ἑπτακόσιοι, κτλ
800	ω′	ὀκτακόσιοι, κτλ
900	ϡ′	ἐνακόσιοι, κτλ
1,000	,α	χίλιοι, κτλ
2,000	,β	δισχίλιοι, κτλ
3,000	,γ	τρισχίλιοι, κτλ
4,000	,δ	τετρακισχίλιοι, κτλ
5,000	,ε	πεντακισχίλιοι, κτλ
10,000	,ι	μύριοι, κτλ

Below are the declensions of the numbers 1 through 4 in Greek, plus the declensions of οὐδείς and μηδείς, *no one, nothing*. Notice that the number 1 has separate forms for all three genders, 3 and 4 have only two sets of endings, and 2 uses the same set for all three genders.

εἷς	μία	ἕν	δύο
ἑνός	μιᾶς	ἑνός	δυοῖν
ἑνί	μιᾷ	ἑνί	δυοῖν
ἕνα	μίαν	ἕν	δύο

τρεῖς	τρία	τέτταρες	τέτταρα
τριῶν	τριῶν	τεττάρων	τεττάρων
τρισί	τρισί	τέτταρσι	τέτταρσι
τρεῖς	τρία	τέτταρας	τέτταρα

οὐδείς	οὐδεμία	οὐδέν
οὐδενός	οὐδεμιᾶς	οὐδενός
οὐδενί	οὐδεμιᾷ	οὐδενί
οὐδένα	οὐδεμίαν	οὐδέν

μηδείς	μηδεμία	μηδέν
μηδενός	μηδεμιᾶς	μηδενός
μηδενί	μηδεμιᾷ	μηδενί
μηδένα	μηδεμίαν	μηδέν

Both οὐδείς and μηδείς mean *no one, nothing; not one;* οὐδείς is used where the negative οὐ is appropriate, and μηδείς where the negative μή is appropriate.

Appendix C

The Principal Parts of Several Important Greek Verbs; a Synopsis of γράφω

Principal Parts

ἀγγέλλω, ἀγγελῶ, ἤγγειλα, ἤγγελκα, ἤγγελμαι, ἠγγέλθην (imperfect
 ἤγγελλον) *announce, report*

ἄγω, ἄξω, ἤγαγον, ἦχα, ἦγμαι, ἤχθην (imperfect ἦγον) *lead, drive*

αἱρέω, αἱρήσω, εἷλον, ᾕρηκα, ᾕρημαι, ᾑρέθην (imperfect ᾕρουν) *take,
 seize; choose*

ἀκούω, ἀκούσομαι, ἤκουσα, ἀκήκοα, ἤκουσμαι, ἠκούσθην (imperfect
 ἤκουον) *hear, listen*

ἁλίσκομαι, ἁλώσομαι, ἑάλων, ἑάλωκα, —, — (imperfect ἡλισκόμην)
 be captured (passive of αἱρέω)

ἁμαρτάνω, ἁμαρτήσομαι, ἥμαρτον, ἡμάρτηκα, ἡμάρτημαι,
 ἡμαρτήθην (imperfect ἡμάρτανον) *miss, make a mistake*

ἀμείβω, ἀμείψω, ἤμειψα, —, ἤμειμμαι, ἠμείφθην (imperfect ἤμειβον)
 change, alter

ἀποθνῄσκω, ἀποθανοῦμαι, ἀπέθανον, τέθνηκα, —, — (imperfect
 ἀπέθνῃσκον) *die*

ἀποκτείνω, ἀποκτενῶ, ἀπέκτεινα, ἀπέκτονα, —, — (imperfect
 ἀπέκτεινον) *kill*

ἄρχω, ἄρξω, ἦρξα, ἦρχα, ἦργμαι, ἤρχθην (imperfect ἦρχον) *rule,
 govern; begin*

βαίνω, βήσομαι, ἔβην, βέβηκα, —, — *walk, step, go*

βάλλω, βαλῶ, ἔβαλον, βέβληκα, βέβλημαι, ἐβλήθην *throw*

βλέπω, βλέψομαι or βλέψω, ἔβλεψα, βέβλεφα, βέβλεμμαι, ἐβλέφθην
 see, look

βούλομαι, βουλήσομαι, —, —, βεβούλημαι, ἐβουλήθην *want, wish*

γαμέω, γαμῶ, ἔγημα, γεγάμηκα, γεγάμημαι, ἐγαμήθην *marry*

γελάω, γελάσομαι, ἐγέλασα, —, γεγέλασμαι, ἐγελάσθην *laugh*

γίγνομαι, γενήσομαι, ἐγενόμην, γέγονα, γεγένημαι, ἐγενήθην *become,
 come into being*

γιγνώσκω, γνώσομαι, ἔγνων, ἔγνωκα, ἔγνωσμαι, ἐγνώσθην *know,
 recognize*

γράφω, γράψω, ἔγραψα, γέγραφα, γέγραμμαι, ἐγράφην *write*

δείκνυμι, δείξω, ἔδειξα, δέδειχα, δέδειγμαι, ἐδείχθην *show, point out*

δηλόω, δηλώσω, ἐδήλωσα, δεδήλωκα, δεδήλωμαι, ἐδηλώθην *show, reveal, explain*

διδάσκω, διδάξω, ἐδίδαξα, δεδίδαχα, δεδίδαγμαι, ἐδιδάχθην *instruct, teach*

δίδωμι, δώσω, ἔδωκα, δέδωκα, δέδομαι, ἐδόθην *give*

δοκέω, δόξω, ἔδοξα, δέδοχα, δέδογμαι, ἐδόχθην *seem, seem best; think*

δύναμαι, δυνήσομαι, ἐδυνησάμην, —, δεδύνημαι, ἐδυνήθην *can, be able*

εἰμί, ἔσομαι, —, —, —, — (imperfect ἦν) *be*

ἐλαύνω, ἐλῶ, ἤλασα, ἐλήλακα, ἐλήλαμαι, ἠλάθην (imperfect ἤλαυνον) *drive, march*

ἕπομαι, ἕψομαι, ἑσπόμην, —, —, — (imperfect εἱπόμην) *come after, follow*

ἔρχομαι, ἐλεύσομαι, ἦλθον, ἐλήλυθα, —, — (imperfect ἠρχόμην) *come, go*

ἐσθίω, ἔδομαι, ἔφαγον, ἐδήδοκα, ἐδήδεσμαι, ἠδέσθην (imperfect ἤσθιον) *eat*

ἔχω, ἕξω or σχήσω, ἔσχον, ἔσχηκα, ἔσχημαι, ἐσχέθην (imperfect εἶχον) *have, hold*

ζάω, ζήσω, ἔζησα, ἔζηκα, —, — *live*

ἵημι, ἥσω, ἧκα, εἷκα, εἷμαι, εἵθην (imperfect ἵην) *throw, hurl*

ἵστημι, στήσω, ἔστησα and ἔστην, ἕστηκα, ἕσταμαι, ἐστάθην (imperfect ἵστην) *stand*

καλέω, καλῶ, ἐκάλεσα, κέκληκα, κέκλημαι, ἐκλήθην *call*

λαμβάνω, λήψομαι, ἔλαβον, εἴληφα, εἴλημμαι, ἐλήφθην *take, seize, get*

λανθάνω, λήσω, ἔλαθον, λέληθα, λέλησμαι, ἐλήσθην *deceive, escape notice of*

λέγω, λέξω, ἔλεξα or εἶπον, εἴρηκα, λέλεγμαι, ἐλέχθην *say, speak, tell*

λείπω, λείψω, ἔλιπον, λέλοιπα, λέλειμμαι, ἐλείφθην *leave*

μανθάνω, μαθήσομαι, ἔμαθον, μεμάθηκα, —, — *learn*

μένω, μενῶ, ἔμεινα, μεμένηκα, —, — *remain*

νικάω, νικήσω, ἐνίκησα, νενίκηκα, νενίκημαι, ἐνικήθην *conquer, win*

νομίζω, νομιῶ, ἐνόμισα, νενόμικα, νενόμισμαι, ἐνομίσθην *think, believe; believe in, honor*

οἶμαι, οἰήσομαι, —, —, —, ᾠήθην (imperfect ᾠόμην) *think*

ὁράω, ὄψομαι, εἶδον, ἑόρακα, ἑώραμαι and ὦμμαι, ὤφθην (imperfect ἑώρων) *see*

πάσχω, πείσομαι, ἔπαθον, πέπονθα, —, — *suffer*

πείθω, πείσω, ἔπεισα, πέποιθα and πέπεικα, πέπεισμαι, ἐπείσθην *persuade;* (middle) *obey*

πέμπω, πέμψω, ἔπεμψα, πέπομφα, πέπεμμαι, ἐπέμφθην *send*

πίπτω, πεσοῦμαι, ἔπεσον, πέπτωκα, —, — *fall*
ποιέω, ποιήσω, ἐποίησα, πεποίηκα, πεποίημαι, ἐποιήθην *do, make*
πράττω, πράξω, ἔπραξα, πέπραχα and πέπραγα, πέπραγμαι, ἐπράχθην
    achieve, manage; do, act
τίθημι, θήσω, ἔθηκά, τέθηκα, τέθειμαι, ἐτέθην *place, put, make*
τίκτω, τέξομαι, ἔτεκον, τέτοκα, —, — *give birth to*
τρέπω, τρέψω, ἔτρεψα, τέτροφα, τέτραμμαι, ἐτράπην *turn, turn away;*
    change; defeat
τρέφω, θρέψω, ἔθρεψα, τέτροφα, τέθραμμαι, ἐτράφην *nourish, support,*
    raise
τρέχω, δραμοῦμαι, ἔδραμον, δεδράμηκα, δεδράμημαι, — *run*
τυγχάνω, τεύξομαι, ἔτυχον, τετύχηκα, τέτευγμαι, ἐτεύχθην *meet;*
    happen
φέρω, οἴσω, ἤνεγκον, ἐνήνοχα, ἐνήνεγμαι, ἠνέχθην *bear, carry*
φεύγω, φεύξομαι, ἔφυγον, πέφευγα, —, — *flee, escape*

Synopsis of γράφω

An economical and efficient way to practice and review verbs is through
a *synopsis,* an abbreviated conjugation of a verb in *one person* only. Use
a different person and number for each synopsis, in order to maintain
all the forms of the conjugation. Below is a sample synopsis, of γράφω in
the third-person singular:

ACTIVE

	present	imperfect	future	aorist	perfect	pluperfect
indicative	γράφει	ἔγραφε	γράψει	ἔγραψε	γέγραφε	ἐγεγράφει
subjunctive	γράφῃ			γράψῃ	γεγραφὼς ᾖ	
optative	γράφοι		γράψοι	γράψειε	γεγραφὼς εἴη	
participle	γράφων		γράψων	γράψας	γεγραφώς	
imperative	γραφέτω			γραψάτω	γεγραφὼς ἔστω	
infinitive	γράφειν		γράψειν	γράψαι	γεγραφέναι	

MIDDLE/PASSIVE

	present	imperfect	perfect	pluperfect
indicative	γράφεται	ἐγράφετο	γέγραπται	ἐγέγραπτο
subjunctive	γράφηται		γεγραμμένος ᾖ	
optative	γράφοιτο		γεγραμμένος εἴη	
participle	γραφόμενος		γεγραμμένος	
imperative	γραφέσθω		γεγράφθω	
infinitive	γράφεσθαι		γεγράφθαι	

MIDDLE

	future	aorist
indicative	γράψεται	ἐγράψατο
subjunctive		γράψηται
optative	γράψοιτο	γράψαιτο
participle	γραψόμενος	γραψάμενος
imperative		γραψάσθω
infinitive	γράψεσθαι	γράψασθαι

PASSIVE

	future	aorist
indicative	γραφήσεται	ἐγράφη
subjunctive		γραφῇ
optative	γραφήσοιτο	γραφείη
participle	γραφησόμενος	γραφείς
imperative		γραφήτω
infinitive	γραφήσεσθαι	γραφῆναι

Greek-English Vocabulary

The numbers refer to the lessons, where fuller entries will be found. App. A, App. B, App. C = Appendix A, etc.

A α
ἁ = ἡ (14)
ἀγαθός, -ή, -όν *good, brave, noble* (4, 19)
Ἀγάθων, -ωνος, ὁ *Agathon* (20)
Ἀγαμέμνων, -ονος, ὁ *Agamemnon* (7)
ἄγαν *very much, too much* (13)
ἀγανακτεῖν *showing signs of grief* (21)
ἀγάπη, -ης, ἡ *love* (8)
ἀγγέλλω *announce* (16, App. C)
ἀγορά, -ᾶς, ἡ *marketplace* (15)
ἄγω *lead, drive* (6, 19, App. C)
ἀδάματος, -ον *unconquered, unwedded* (22)
ἀδελφή, -ῆς, ἡ *sister* (6)
ἀδελφός, -οῦ, ὁ *brother* (6)
ἀδήριτος, -ον *unconquerable* (22)
ἀδικέω *do wrong* (17)
ἀδικία, -ας, ἡ *injustice* (17)
ἄδικος, -ον *unjust* (18)
ἀδόκητος, -ον *unexpected* (23)
ἀδυνατεῖ *is unable* (20)
ἀεί *always, forever* (6)
ἀέλπτως *beyond all hope* (23)
Ἀθῆναι, -ῶν, αἱ *Athens* (6)
Ἀθηναῖος, -α, -ον *Athenian* (5)
ἄθλιος, -α, -ον *struggling, wretched* (10)
ἆθλον, -ου, τό *contest prize* (19)
αἰάζειν *to lament* (20)
αἰαῖ (cry of grief or sorrow) (20)
Αἴας, -ντος, ὁ *Ajax* (16)
Αἰγαῖος, -α, -ον *Aegean* (22)
αἴγλα, -ας, ἡ *light, glory* (15)
αἰεί = ἀεί
αἱμάξαι *to stain with blood* (22)

αἴνει *praise* (10)
αἴνιγμα, -ματος, τό *riddle* (8)
αἱρέω *take, seize* (14, App. C)
αἶσα, -ης, ἡ *one's lot, destiny* (22)
αἴσχιστος, -η, -ον *most shameful* (14)
αἰσχρός, -ά, -όν *shameful* (13)
αἰών, -ῶνος, ὁ *lifetime, an age* (9, 15)
ἀκούω *hear, listen to* (15, App. C)
ἀλήθεια, -ας, ἡ *truth* (19)
ἀληθής, -ές, *unconcealed, true, honest* (16)
ἁλίσκομαι *be captured* (App. C)
ἀλλά *but* (11)
ἀλλήλων *each other* (13)
ἄλλος, -η, -ον *another* (14)
ἄλλοτε *another time* (19)
ἀλλότριος, -α, -ον *someone else's* (11)
ἁμαρτάνω *miss the mark, make a mistake* (7, App. C)
ἀμείβω *change, alter* (9, App. C)
ἀμείνων, -ον *better* (10)
ἀμφί *around, about* (App. A)
ἄν (untranslatable particle) (15)
ἀνά *up, along* (App. A)
ἀναγκαῖος, -α, -ον *necessary, indispensable* (10)
ἀνάγκη, -ης, ἡ *necessity* (22)
ἀνάμνησις, -εως, ἡ *memory* (13)
ἄναξ, -κτος, ὁ *lord, master* (19)
ἄναυρος, -ου, ὁ *mountain torrent, river* (22)
ἀνδάνειν *be pleasing* (17)
ἀνέλπιστος, -ον *unexpected*
ἄνεμος, -ου, ὁ *wind* (11)
ἀνεόρταστος, -ον *without holidays* (4)
ἄνευ *without, except* (13, App. A)
ἀνήρ, ἀνδρός, ὁ *man, husband* (8)
ἄνθος, -ους, τό *blossom, flower* (10)
ἀνθρωπεῖος, -α, -ον *human* (24)
ἄνθρωπος, -ου, ὁ *human being, man* (3)
ἀνίημι *send up, let go* (15)
ἀνόμημα, -ματος, τό *transgression, sin* (24)
ἀντάξιος, -α, -ον *worth as much as* (14)
ἀντί *opposite, in place of* (14, App. A)
ἀντία *against* (16)
ἀντιλέγω *say in reply* (24)
ἀντιοστατεῖ *is unfavorable* (15)

ἄξιος, -α, -ον *worthy* (19)

ἀπανδόκευτος, -ον *without an inn* (4)

ἅπας = πᾶς (14, 15)

ἀπεργάσασθαι *to complete* (20)

ἀπέρχομαι *go away* (24)

ἀπό *from, by means of* (19, App. A)

ἀποδίδωμι *give back, return* (24)

ἀποθνήσκω *die* (11, App. C)

ἀποκτείνω *kill* (App. C)

ἀποτίνω *pay, take vengeance* (19)

ἀποτυγχάνειν *to lose* (11)

ἀποφεύγω *escape, be acquitted* (17, 21)

ἅπτω *bind, join, grasp* (20)

ἄρα *then, so then, it seems* (23)

ἀργύριον, -ου, τό *silver, money* (15)

ἀρετή, -ῆς, ἡ *virtue* (13, 19)

ἀρθήσεται *shall be taken away* (24)

ἀριθμός, -οῦ, ὁ *number* (21)

ἄριστος, -η, -ον *best* (3)

ἁρπάσαι *to carry off* (18)

ἄρτι *just now, right now* (8)

ἄρτιος, -α, -ον *complete* (20)

Ἀρταξέρξης, -ου, ὁ *Artaxerxes* (14)

ἀρχαῖος, -α, -ον *old, ancient* (22)

ἀρχή, -ῆς, ἡ *beginning, origin* (8)

ἄρχω *begin, rule* (10, App. C)

ἄρχων, -οντος, ὁ *ruler* (7)

ἀσκοῦσιν *practice, exercise* (14)

ἀσπίς, -ίδος, ἡ *shield* (14)

ἀστράγαλος, -ου, ὁ *knucklebone*, (pl.) *dice* (13)

ἄστρον, -ου, τό *star* (22)

ἄστυ, -εως, τό *town* (16)

ἀσφαλῶς *firmly, with certainty* (12)

ἀσχολία, -ας, ἡ *business, being busy* (22)

αὖ *on the other hand, moreover* (22)

αὐτός, -ή, -ό *same, -self, him, her, it* (6)

ἀφίημι *allow, forgive, dismiss* (12)

ἄφωνος, -ον *voiceless, mute* (16)

ἀχάριτα *unpleasant, disagreeable* (22)

Β β

βαίνω *walk, step* (App. C)

βάλλω *throw* (9, App. C)

βάρβαρος, -ου, ὁ *foreigner, Persian* (14)
βάρος, -ους, τό *weight* (8)
βαρύς, -εῖα, -ύ *heavy, wearisome* (15, 16)
βασιλεία, -ας, ἡ *kingdom* (24)
βασιλεύς, -έως, ὁ *king* (8)
βασιλεύω *be king* (14)
βέβηκεν *has stepped* (16)
βέλτιστος, -η, -ον *noblest* (10)
βελτίων, -ον *nobler* (10)
βίος, -ου, ὁ *life* (4)
βλάπτω *mislead, damage* (21)
βλέπω *see, look* (8, App. C)
βοηθέω *run to help* (21)
βοτόν, -οῦ, τό *beast* (22)
βουλεύω *deliberate, plan* (20)
βούλομαι *want, wish* (19, App. C)
βοῦς, βοός, ὁ or ἡ *ox, bull, cow* (16)
βραδύς, -εῖα, -ύ *dull, slow* (16)
βραχύς, -εῖα, -ύ *short, small, few* (16)
βροτός, -οῦ, ὁ *mortal* (4)

Γ γ

γαμέω *marry* (App. C)
γάρ *for, because* (3)
γε *at least, anyway, indeed* (21)
γεγονώς, -υῖα, -ός *total* (with numbers) (21)
γελάω *laugh* (13, App. C)
γέλοιος, -α, -ον *funny* (15)
γέλως, -ωτος, ὁ *laughter* (13)
γένεσις, -εως, ἡ *origin, source, creation* (8)
γέννημα, -ματος, τό *offspring* (19)
γέρων, -οντος, ὁ *old man* (19)
γῆ, γῆς, ἡ *earth, country, land* (14)
γίγνομαι *become, come to be* (19, App. C)
γιγνώσκω *know, recognize* (15, App. C)
γλυκύς, -εῖα, -ύ *sweet, pleasant* (16)
γλῶττα, -ης, ἡ *tongue, language* (6)
γνῶθι *know* (24)
γνώμη, -ης, ἡ *opinion, intelligence* (4)
γονεύς, -έως, ὁ *begetter,* (pl.) *parents* (24)
γοργῶπις *fierce-eyed* (22)
γράφω *write* (6, App. C)
γυμνός, -ή, -όν *naked, nude* (14)

γυνή, γυναικός, ἡ *woman, wife* (8)

Δ δ
δαιμόνιον, -ου, τό *divinity, divine power* (23)
δαίμων, -ονος, ὁ *divinity, god* (7)
δακρύειν *to lament* (21)
δάκρυον, -ου, τό *tear, teardrop* (14)
δαπανάω *consume, use up* (23)
δέ *and, but* (8)
δέδοικα *fear* (22)
δεῖ *it is necessary, one must* (13, 23)
δείκνυμι *show, point out* (12, App. C)
δεινός, -ή, -όν *fearful, terrible, marvelous* (5)
δεῖπνον, -ου, τό *meal, dinner* (17)
δέκα *ten* (App. B)
Δελφοί, -ῶν, οἱ *Delphi* (7)
δένδρος, -ους, τό *tree* (22)
δέοντα *what is necessary* (17)
δεσπότης, -ου, ὁ *master, chief* (16)
δεύτερος, -α, -ον *second* (10)
δηλόω *show, reveal, explain* (13, App. C)
δημοκρατία, -ας, ἡ *democracy* (10)
Δημοσθένης, -ους, ὁ *Demosthenes* (23)
δηνάριον, -ου, τό *denarius* (24)
δήπου *I presume, surely* (19)
διά *through, because of* (8, App. A)
διάδηλος, -ον *distinguishable* (10)
διαμείβω *purchase, exchange* (19)
διαπτυχθέντες *when they are opened up* (23)
διατίθημι *distribute, manage, arrange* (12)
διαφέρειν *are different from* (10)
διδάσκω *teach* (App. C)
δίδωμι *give* (12, App. C)
δίκαια, -ων, τά *rights* (13)
δίκαιος, -α, -ον *just* (10)
δίκη, -ης, ἡ *right, justice, satisfaction* (18)
  δίδωμι δίκην *pay a penalty* (18)
  δίκῃ = δικαίως (21)
διόσδοτος, -ον *given by Zeus* (15)
δίπους *two-footed* (8)
δίς *twice* (7, 19)
διώκω *pursue, chase* (18)
δοκέω *expect, think, seem, seem best* (13, App. C)

δόκιμος, -ον *trustworthy* (24)
δολιχός, -ή, -όν *long* (9)
δόξα, -ης, ἡ *opinion, reputation* (4)
δρᾶμα, -ματος, τό *deed, action, drama* (8)
δράω *do, accomplish* (14)
δρομικός, -ή, -όν *good at running, swift* (19)
δύναμαι *be able* (19, App. C)
δύναμις, -εως, ἡ *strength, power, influence* (21)
δύο *two* (App. B)
δυσπραξία, -ας, ἡ *bad luck* (24)
δῶρον, -ου, τό *gift* (3)

Ε ε
ἐάν = εἰ + ἄν (15)
ἔαρ, ἔαρος or ἦρος, τό *spring, springtime* (13)
ἑαυτοῦ, -ῆς, -οῦ *himself, herself, itself* (15)
ἐγγυητής, -οῦ, ὁ *guarantor, guarantee* (13)
ἐγγύθεν *from close at hand* (19)
ἔγχος, -ους, τό *spear, lance* (14)
ἐγώ *I* (13)
ἔγωγε = ἐγώ + γε
ἐθέλω *want, wish* (6)
εἰ *if*
εἰ μή *if not, unless* (15)
εἰδῆς *you may know* (23)
εἶδος, -ους, τό *form, shape, appearance* (8, 19)
εἰκῆ *with no purpose, at random* (20)
εἰκών, -όνος, ἡ *image, likeness, picture* (24)
εἰμί *be* (6, App. C)
εἶμι *shall go* (22)
εἶπον *said* (14)
εἰρήνη, -ης, ἡ *peace* (22)
εἴρηται *has been said* (22)
εἰς *into, in the presence of* (6, 13, App. A)
εἷς, μία, ἕν *one* (App. B)
ἐκ (ἐξ) *out of, from* (9, App. A)
ἕκαστος, -η, -ον *each* (3)
ἑκάτερος, -α, -ον *each (of two)* (21)
ἐκβάλλω *throw out, cast aside, produce* (9)
ἐκεῖνος, -η, -ον *that* (11)
ἐκλαλέω *blurt out, blab* (16)
ἐκφεύγω *escape, be acquitted* (20)
ἑκών, -οῦσα, -όν *readily, willing, willingly* (21)

ἔλαιον, -ου, τό *olive oil* (19, 23)
ἐλάττων, -ον *smaller, less, worse* (10)
ἐλαύνω *drive, march* (16, App. C)
ἐλάχιστος, -η, -ον *smallest, least, worst* (10)
Ἕλληνες, -ων, οἱ *the Greeks, Hellenes* (12)
ἐλπίς, -ίδος, ἡ *hope* (7)
ἐμβάλλω *inflict, lay upon* (22)
ἐμός, -ή, -όν *my, mine* (11, 20)
ἔμπεδος, -ον *fixed, firm, secure* (19)
ἐμπίπτω *fall in or on, fall in with* (15)
ἐμφανῶς *openly, visibly* (22)
ἐν *in, among* (3, App. A)
ἔνδοθεν *from within, on the inside* (17)
ἕνεκα *on account of* (App. A)
ἔνθα *there, then* (14)
ἐνί = ἐν (14)
ἐνοικέω = οἰκέω (14)
ἐνταῦθα *here, there* (3)
ἐντός *within, inside* (17)
ἐντυγχάνω *meet with* (20)
ἐξαμαρτεῖν *to fail* (19)
ἐξανευρίσκω *invent* (23)
ἐξαπατάω *deceive, cheat* (13)
ἔξεστι *it is allowed, it is possible* (24)
ἔξωθεν *without, on the outside* (17)
ἔοικε *it seems* (21)
ἐπαινέω *praise* (13)
ἐπαίρεται *is lifted up* (19)
ἐπάμερος *ephemeral, short-lived* (15)
ἐπεγγελάω *laugh at* (21)
ἐπεί *when, since* (12)
ἐπειδάν = ἐπειδή + ἄν (15)
ἐπειδή *when, since* (15)
ἔπειμι (εἰμί) *remain, last; be present* (15)
ἔπειμι (εἶμι) *come upon, approach, come after* (22)
ἔπειτα *then, next* (19)
ἐπεντύνοντα *preparing, arming* (22)
ἐπί *on, at, upon, toward, for* (12, 14, 17, App. A)
ἐπιγραφή, -ῆς, ἡ *inscription, name* (24)
ἐπιδείκνυμι *show, point out* (24)
ἐπισκοπέω *observe, consider, reflect* (19)
ἐπιτελεῖ *finishes, completes* (20)

ἕπομαι *follow* (20, App. C)
ἐπώνυμος, -ον *significant, as a significant name* (20)
ἐράω *love, be in love with* (13)
ἔργον, -ου, τό *work, deed* (22)
ἐρίζων *quarreling, wrangling* (16)
ἔριον, -ου, τό *wool* (20)
ἔρχομαι *come, go* (App. C)
ἐρῶ *shall say* (16)
ἐρωτάω *ask* (a question) (23)
ἐσθίω *eat* (15, App. C)
ἐσθλός, -ή, -όν *good, brave, noble* (12)
ἔσοπτρον, -ου, τό *mirror* (8)
ἔστι *there is, it is possible* (4, 7)
ἑταῖρος, -ου, ὁ *companion* (22)
ἕτερος, -α, -ον *another, other* (3)
ἔτι *still, yet* (22)
ἔτος, -ους, τό *year* (8)
εὖ *well* (13)
    εὖ ἔχει *it is well* (20)
εὐγενής, -ές *wellborn, highborn* (22)
εὐδαίμων, -ον *blessed, fortunate, happy* (10)
εὐήθης, -ες *simple, foolish, absurd* (24)
εὐθύς, -εῖα, -ύ *straight, direct* (20)
εὔκλεια, -ας, ἡ *good reputation, glory* (6)
Εὐριπίδης, -ου, ὁ *Euripides* (8)
εὑρίσκω *find, discover* (23)
εὐσεβής, -ές *pious, righteous, holy* (17)
εὐτέλεια, -ας, ἡ *little expense* (13)
εὔχομαι *pray, long for* (24)
ἔφη *he, she said* (7, 23)
ἐφικτός, -ή, -όν *accessible, attainable* (15)
ἐχθαίρομαι *I am hated* (22)
ἔχθω *hate* (22)
ἐχθρός, -οῦ, ὁ *enemy* (13)
ἔχιδνα, -ης, ἡ *viper* (19)
ἔχω *have, hold* (8, App. C)

Ζ ζ
ζάω *live* (15, App. C)
Ζεύς, Διός, ὁ *Zeus* (17)
ζημία, -ας, ἡ *loss, expense, penalty* (19)

H η

ἤ *or, than* (3)
ἡγεμών, -όνος, ὁ *leader, commander* (7)
ἡγέομαι *think, believe* (19)
ἠδέ *and* (9)
ἤδη *already, by this time* (22)
ἥδιστος, -η, -ον *sweetest, very sweet* (13)
ἡδύς, -εῖα, -ύ *pleasant, welcome, pleasing* (16)
ἥκιστα *least* (10)
ἦλθον *came, went* (15)
ἥλιος, -ου, ὁ *sun* (22)
ἡμέρα, -ας, ἡ *day* (7)
ἥμισυ, -εος, τό *half* (10)
ἤν = ἐάν (15)
ἦν *there was* (5)
ἦν δ' ἐγώ *said I* (19)
ἧττον *less* (13)

Θ θ

θάλαττα, -ης, ἡ *sea* (11)
θάνατος, -ου, ὁ *death* (9)
θάττων, -ον *swifter* (20)
θαυμάζω *wonder, marvel at* (11)
θεά, -ᾶς, ἡ *goddess*
θελκτήριον, -ου, τό *charm, spell* (4)
θέλω = ἐθέλω
θεός, -οῦ, ὁ or ἡ *god, goddess* (3)
θέω *run* (20)
θησαυρός, -οῦ, ὁ *treasure-house, treasury* (9)
θνήσκω = ἀποθνήσκω
θυροκοπῆσαι *breaking and entering* (19)
θύω *sacrifice* (14)

I ι

ἰάπτων *wounding, piercing* (16)
ἰατρός, -οῦ, ὁ *physician* (3)
ἴδετε *behold!* (16)
ἱερεύς, -έως, ὁ *priest* (8)
ἱερόν, -οῦ, τό *temple* (3)
ἵημι *throw, hurl* (12, App. C)
Ἰησοῦς, -οῦ, ὁ *Joshua, Jesus* (16)
Ἰλιάς, -άδος, ἡ *Iliad* (7)
Ἴλιος, -ου, ἡ *Ilios, Troy* (22)

ἵνα *in order, so that* (18)
ἵππος, -ου, ὁ or ἡ *horse*
ἵστημι *stand, erect, make a stand* (12, App. C)
ἰσχύς, -ύος, ἡ *strength* (16)
ἴσως *probably, perhaps* (17)
ἰχθύς, -ύος, ὁ *fish* (16)
ἴχνος, -ους, τό *track, footstep* (16)
ἴωμεν *let's go* (17)

Κ κ

καθάπερ *just as, exactly as* (15)
καί *and, also, even* (3, 9)
καινός, -ή, -όν *new, fresh* (6)
καίπερ *even though, although* (14)
καιρός, -οῦ, ὁ *critical time, right time, season* (16)
Καῖσαρ, -αρος, ὁ *Caesar* (24)
κακία, -ας, ἡ *badness,* (pl.) *vices* (19)
κακοδαίμων, -ον *unfortunate, unhappy* (19)
κακόν, -οῦ, τό *trouble, problem* (11)
κακός, -ή, -όν *bad, evil* (4, 19)
κακῶς ἔχω *be badly off, be ill* (15)
καλέω *call, summon* (13, App. C)
κάλλος, -ους, τό *beauty* (14)
καλός, -ή, -όν *pretty, fine, beautiful* (3)
καλῶς ἔχει *it is well* (20)
Καμβύσης, -ου, ὁ *Cambyses* (15)
κἄν = καὶ ἄν
κἂν = καὶ ἐν
καρδία, -ας, ἡ *heart* (19)
κατά *down from, against, over* (10, App. A)
καταβαύζω *bark at* (15)
καταλείπω *leave behind* (21)
κατατίθημι *place down, deposit* (12)
καταψηφίζομαι *vote to condemn* (21)
κατέκαυσεν *he burned completely* (18)
κατθανεῖν = ἀποθανεῖν
κάτοπτρον, -ου, τό *mirror* (8)
κεῖμαι *lie, lie down* (19)
κεῖνος = ἐκεῖνος
κέκρανται *has been cast* (22)
κελεύω *order, command* (13)
κενός, -ή, -όν *empty* (20)
κέρατα *horns* (14)

κέρδος, -ους, τό *profit, advantage, gain* (19)
κῆνσος, -ου, ὁ *census, census tax* (24)
κῆρυξ, -κος, ὁ *messenger* (7)
κίνδυνος, -ου, ὁ *danger, hazard, risk* (17)
Κνίδος, -ου, ἡ *Cnidus* (14)
κοινός, -ή, -όν *common, shared* (17)
κόλαξ, -κος, ὁ *flatterer* (15)
κομίζω *take care of, convey* (16)
κόραξ, -κος, ὁ *raven, crow* (15)
κόρος, -ου, ὁ *one's fill, abundance* (20)
κοσμέω *order, arrange, embellish, honor* (22)
κόσμος, -ου, ὁ *ornament, decoration, world* (17)
κραίνω *accomplish, fulfill* (23)
κραιπάλη, -ης, ἡ *drinking party, hangover* (19)
κρατέω *rule over* (20, 23)
κρίνω *separate, choose, decide* (16)
κρίσις, -εως, ἡ *decision, judgment* (16)
κρυπτός, -ή, -όν *hidden* (3)
κτῆμα, -ματος, τό *possession* (10)
κτλ = καὶ τὰ λοιπά *et cetera* (14)
κυβερνήτης, -ου, ὁ *pilot, helmsman* (16)
κύλιξ, -κος, ἡ *cup, wine-cup* (20)
Κύπρις, -εως, ἡ *Cypris, Aphrodite* (14)
κύριος, -α, -ον *authoritative, with power over* (9)
Κῦρος, -ου, ὁ *Cyrus* (14)
κύων, κυνός, ὁ or ἡ *dog* (7)
κωλύω *hinder, prevent* (24)

Λ λ
λαγωοῖς *hares, rabbits* (14)
Λακεδαιμόνιος, -ου, ὁ *a Spartan, Lacedaemonian* (19)
λαλέω *talk, prattle, chirp* (16)
λαμβάνω *take, seize, get* (15, App. C)
λαμπρός, -ή, -όν *shining* (15)
λανθάνω *deceive, escape notice of* (14, App. C)
λαός, -οῦ, ὁ *people* (7)
λέγω *say, tell, mean* (6, App. C)
λείβων *pouring forth* (14)
λείπω *leave* (21, App. C)
λέμβος, -ου, ὁ *boat, fishing boat* (18)
λέων, -οντος, ὁ *lion* (14)
λήθη, -ης, ἡ *forgetfulness* (22)
ληπτέος, -α, -ον *must be taken* (23)

λίαν *too, too much* (10)
λόγος, -ου, ὁ *account, word, speech, story* (3)
   λόγοι (without article) *talk, dialogue* (19)
   λόγος (ἐστί) = λέγουσι (11)
λύπη, -ης, ἡ *pain* (4)
λυσιτελής, -ές *useful, profitable* (16)
λυσσώδης, -ες *stark-raving* (22)
λύω *set free, destroy* (6)
λῷστος, -η, -ον *most desirable* (13)

Μ μ

μάθημα, -ματος, τό *lesson* (8)
μάθησις, -εως, ἡ *learning, education* (8)
μακάριος, -α, -ον *blessed, happy* (13)
μακρός, -ά, -όν *long* (4)
μακύνων *delaying, putting off* (16)
μαλακία, -ας, ἡ *softness, moral weakness* (13)
μᾶλλον *rather* (13)
μανθάνω *learn* (6, App. C)
Μαραθών, -ῶνος, ὁ *Marathon* (12)
μάρνασθαι *to fight* (20)
μάχομαι *fight* (22)
μεγάλως *greatly* (10)
μέγας, μεγάλη, μέγα *big, great, large* (14)
μέγιστος, -η, -ον *biggest, greatest* (10)
μεθύω *be drunk* (20)
μείγνυμι (see μίγνυμι)
μείζων, -ον *bigger, greater* (10)
μείλιχος, -α, -ον *soothing, gracious* (15)
μέλαινα *dark, black* (22)
μελέτη, -ης, ἡ *practice, exercise* (10)
μέλλω *be destined to, likely to, about to* (23)
μέλος, -ους, τό *song, poem* (12)
μέμνησο *remember* (24)
μέν *on the one hand* (10)
μένω *remain* (8, App. C)
μετά *with, after* (13, App. A)
μεταπίπτω *fall differently* (21)
μετεωρίζεται *is raised high* (19)
μέτρον, -ου, τό *measure* (15)
μή *no, not* (11)
μηδείς, μηδεμία, μηδέν *no one, nothing* (15, App. B)
μηκυνοῦμεν *we will prolong, extend* (18)

μήτηρ, μητρός, ἡ *mother* (6)
μίγνυμι *join, bring together, mix with* (19)
μικρός, -ά, -όν *small* (9)
μιμέομαι *imitate* (20)
μισέω *hate* (16)
μῖσος, -ους, τό *hatred, object of hate* (23)
μνημονεύω *call to mind, remember* (21)
μοῖρα, -ας, ἡ *lot, portion, destiny, fate* (4)
μοναρχία, -ας, ἡ *monarchy* (12)
μόνον *only* (17)
μόνος, -η, -ον *alone, only* (4)
μορφή, -ῆς, ἡ *shape, form* (9)
Μοῦσα, -ης, ἡ *Muse* (13)
μυρίος, -α, -ον *numberless, countless* (11)
μῦς, μυός, ὁ *mouse* (16)
μῶρος, -ου, ὁ *fool* (15)

N ν
ναῦς, νεώς, ἡ *ship* (16)
νεκρός, -οῦ, ὁ *corpse* (15)
νέος, -α, -ον *new, young* (10)
νεανίας, -ου, ὁ *young man* (4)
νηκτόν, -οῦ, τό *the skill of swimming* (14)
νῆσος, -ου, ἡ *island* (22)
νίζω *wash, cleanse* (24)
νικάω *win, conquer* (13, App. C)
νίκη, -ης, ἡ *victory* (4)
νομίζω *think, consider* (6, App. C)
νόμισμα, -ματος, τό *coin* (24)
νόμος, -ου, ὁ *law, custom* (6)
νόσος, -ου, ὁ *sickness* (22)
νοῦς, -οῦ, ὁ *mind* (3)
νῦν *now* (8)
νύξ, -κτός, ἡ *night* (7)

Ξ ξ
ξένος, -ου, ὁ *stranger, friend* (19)
ξένος, -η, -ον *strange, foreign, unusual* (3)
Ξενοφῶν, -ῶντος, ὁ *Xenophon* (5)

O o
ὁ, ἡ, τό *the* (3)
    ὁ μὲν . . . ὁ δέ *the one . . . the other* (15)

ὅδε, ἥδε, τόδε *this, that* (11)

ὁδός, -οῦ, ἡ *road* (3)

ὀδούς, ὀδόντος, ὁ *tooth* (14)

ὅθεν *whence* (10)

οἶδα *know* (9)

Οἰδίπους, -ποδος or -που, ὁ *Oedipus* (8)

οἴκαδε *home, homeward* (14)

οἰκεῖος, -α, -ον *kindred, dear, one's own* (10)

οἰκέω *live in, inhabit* (13)

οἰκτρός, -ά, -όν *pitiable, lamentable* (21)

οἶμαι *think* (20, App. C)

οἴμοι *oh! ah!* (19)

οἶνος, -ου, ὁ *wine* (8)

οἴομαι (see οἶμαι)

οἶον *as for example* (22)

οἶος, -α, -ον *such, such a* (13, 23)

   οἶός τ' εἰμι *be able, be possible*

ὄλβιος, -α, -ον *blessed, happy* (15)

ὄλβος, -ου, ὁ *happiness, wealth* (20)

ὀλίγος, -η, -ον *little, small, short, few* (13)

ὅλως *in short, generally* (20)

ὁμευνέτιν *sleeping partner, bedmate* (16)

Ὅμηρος, -ου, ὁ *Homer* (7)

ὄμμα, -ματος, τό *eye* (16)

ὁμοιοῦσθαι *to become like* (19)

ὅμοιος, -α, -ον *like, similar to* (16)

ὅμως *nevertheless, all the same* (22)

ὄναρ, τό (only nominative and accusative) *dream* (15)

ὄνομα, -ματος, τό *name* (9)

ὀνομάζω *name, call* (7)

ὀξύς, -εῖα, -ύ *sharp, keen, quick* (16)

ὅπερ *the very thing which* (24)

ὁπλή, -ῆς, ἡ *hoof* (14)

ὁπλίσαι *to outfit, prepare* (18)

ὁπότε *when, whenever* (17)

ὅπως *so, in order that, however* (18, 20)

ὁράω *see* (14, App. C)

ὀργή, -ῆς, ἡ *anger, wrath, mood, temperament* (5, 19)

ὅρκος, -ου, ὁ *oath* (13)

ὀρνέοις *birds* (14)

ὅς, ἥ, ὅ *who, which, that* (11)

ὅσος, -η, -ον *how much, how great, as much as* (17, 19)

ὅστις, ἥτις, ὅτι *who(ever), what(ever)* (14)

ὅταν = ὅτε + ἄν

ὅτε *when* (15)
ὅτι *that* (11)
οὐ *no, not* (4)
οὐδέ *and not, nor, not even* (10)
οὐδείς, οὐδεμία, οὐδέν *no one, nothing* (15, App. B)
οὐκέτι *no longer, no more* (14)
οὔκουν . . . ; (excited interrogative particle) (13)
οὐκοῦν *very well, yes, surely* (15)
οὖν *well, then, so* (14)
οὐρανός, -οῦ, ὁ *heaven, sky* (22)
οὖς, ὠτός, τό *ear* (19)
οὔτε . . . οὔτε *neither . . . nor* (15)
οὗτος, αὕτη, τοῦτο *this* (11)
οὕτω (οὕτως) *thus, so* (13)
   οὕτως ἔχει *it is so* (20)
ὀφείλεται *is required, is our destiny* (22)
ὀφθαλμός, -οῦ, ὁ *eye* (19)
ὄψις, -εως, ἡ *appearance, face* (8)

Π π

πάθημα, -ματος, τό *experience, suffering* (22)
παιδεία, -ας, ἡ *education* (16)
παιδεύω *teach, educate* (6)
παιδίον, -ου, τό *child (under 7)* (3)
παῖς, παιδός, ὁ or ἡ *child (over 7)* (8)
παλαιός, -ά, -όν *old, aged, ancient* (10)
Πάν, Πανός, ὁ *Pan* (17)
πανταχοῦ *everywhere* (24)
πάππος, -ου, ὁ *grandfather* (6)
παρά *from, beside, near, by* (21, App. A)
παραλαμβάνω *call in, get control of, invite* (15)
πάρειμι *be present* (12)
πάρεστι *it is possible* (20)
παρέχομαι *furnish, present, display* (23)
πᾶς, πᾶσα, πᾶν *all, every, the whole* (14)
πάσχω *suffer, experience* (13, App. C)
πατάξαι *assault and battery* (19)
πατήρ, πατρός, ὁ *father* (6)
παύω *put an end to, stop, cease* (22)
πεδίον, -ου, τό *plain* (7)
πείθω *persuade* (11, 19, App. C)
πεῖρα, -ας, ἡ *trial, attempt* (8)
πειράζω *put to the test, tempt* (24)
πειστέον *one must obey* (23)

πέλαγος, -ους, τό *sea* (22)
πέλεκυς, -εως, ὁ *twin-blade axe, battle-axe* (16)
πέμπω *send* (6, App. C)
πενία, -ας, ἡ *poverty* (10)
πένομαι *be poor* (19)
πέντε *five* (App. B)
πεπορθηκέναι *to have sacked, plundered* (22)
πεπρωμένος, -η, -ον *fated* (22)
περί *around, about* (23, 24, App. A)
περιγίγνομαι *be superior* (23)
περίσσευμα, -ματος, τό *abundance* (19)
Πέρσης, -ου, ὁ *a Persian* (12)
πέτασθαι *to fly* (14)
πέφυκα *be inbred, be by nature* (21)
πιθανός, -ή, -όν *persuasive, credible* (23)
πικρός, -ά, -όν *sharp, bitter* (16)
πίνω *drink* (19)
πίπτω *fall* (15, App. C)
πιστεύω *trust* (6)
πίστις, -εως, ἡ *faith, trust* (8)
Πλάτων, -ωνος, ὁ *Plato* (13)
πλεῖστος, -η, -ον *most, greatest* (19)
πλείων (or πλέων), -ον *more, greater* (10)
πληγή, -ῆς, ἡ *blow, impact* (19)
πλῆθος, -ους, τό *great number, multitude* (16)
πλήν *except, besides* (App. A)
πλήρης, -ες *full* (20)
πλοῦς, -οῦ, ὁ *sailing, voyage* (15)
πλούσιος, -α, -ον *rich, wealthy* (17)
πλουτέω *be rich* (19)
πλοῦτος, -ου, ὁ *wealth* (15)
πνεῦμα, -ματος, τό *wind, breath* (15)
ποδαπός, -ή, -όν *from what country? of what sort?* (5)
ποδωκίαν *swiftness of foot* (14)
ποθέω *long for, yearn to* (21)
ποιέω *do, make* (13, App. C)
ποίησις, -εως, ἡ *production, creating* (8)
ποιητέος, -α, -ον *must be done, must be considered* (23)
ποιητής, -οῦ, ὁ *poet* (7)
ποιμήν, -ένος, ὁ *shepherd* (7)
πολεμέω *fight, make war on* (13)
πολέμιοι, -ων, οἱ *the enemy (military)* (6)

πόλεμος, -ου, ὁ *war* (7)
πόλις, -εως, ἡ *city, state* (8)
πολιτεία, -ας, ἡ *government* (12)
πολίτης, -ου, ὁ *citizen* (4)
πολιτικός, -ή, -όν *pertaining to the* πόλις (21)
πολλάκις *often* (6)
πολυπραγμοσύνη, -ης, ἡ *curiosity* (11)
πολύς, πολλή, πολύ *much, many* (14)
πονηρία, -ας, ἡ *wickedness, cowardice* (20)
πονηρός, -ά, -όν *wicked, evil* (9)
πόνος, -ου, ὁ *work, toil, pain* (3)
πορευτέος, -α, -ον *must be traversed* (23)
πόρος, -ου, ὁ *path, way* (23)
ποτέ *at any time, ever* (20)
ποῦ *where?* (3)
πούς, ποδός, ὁ *foot* (16)
πρᾶγμα, -ματος, τό *thing, matter, affair* (19)
πρᾶξις, -εως, ἡ *action, doing* (8)
Πραξιτέλης, -ους, ὁ *Praxiteles* (14)
πράττω *achieve, manage, effect* (13, App. C)
πρέπει *it is fitting* (19)
πρίν *before, formerly* (17)
πρό *before, in front of, rather than* (App. A)
προαιρετός, -ή, -όν *chosen, planned* (22)
προαιρέω *choose beforehand* (22)
προδίδωμι *betray, forsake, abandon* (12)
πρόνοια, -ας, ἡ *foresight, forethought* (20)
πρός *from, in the eyes of, toward* (3, 16, 24, App. A)
προσέχω *turn toward* (24)
προσήκων, -ουσα, -ον *one's own* (21)
προσφέρω *bring to* (24)
πρόσφθεγμα, -ματος, τό *greeting* (16)
πρόσωθεν *from afar* (19)
πρόσωπον, -ου, τό *face, mask, dramatic character* (8)
προτείνω *hold out, offer* (23)
πρότερος, -α, -ον *former, preceding* (21)
προφήτης, -ου, ὁ *prophet, interpreter* (18)
πρῷρα, -ας, ἡ *prow* (15)
πρῶτον *first* (23)
πτερόν, -οῦ, τό *feather* (11)
πῦρ, πυρός, τό *fire* (10)
πῶς *how?* (17)
πως *somehow* (10)

Ρ ρ

ῥᾴδιος, -α, -ον *easy* (10)
ῥᾷστος, -η, -ον *easiest* (10)
ῥᾴων, -ον *easier* (10)
ῥέω *flow, stream* (20)
ῥῆμα, -ματος, τό *word* (19)
ῥητορικός, -ή, -όν *rhetorical, oratorical* (23)
ῥήτωρ, -ορος, ὁ *public speaker, orator* (24)

Σ σ

σαυτοῦ, -ῆς, -οῦ *yourself* (24)
σαφής, -ές *clear, plain, distinct* (20)
σαφῶς *clearly, plainly, distinctly* (18)
σελήνη, -ης, ἡ *moon* (22)
σημαίνω *give signs* (24)
σθένος, -ους, τό *strength, power* (22)
σιγάω *be silent* (16, 24)
σιγῇ *in silence, silently* (24)
σίδηρον, -ου, τό *iron* (14)
σιωπάω *keep silent* (24)
σκιά, -ᾶς, ἡ *shade, shadow* (15)
σκοπέω *consider, look closely* (22)
σοφία, -ας, ἡ *wisdom, skill, cleverness* (7)
Σοφοκλῆς, -έους, ὁ *Sophocles* (8)
σοφός, -ή, -όν *wise, skilled, clever* (3)
στείχοντα *walking* (20)
στελοῦμεν *we will set out* (15)
στέφανος, -ου, ὁ *crown* (3)
στεφανόω, *wreathe, reward with a crown* (19)
στόμα, -ματος, τό *mouth* (19)
στρατιά, -ᾶς, ἡ *army* (5)
στρατιώτης, -ου, ὁ *soldier* (5)
στρατόπεδον, -ου, τό *military camp* (14)
στρατός, -οῦ, ὁ *army* (22)
σύ *you* (13)
συγγενές, -οῦς, τό *kinship* (10)
συμβάλλεται *contribute to* (21)
συμπαθής, -ές *sympathetic* (10)
συμφέρω *bring together* (20)
συμφήσουσι *will agree with* (13)
σύν *with* (App. A)
σύνειμι *be with* (15)
συνθήκη, -ης, ἡ *agreement, covenant* (13)

συνίστημι *organize, put together, come together* (12)
σφαλερός, -ά, -όν *slippery, perilous* (16)
σφάλλω *trip up, overthrow* (22)
Σφίγξ, Σφιγγός, ἡ *Sphinx* (8)
σχολή, -ῆς, ἡ *leisure, rest* (22)
Σωκράτης, -ους, ὁ *Socrates* (8)
σῶμα, -ματος, τό *body* (8)
σωτήρ, -ῆρος, ὁ *savior* (16)
σωφρονοῦντος *of one who is sound of mind* (24)

T τ
τάλας *wretched, miserable* (23)
ταμίας, -ου, ὁ *treasurer* (5)
τάν = τήν (14)
τᾶν = τοι ἄν
ταρασσέσθω *let it be troubled* (24)
ταῦρος, -ου, ὁ *bull* (14)
ταχύς, -εῖα, -ύ *swift, quick, rapid* (16)
τε *and* (5)
τείνω *stretch out, hold out* (23)
τεῖχος, -ους, τό *wall* (17)
τελευτάω *die* (15)
τελέω *bring to an end, accomplish* (23)
τέλος, -ους, τό *end, goal, obligation* (9, 16)
τετράπους, -ουν *four-footed* (8)
τετρωμένος, -η, -ον *wounded* (18)
τέτταρες, τέτταρα *four* (App. B)
τέχνη, -ης, ἡ *skill, art, craft* (15)
τῇδε *here* (17)
τίθημι *place, establish* (12, App. C)
τίκτω *give birth to* (14, App. C)
τιμάω *honor* (17)
τιμή, -ῆς, ἡ *honor, dignity* (16)
τίν = σοί
τίς, τί *who? what?* (5)
τις, τι *someone, something, anyone, anything* (5)
τοι *let me tell you* (8)
τοιόσδε, τοιάδε, τοιόνδε *such as this* (22)
τοιοῦτος, τοιαύτη, τοιοῦτο *such, so* (20)
τόλμα, -ης, ἡ *courage, nerve* (9)
τολμάω *dare to* (21)
τότε *then* (8)
τοὐκ = τὸ ἐκ (15)

τρεῖς, τρία *three* (App. B)
τρέπω *turn* (App. C)
τρέφω *nourish* (19, App. C)
τρέχω *run* (App. C)
τριάκοντα *thirty* (21, App. B)
τρίπους, -ουν *three-footed* (8)
τρίς *three times* (19)
Τροία, -ας, ἡ *Troy* (22)
τυγχάνω *meet, happen* (13, 14, App. C)
τυραννίς, -ίδος, ἡ *tyranny* (10)
τύραννος, -ου, ὁ *tyrant, king, absolute ruler* (10)
τυφλός, -ή, -όν *blind* (5)
τύχη, -ης, ἡ *luck, fortune* (9)

Υ υ

ὑβρίζω *commit outrage, injure wantonly* (16)
ὕβρις, -εως, ἡ *wanton insolence, hubris* (20)
ὑγιαίνειν *to be healthy* (13)
ὕδωρ, ὕδατος, τό *water* (10)
υἱός, -οῦ, ὁ *son* (16)
ὕμνος, -ου, ὁ *hymn of praise, ode* (10)
ὑπακούω *obey, heed* (11)
ὑπέρ *over, above, beyond, for* (17, App. A)
ὑπηρετῶ *I am a servant* (23)
ὑπῆρχε *preferred* (14)
ὕπνος, -ου, ὁ *sleep* (9)
ὑποκριτής, -οῦ, ὁ *actor, pretender, hypocrite* (24)
ὑπό *beneath, by, about* (14, 19, App. A)
ὑποθήκη, -ης, ἡ *suggestion* (21)

Φ φ

φαίνω *show, reveal, appear* (19)
φανερός, -ά, -όν *visible, open* (3)
φέγγος, -ους, τό *light, splendor, joy* (15)
φέρω *bear, carry* (6, App. C)
φεῦ *oh! ah!* (14)
φεύγω *flee, escape* (15, App. C)
φημί *say, tell, say so* (23)
φιλέω *love* (14)
φίλιος, -α, -ον *friendly, compatible* (17)
φιλίων, -ον *dearer, more beloved* (10)
φιλοκαλέω *love beauty* (13)
φιλομάθεια, -ας, ἡ *love of learning* (11)
φίλος, -η, -ον *dear, beloved* (17)

φίλος, -ου, ὁ *a friend* (3)
φιλοσοφέω *love knowledge* (13)
φιλοσοφία, -ας, ἡ *love of knowledge, philosophy* (16)
φίλτατος, -η, -ον *dearest, most beloved* (10)
φοβέομαι *be afraid* (20)
φρονέω *intend, think, plan* (16)
φρόνημα, -ματος, τό *spirit, pride, arrogance* (14)
φροντίς, -ίδος, ἡ *thought* (10)
φυά, -ᾶς, ἡ *inborn nature* (20)
φύσις, -εως, ἡ *nature* (9)

Χ χ

χαλεπός, -ή, -όν *difficult, harsh* (3)
χαλκός, -οῦ, ὁ *copper, bronze, a metal mirror* (8)
χάρις, -ιτος, ἡ *favor, grace* (7)
χάσμα, -ματος, τό *yawning chasm, gulf* (14)
χείρ, χειρός, ἡ *hand* (22)
χελιδών, -όνος, ἡ *swallow* (13)
χρέμπτεται *she is clearing her throat* (24)
χρή *it is necessary, one must* (10)
χρῆμα, -ματος, τό *thing*, (pl.) *money* (15)
χρηστός, -ή, -όν *good, kind, useful* (4)
χριστός, -ή, -όν *anointed*, (cap.) *Christ* (16)
χρόνος, -ου, ὁ *time* (3)
χρυσός, -οῦ, ὁ *gold* (8)
χρυσοῦς, -ῆ, -οῦν *golden* (16)
χῶ = καὶ ὁ
χώρα, -ας, ἡ *place, land, country* (4)
χωρίς *without* (4)

Ψ ψ

ψευδής, -ές *false* (16)
ψηφίζομαι *vote* (21)
ψῆφος, -ου, ἡ *pebble, ballot* (3, 21)
ψυχή, -ῆς, ἡ *soul* (4)

Ω ω

ὦ *O* (with vocative) (17)
ὧδε *in this way, thus* (20)
ὥρα, -ας, ἡ *hour, season, time* (22)
ὡς *as, that, in order, so that, how* (6, 10, 11, 15, 18)
ὥσπερ *just as* (7)
ὥστε *so as, so that* (20)

English-Greek Vocabulary

A a
able οἶος
  be — οἶός τ' εἰμι, δύναμαι
accessible ἐφικτός
advantage κέρδος
Agamemnon Ἀγαμέμνων
Ajax Αἴας
all πᾶς
always ἀεί
and καί, τε
appear φαίνομαι
army στρατιά
Athenian Ἀθηναῖος
Athens Ἀθῆναι
  to — Ἀθήναζε

B b
badly off, be κακῶς ἔχω
band together συνίστημι (*intransitive*)
barbarian βάρβαρος
be εἰμι
  — with σύνειμι
beast βοτόν
beautiful καλός
become γίγνομαι
believe νομίζω
beloved φίλος
beside πρός
best ἄριστος, βέλτιστος, κράτιστος
betray προδίδωμι
book βιβλίον
both καί, τε
boy ὁ παῖς
brave ἀγαθός
bring to an end τελέω
but ἀλλά, δέ

by ὑπό
— far: see *far*

C c
call καλέω (summon), ὀνομάζω (name)
camp στρατόπεδον
carry φέρω
certain τις, τι
change ἀμείβω
characteristic: (*use genitive*)
charm θελκτήριον
child παῖς (over seven), παιδίον (under seven)
choose, we must ληπτέον (ἡμῖν)
citizen πολίτης
city πόλις
come ἔρχομαι
commander ἄρχων
compatible with φίλιος + *dative*
condemn: see *vote to condemn*
consider:
    must be —ed more important περὶ πλείονος (or πλέονος) ποιητέα
crown στέφανος
custom νόμος

D d
dangerous σφαλερός, χαλεπός
dare τολμάω + *infinitive*
decide κρίνω
destroy λύω
die ἀποθνῄσκω
different ἄλλος, ἕτερος
difficult χαλεπός
distribute διατίθημι
divinity δαίμων
dog κύων
drama δρᾶμα
drinking τὸ πίνειν
during: use *genitive* of time

E e
each ἕκαστος
— other ἀλλήλων
eat ἐσθίω

education παιδεία
enemy πολέμιοι (military), ἐχθρός (personal)
escape φεύγω, ἐκφεύγω
establish κατατίθημι
even though καίπερ + *participle*
everyone πάντες
everything πάντα
evil κακός, πονηρός

F f
face πρόσωπον
false:
   the — τὸ ψευδές
far:
   by — μακρῷ
father πατήρ
fear φοβέομαι, δέδοικα + μή + *subjunctive* or *optative*
fight πολεμέω, μάχομαι + *dative*
find εὑρίσκω
fine καλός
for (*conjunction*) γάρ
for (*preposition*): use *dative*
forgive ἀφίημι
friend φίλος
frightened, be φοβέομαι

G g
gift δῶρον
give δίδωμι
glory εὔκλεια
goal τέλος
go away ἀπέρχομαι
god θεός
goddess θεά, ἡ θεός
gold χρυσός
good καλός, ἀγαθός
government πολιτεία
grant δίδωμι

H h
happen κυρέω, τυγχάνω + *participle*
have ἔχω
hear ἀκούω

helmsman κυβερνήτης
help: see *run to help*
here τῇδε, ἐνταῦθα
himself ἑαυτοῦ
home (homeward) οἴκαδε
honor τιμάω
hope ἐλπίς
human being ἄνθρωπος

I i

I ἐγώ
if εἰ + *indicative, optative;* ἐάν (ἤν, ἄν) + *subjunctive*
imitate μιμέομαι
immortal ἀθάνατος
important: see *consider*
in ἐν
into εἰς
is: see *be*
it: (*omit*)

J j

just δίκαιος

K k

keep ἔχω
king βασιλεύς, τύραννος
know οἶδα, γιγνώσκω

L l

lament δακρύω
language γλῶττα
laugh γελάω
law νόμος
lead ἄγω
learn μανθάνω
lesson μάθημα
Let's: use hortatory *subjunctive*
live ζάω (exist), οἰκέω (inhabit)
long μακρός, δολιχός
longer, no οὐκ ἔτι
lose ἁμαρτάνω
love, be in ἐράω
luck τύχη

M m

make war: see *war*
man ἀνήρ (male), ἄνθρωπος (human)
Marathon Μαραθών
marketplace ἀγορά
master ἄναξ
may: use *optative* of wish or *subjunctive/optative* of purpose
messenger κῆρυξ, ἄγγελος
might: use potential *optative*
mind νοῦς
mirror ἔσοπτρον, κάτοπτρον
mix with μίγνυμαι (middle)
money χρήματα, ἀργύριον
more: use *comparative*
mortal βροτός
mother μήτηρ
must: use *verbal*
my: use *definite article*

N n

name ὄνομα
nature φύσις
neither . . . nor οὔτε . . . οὔτε
new καινός, νέος
night νύξ
no, not οὐ, μή
noble ἀγαθός
nor οὐδέ, οὔτε . . . οὔτε
not οὐ, μή
nothing οὐδέν
nourish τρέφω
now νῦν, ἤδη

O o

obey ὑπακούω, πείθομαι (middle)
obligation τέλος
observe ἐπισκοπέω
of: use *genitive*
often πολλάκις
opinion γνώμη
or ἤ
order:
    in — to ἵνα, ὡς, or ὅπως + *subjunctive* or *optative*
our: use *definite article*

P p

passage:
  the — of time τὸ χρόνον γεγενῆσθαι πολύν
pay attention προσέχω τὸν νοῦν
peace εἰρήνη
people ἄνθρωποι (often unexpressed)
Persian Πέρσης, βάρβαρος
persuade πείθω
physician ἰατρός
play δρᾶμα
poet ποιητής
present, be πάρειμι
presume:
  I — δήπου
problems κακά
pursuit of wisdom φιλοσοφία
put an end to παύω

R r

rather μᾶλλον
remain μένω
remember μνημονεύω
report ἀγγέλλω
reputation δόξα
rhetoric ἡ ῥητορική
riddle αἴνιγμα
right now ἄρτι
road ὁδός
ruler ἄρχων
run θέω, τρέχω
  — to help βοηθέω

S s

sacrifice θύω
same αὐτός
say λέγω, φημί, ἐρῶ (*future*)
  said I ἦν δ' ἐγώ
see ὁράω
seem δοκέω
  it —s (parenthetic) ἄρα
  —best δοκεῖ + *infinitive*
send πέμπω
sharp ὀξύς
she: (*omit*)

shepherd ποιμήν
should: use *optative*
show δηλόω
silence, in σιγῇ
sister ἀδελφή, κασιγνήτη
sleep ὕπνος
small μικρός
Socrates Σωκράτης
soldier στρατιώτης
some τις, τι
something τι
Sophocles Σοφοκλῆς
so that ἵνα, ὡς, or ὅπως + *subjunctive* or *optative*
soul ψυχή
speak λέγω
   —ing τό λέγειν
speech λόγος
still, be σιγάω
strange ξένος
strength ἰσχύς, σθένος
stronger κρείττων
summon καλέω
swiftly ταχέως
  more — θᾶττον

T t
teach παιδεύω
tell λέγω, φημί
temple ἱερόν
than ἤ (or use *genitive* of unequal comparison)
that (*conjunction*) ὅτι, ὡς + *indicative; accusative/infinitive* alone; or ἵνα,
   ὡς, or ὅπως + purpose clause
that (*demonstrative*) ἐκεῖνος, ὅδε
that (*relative*) ὅς, ἥ, ὅ
the ὁ, ἡ, τό
their: use *definite article*
there ἐνταῦθα
there is ἔστι
  — nothing οὐκ ἔστιν οὐδέν
these: see *this*
they: (*omit*)
thing χρῆμα (often understood)
think νομίζω, οἶμαι
this ὅδε, οὗτος

those: see *that*
through διά
thy σου
time:
   it is — to ὥρα ἐστί + *infinitive*
to: use *dative*
together: see *band together*
too: use *comparative*
town ἄστυ
trip up σφάλλω
true:
   is it not — that . . . ? οὔκουν . . . ;
   the true τἀληθές
trust πιστεύω
tyranny τυραννίς

U u
unexpected:
   all the — things πάντα τὰ ἀδόκητα
us: see *we*
used to: use *imperfect*
useful χρηστός

V v
very: use *superlative*
victory νίκη
virtue ἀρετή
vote to condemn καταψηφίζομαι

W w
want ἐθέλω, βούλομαι
war πόλεμος
war, make πολεμέω
was: see *be*
way πόρος
we ἡμεῖς
welcome ἡδύς
well εὖ, καλῶς
   be — εὖ ἔχει (impersonal)
   —born εὐγενής
what . . . ? τί . . . ;
what (that which) ὅτι, ἅτινα
when, whenever ἐπεί, ἐπειδή, ὅτε
which ὅς, ἥ, ὅ

who . . . ? τίς . . . ;
whoever ὅς, ὅστις
wife γυνή
will: use *future*
wind ἄνεμος
wise σοφός
wish ἐθέλω
with μετά, σύν (see also *be with*)
without ἄνευ, χωρίς
woman γυνή
word λόγος, ῥῆμα
world:
    who in the — . . . ? τίς ποτε . . . ;
worst κάκιστος
worthy ἄξιος
would: use formula for *future-less-vivid* or *contrary-to-fact condition*
write γράφω

X x
Xenophon Ξενοφῶν

Y y
you σύ, ὑμεῖς
young νέος, καινός
    — man νεανίας
your: use *definite article*
yourselves:
    for —: use *middle voice*

Subject Index

Author Index